A Last Survivor
— *of the* —
Orphan Trains

A Last Survivor
— *of the* —
Orphan Trains

A Memoir

William Walters *and*
Victoria Golden

Published by Orphan Books, victoriagoldenauthor.com

Edited by Linda Gunnarson

 Designed by Girl Friday Productions
www.girlfridayproductions.com

Interior Design: Paul Barrett
Cover Design: Kathleen Lynch
Image Credits: Cover image © Steven Liveoak/Alamy Stock Photo

ISBN (Paperback): 9780999768501
e-ISBN: 9780999768518

First Edition

Printed in the United States of America

For Dorothea, Will, and Gerald

CONTENTS

Introduction

Orphan Trains in America? Like most people I was unaware. Then I came to know eighty-six-year-old William Walters. As little more than a toddler, William was placed on one of the countless trains that delivered an estimated 200,000 to 250,000 American children into the hands of strangers living along the nation's rail lines from 1854 to the early 1930s. In 2012, William enrolled in a hospice-sponsored support group for grieving spouses attended by a friend of mine. When she told me what William had shared with their grief group, it became clear that William Walters' journey on an Orphan Train marked only the beginning of his extraordinary trajectory through nine decades of American history—a story that clearly deserved to be recorded.

Shortly after his mother died in 1930, four-year-old William Delos VanSteenburgh and his seven-year-old brother, Jared, were removed from their home in Pennsylvania and placed by a relative on an Orphan Train with Southwest destinations. This made William and his brother two of the last participants in the Orphan Train movement in America that relocated homeless or impoverished children westward from eastern cities to homes in rural regions. At one of many towns along his train's southwestern route, strangers chose William's brother from among the assembled children. Some stops later William was removed from the station platform in Gallup, New Mexico, by a childless couple who gave him the name William Walters and who would abuse him for the next five years.

So began the saga that made William into a repeat runaway, provided brief respite and his first schooling at Father Flanagan's Boys Town
in Nebraska, pulled him onto the road and the rails as a twelve-year-old
during the Great Depression, found him refuge as a sixteen-year-old
at Newsboys' Home in New York, and drew him to special service as a
teenage Marine scout on Japanese-occupied islands in the Pacific during
World War II.

William's journey is remarkable for the threats he faced and survived, the hopeful attitude he maintained throughout, his adaptability
in learning whatever form of work came his way, the mental ability
recognized in him by the Marine Corps, and his eventual emergence as a
successful adult in postwar America. His story is extreme in terms of early
deprivation and violence, for which he showed emotional scars, but also
is emblematic of American mobility: the potential, provided you survive childhood intact, to pick yourself up and move on from crisis. As his
fortunes plummeted and rose repeatedly, William gradually transformed
from victim to victor. Along the way, his personal journey intersected with
some major moments in national and world history, including his arrival
in Nagasaki two weeks after the atom bomb dropped.

William sat down to tell me his life story soon after losing the love
of his life, his wife of sixty-five years. By that telling, he had been a farm
manager, plumber, upholsterer, factory worker, fire engineer, shop owner,
and finally manager of the design department for Macy's San Francisco.
During that last job, Macy's sent him to Africa, the Amazon, and Papua
New Guinea on scouting trips for design studio artifacts, igniting in
William a love of world travel that took him to myriad foreign destinations until cancer slowed him at age ninety. He died at home in Santa
Rosa, California, on January 21, 2017.

You cannot understand William without knowing the importance
of his sixty-five-year-long love story and his hunger for the affection and
reassurance it provided. The idea of marrying came as a surprise to both
William and his intended, and the girl must have been just as surprised
after their marriage to discover the key role she needed to play in protecting and preserving the fragile ego of this otherwise strong young man. As

William unfolded for me his many adventures, he didn't say this is what his wife did for him, but that is what was revealed.

Throughout his life, William demonstrated a spectacular ability to absorb and remember. If you had met him, you would not have suspected that his formal schooling amounted to approximately two years, with most of his education gained via experience and voracious reading. Although at times during my interviews William worried over the accuracy of his memory for events that had transpired seventy or eighty years ago, he was able to summon and quote material learned as a child and demonstrated fluency in spoken Japanese, which he learned as a teenager during six months of classes following graduation from Marine Corps boot camp. However, it was natural that the passage of time had blurred William's recollections about his youth. Also, the nature of William's childhood experiences made it hard to remember the exact sequence of events and his precise age when certain incidents unfolded; for most of his youth he did not live with a family that marked his birthdays or noted the timing of important milestones. As a result, this telling is bound to include mistakes in recollection as well as the subjective coloring of his perspective. Nevertheless, whatever imperfections this book possesses, the powerful story of William Delos VanSteenburgh, AKA William Walters, calls out to be told.

The main chapters of this book are narrated in William's voice, the result of his conversations with me over a period of four years. In between are flash-forwards to events in William's life written from my perspective, some of them critical of William. (It says a lot about William that he approved these commentaries.) An appendix provides information we found about William's biological parents and about the couple who adopted him; background information on the Orphan Trains; and a brief profile of Isidor Goldberg, the colorful inventor/entrepreneur who became William's employer soon after World War II.

—Victoria Golden

CHAPTER ONE

Memories of My Mother's Death and of Home

I don't remember my mother but I remember her coffin.

She died in 1930 when I was four. The practice in those days was to pack a body in ice and set the casket in the parlor. In my mother's case, the big narrow box was made of dark wood. My big sister, Marian, held my hand as I stood in the downstairs hallway and peered into the parlor. I didn't want to go in.

The parlor curtains were drawn, and the room was dimly lit. From the doorway you could see the coffin. It had a heavy cloth arranged around one end, which must have been the opening where my mother could be viewed. A number of strangers were gathered in the room. Marian, who was about eighteen at the time and actually my half-sister, led me by the hand into the parlor. I was crying, terrified. I understood that my life was going to change, and I didn't know what was going to happen.

We lived in Susquehanna Depot, Pennsylvania—my mother, my siblings and me, and maybe my father. My mother had been sick for what seemed like a long time. I wasn't allowed to enter the room where she lay upstairs because she was terribly ill and could not be disturbed.

Marian had taken care of me and my brother when our mother no longer could, and she was good to us. Until I saw that coffin, there was a feeling of safety and love in our home.

Other bits of memory hang on. Not my father; he's an enigma, but tax records say the property was owned in his name. We lived alongside a river in a big old house. The area around our home was heavily wooded and the backyard verdant. Trees lined the waterway, with few other houses nearby. I could play in the backyard but was warned not to go near the riverbank because the river was dangerous.

Around the time of my mother's funeral there was much shuttling to and fro making arrangements, including me coming and going from the house with grown men. We were riding in a car through a covered bridge when an accident occurred, either our car or someone else's. We stopped at the far side of the bridge. A man's arm was bleeding badly. Broken window glass had cut him. Someone wrapped a cloth around the wound.

And that's it. That's all I have of my life before everything changed.

Boot camp

In 1942, as the Marine Corps whipped into shape tens of thousands of young men for the Allied war effort, he may have been the only recruit to find boot camp a breeze. A cakewalk, as he later said. Like sitting home in a rocking chair. William was a gangly sixteen-year-old, about six feet tall and slender enough that you might have expected a strong wind to fold him in half. Beneath his baggy Marine greens, though, William was tough. Tough and muscular from years of farm work. And from other things that gave him an edgy quality, a barely contained volatility.

Looking at this kid, you might have figured that he'd lived the American dream. He was white, blond, healthy, and smart.

Lying about his age, enlisting with other young men to fight in World War II, he'd known that it had to be the Marines, the best of the best. No one had ever told him he was the best at anything.

From the moment the new recruits arrived at Parris Island, South Carolina, the drill instructor screamed in their faces. Blasted them with harangues day after day. There were only seven weeks to hurl the boys through relentless physical and mental training, only seven weeks to transform them into effective fighters badly needed in multiple war arenas.

Shrieking and cursing? Physical punishment? William was used to that. He was also a good marksman.

One night during boot camp, he heard one of the kids in his barracks sobbing. That morning the DI had felt the boy's face to see if he'd shaved properly and decided he hadn't. It's possible the kid may have shaved just fine, but that didn't enter into it. The DI had put a bucket over the boy's head and told him to shave. Seeing this, William had blown up. "Why are you picking on him? Can't you see he can't take it? Why don't you try that on me!" You did not sass a DI, but the DI didn't flare up. All he said was to see him later. William did.

"All right," said his DI. "I'm going to tell you why I'm doing that to him. I know you can take that kind of treatment, but he can't. How would you like to have him in the foxhole next to you?"

William thought about it. He said nothing.

"This is nothing personal," said the DI. "I don't dislike the kid. I'm trying to make a man of him."

To the crying boy that night, William tried to explain the DI only wanted to toughen him up. That he shouldn't take it so hard, that in six weeks it would be over with. But the boy was distraught. He said he couldn't stand the treatment.

In the end, that recruit didn't make it. They labeled him "Section 8." Mentally unfit. He was sent home. William wasn't. They made him an officer, taught him Japanese, and sent him into the Pacific on intelligence missions as part of a small, hand-picked unit of Marines.

The Corps suited him. William was tough and competent and even tenderhearted. However, say the wrong word or make the wrong move, and he might strike. At William's core there was an aching wound, and it would be some years before anyone would soothe it.

CHAPTER TWO

The Shock of Life with the Walters

I boarded the Orphan Train with my brother at a train station in a big city. Around us, children were crying. Even the older boys were inconsolable. The two of us were weeping, too. The situation was a mystery; we were surrounded by people we didn't know. Along with the other children we were led to a coach car up front near the engine, away from the rest of the passengers. Marian saw us onto the train to settle us and instructed my brother to watch out for me, which was asking a lot of a kid his age; he wasn't much older than me. In what city we boarded, I can't say, but the way I felt as we found a seat on the Pullman car is easy to summon up. A knot in my gut. Grief and fear, loss. It was as if we'd fallen into the river near our house and been swept away from everything we knew.

Anger at Marian was not part of it. She was kind. My impression was that events were moving along with no way to stop them. It didn't seem like my sister had a choice when she put us on the train.

My brother was seven or eight years old and named Jared (per the 1930 U.S. Census) or Gerald (what he told me when I met him as an adult). The April 1930 Census shows my mother alive and us boys living with her, but I later put together that I turned five on September 27 in Gallup, New Mexico, in fall of that same year.

After the train got going and time passed, we kids began to play and horse around. The chaperones didn't control us very well. There were too many of us for the number of adults.

The journey felt long. Coal smoke from the engine blew back at us through the open windows. It was so thick you could feel it on your tongue as well as smell it. The coach car had wooden seats with backs that were only slightly padded. We had to sleep on the hard benches, leaning against each other or the car wall to doze. In a small restroom at one end of the car, the toilet opened to the track. The sight of railroad ties racing by beneath the toilet seat fascinated and worried me. Our chaperones fed us when the train pulled into stations. They purchased sandwiches or other quick food and handed it out while we stood on train platforms.

After a while, each time the train stopped in a town, we filed out of the train to line up on the station platform so locals could take a look and decide whether they wanted to take us home with them. This was where the crying started up again. We'd formed attachments with other kids while playing together, and when we got out, we feared these attachments would be severed—and, of course, our bonds with our brothers and sisters. On the station platform it was like a horse auction. Some people asked us to open our mouths so they could see our teeth. My brother gripped my hand to keep me from bolting.

Much later I learned that Orphan Train chaperones carried documentation regarding date of birth, parents' names, religion, and nationality, which they passed along to the strangers who stepped forward to claim us.

At one stop my brother was chosen by a family and I wasn't. I didn't notice what city it was; my main response was panic. Returning to the train without him came as a bad blow. No one tried to comfort me. Back on the hard wooden seat, I had no one to hold on to.

There were still quite a few kids in our car when we clattered across the desert leading to Gallup, New Mexico. As we stepped off the train and onto the platform, I came out of my fog and was filled with wonder. It looked like I had arrived in real, live, Indian country.

Most of the western railroad stations in those days had elaborate hotels and restaurants attached, thanks to an Englishman named Fred Harvey who made a deal with the Atchison, Topeka and Santa Fe Railway: The railroad would build hotels and restaurants at stops along its routes and he would manage them, offering clean lodgings and tasty sit-down meals. This was a big departure from what was previously available in the West and brought many more tourists. Eventually the Harvey Company hired a young architect named Mary Colter to create buildings and interior design that captured the flavor of the region by paying homage to the earliest inhabitants of the Southwest, both Native American and Spanish.

Not knowing all that, I was especially struck by what I saw when I stepped off the train in Gallup. A large, sand-colored building faced the train. Its color and stony texture matched the surrounding desert. Off to the side, across a stretch of dusty ground, an Indian woman sat near a small hut weaving on a wooden frame. Later I learned that she was a Navajo, that she made rugs, and that her packed-earth dwelling was called a *hogan*. The wind swept the air free of coal smoke at least briefly, because I smelled a spicy perfume that was sagebrush.

A man and woman came forward from the crowd of people eyeing us kids. They pointed at me. The stucco station building and the Indian woman had distracted me, but my anxiety returned when I saw these two. Their manner was austere and formal. They did not smile. The best description I can give is that they had that stern, pinched quality of the man and wife in the Grant Wood painting *American Gothic*.

These were the Walters. As we walked away from the train, they said or did nothing to make me feel safe or welcome. Mr. Walters may have smiled at others on the street, because he often put on a good face in public. I soon learned he was mayor of Gallup. However, he and his wife were cold toward me from the outset, and that didn't change as I got to know them. In fact, they became far worse.

Henry Albert Walters was a bald-headed man, tall and husky, impressive in size and demeanor. He always carried himself erect. His wife, Eleanor, was medium height and slender. Without exception, she wore her grey hair pulled back in a bun or coiled on top of her head, and always her mouth was set in a grim line.

We drove up into the hills that edged Gallup. The Walters lived in a yellow stucco house surrounded by lawn and a low-lying brick wall. Their home sat on an acre or two and seemed like a mansion. I thought maybe I had arrived in heaven and everything would be fine. The couple had a cook and a maid working for them. There were no other children.

The Walters showed me a room that would be mine. It was furnished with a bed, a nightstand, a dresser, and a straight-backed chair. They assigned me a few basic chores, including making my bed, keeping my room neat, and carrying in firewood each morning.

They also bought me new clothes: a fancy white sailor suit plus shirts and overalls. It was important not to let the sailor suit get dirty, not even a smudge. They had me wear it when we were out in public together or when guests came to the house, which wasn't often.

From the outset the Walters told me to call them "Aunt Eleanor" and "Uncle Henry." They let me keep the name William and said I should call myself by the last name of Walters. At some point, they formally adopted me but didn't tell me. They never opened their arms to me, and my behavior at first didn't make that any more likely. I often cried for my family and for home. I cried until it became clear that tears only led to bad things.

The Walters' cook was a large, heavyset black woman who also did housekeeping. She was neutral in her approach to me, not benevolent and not mean. We didn't have much contact. The young Latina maid treated me about the same. Neither employee lived on the premises but worked for the Walters full time. If the cook or maid saw how I was treated, they never let on. I was told not to associate with them, and they may have been told not to talk with me. After a short while both the cook and the maid were let go.

That first autumn in the Walters' home was a relative grace period, until Christmas arrived. That was my first bad shock. The Walters put up a Christmas tree and invited some friends over on Christmas day. As I watched and waited, they gave presents to everyone but me. Being a little kid, I was in tears by the time their guests left.

"Oh yes," they said, "we have something for you." They handed me a big box covered with wrapping paper. I tore through the paper and opened the box. It contained a horsewhip.

I've never seen another whip like that one. It was peculiar. The whip handle was made of woven strips of leather and was about an inch and a half in diameter and a foot long. Three long, wide leather straps were attached. The Walters made sure I had a good look at the whip and then hung it on a wall in the kitchen. It was kept there from that day onward, except when the Walters took it down to beat me.

As I settled into life in the Walters' home, my daily life consisted of doing chores and then staying out of the way. My responsibilities grew as time went by. Each morning I carried in cedar firewood for the cook stove and pine for the fireplace. The cook stove in the kitchen was both wood- and coal-fired, so I also kept the coal bucket full. At the time of year when the garden was going, I watered it. After the help was let go, Mrs. Walters did the cooking and cleaning, and I did the dishes after meals. Upon completion of chores, I was either sent to my room or allowed to play in the yard unless we were going somewhere for the day. Mrs. Walters liked to visit a friend named Mrs. Miksch, and at her house I was banished to a room by myself, handed a few picture books, and told to keep quiet; those hours felt interminable.

It often seemed like I was handed chores that were impossible for a kid my age. Early on, dishwashing and drying was one of them. Inevitably I dropped or chipped a glass or plate, and then there was hell to pay. My take is that the Walters got a perverse pleasure from demonstrating how incompetent I was. Whatever task I completed, they said that the result was unsatisfactory. That I was useless and stupid. There was never praise, only criticism and often punishment.

One assignment I found hard to get right was trimming the tamarack hedge. A dwarf variety of the pine bordered the yard and needed frequent tending. I was given hand clippers and told to get to it. Tamarack is a rough kind of plant, and the results were never smooth or even. I always left ins and outs in the hedge that were unacceptable. What this and other tasks taught me was to persevere and work out solutions. To tough it out and take the inevitable reprimands.

Very few things in people's homes were electric-powered in the 1920s and 1930s. For example, Mrs. Walters operated her sewing machine with foot-powered treadles. The refrigerator was literally an icebox, with a chunk of ice kept in a compartment near the top and a drip tray under to catch the melt. We did have electric lights and radio. In most big towns there was electricity for telephones and lights.

Firewood came to us almost in log form, and by the time I was about eight, it was my job to chop and split the wood as well as keep the axe sharp. The latter was a formidable task. Down in the basement the Walters had an old sharpener. You rested the axe on a stand to face a big sandstone wheel. Connected to the wheel was a pulley leading to foot pedals, almost like those on old sewing machines. I sat on a board attached to the stand and pedaled with both feet to keep the wheel turning. The process was tedious and slow. For one thing, the wheel was sandstone, and over the years, certain areas of the sandstone had worn down unevenly, causing the wheel to wobble as it turned. Holding a blade steady against that wheel was a real problem, especially since it was a double-edged blade, but that's the way it had to be done. After a while, I developed a technique. Still, it could take a couple of hours of pedaling at the grindstone before the axe was sharp.

In a way, you could say that the Walters were training me to become a successful runaway. I don't think they were trying to do me any favors, but they encouraged an attitude toward work that prepared me for survival on the road. Whatever it was that needed doing, they expected me to do it without much explanation and to do it well. It was up to me to figure it out. After I escaped their house, that training made me bold enough to take on any job that might provide food, shelter, and possibly money.

One day while splitting firewood, I came down on my leg with the newly sharpened axe and hacked open my instep. There was a lot of blood, and the gash was deep. The Walters took me to a doctor who sewed me up. Mr. and Mrs. Walters shrugged off the injury and cut me no slack in my chores while the wound healed. At the time I didn't appreciate that stoicism would come in handy once I escaped down the road and faced physical challenges of various sorts. Instead, every insult, every impossible task, and every cold response made me crave home. I yearned for my family. This was not family. Not in the way I had known it.

From the start, I was told not to ask about my past or my family left behind. The Walters also told me nothing about theirs. I became afraid to ask questions because the couple reprimanded me for addressing them in any way other than what was necessary. They did inform me that my father died before I was born. Maybe he actually was dead or maybe they didn't want to acknowledge that my father was still around and give me hope of any kind. If I raised the subject of my family after that brief mention, I was told they were no longer of any interest to me.

It's possible that the Walters had lost a child or that Mrs. Walters had lost a younger brother. She often scolded me with, "If only you were like your Uncle Clifford" or "Uncle Clifford never would have done that." There was no explanation of who Uncle Clifford was. Every once in a while she visited the Gallup cemetery, and my guess is that she was visiting the grave of a relative there. I accompanied her to the cemetery once and waited a short distance away as she stood before a gravestone. Mrs. Walters said nothing and showed no sign of emotion. She didn't offer a reason for her visit. She took me along to the graveyard that one time because we were out on an errand and it wasn't convenient to drop me at home. Otherwise I knew about her visits to the cemetery only because she made passing reference to them to Mr. Walters.

The only overt emotion I saw expressed in the Walters' home was anger. There was no obvious affection between husband and wife. Never did I see one put an arm around the other or even touch the other's shoulder in acknowledgement. Their relationship seemed pragmatic. They talked with each other and conducted their lives together with no sign of fondness. There were no expressions of other kinds of warmth in their home. They didn't seem to have family nearby and didn't appear to have many close friends, apart from Mrs. Walters' friend Mrs. Miksch.

Meals at the Walters' house varied. We ate breakfast together, but lunch was a haphazard thing. Mr. Walters was rarely at home midday, and often Mrs. Walters did not eat lunch at home either, many times eating that meal elsewhere with a lady friend, usually Mrs. Miksch. If no lunch had been prepared for me, I made myself a peanut butter sandwich. I have fond memories of that old-fashioned peanut butter, the kind that sticks to the top of your mouth and teeth. It was simply ground nuts with salt added and was pretty good.

Dinner at night was not formal in dress but was formal in manner. I had to eat whether I wanted to or not, finish everything I was served, and remain at the table until dismissed. This, I think, was the standard expectation for children then. At dinner, if Mr. Walters was home, the two of them discussed the day's doings, but I was not allowed to talk. Frequently Mr. Walters stayed away from home for days at a time; this was never explained to me. If Mrs. Walters and I ate dinner alone, I was expected not to talk unless spoken to.

A big radio in the Walters' living room served as a major treat in the evening during occasions when I was allowed to stay up and listen to a program with them, but this didn't happen often. Usually I was sent to my room after dinner or after dinner cleanup. The Walters were able to receive shortwave from overseas, so the two of them sat in the living room in the evening listening to broadcasts from near and far. My favorites were Shakespearean performances from overseas, which gave me a lifelong love of Shakespeare. Back in my room, I could also hear snatches of *Amos 'n' Andy* and some kind of radio theater and eventually President Roosevelt during his fireside chats. I didn't pay much attention to politics, but I found the sound of the president's voice comforting.

It would be a couple of decades before the first television sets appeared in U.S. living rooms. In the 1930s, radio was a major form of entertainment in American homes. I learned later that it was customary for American families to gather around the radio in the evenings to hear their favorite shows.

My bedtime routine at the Walters' home was simple. I did everything for myself.

If sent to my room during the day, I read or played with puzzles. Mrs. Walters taught me to read soon after I came to live with them. This had to be a defensive move on her part, since I was often sent to my bedroom, out of the way. Somewhere along the line I learned that Mrs. Walters had been a teacher at Fort Wingate, southeast of Gallup, so teaching me to read may have been an easy task. The Walters gave me a jigsaw of the United States that I learned to assemble. Knowledge of U.S. geography gained from that puzzle helped considerably when I was a twelve-year-old on the road looking for work. There was a time when I could name the capitals of all the states in the nation, and I knew the position of each state in relation to the others. As a runaway with little education, if I heard of a job in another state, I could still figure out which train to catch depending on its direction of travel. The Walters also provided a puzzle map of the world, so I learned

major capitals across the globe. In addition, I had picture
books on Greek mythology, and Mrs. Walters would hand me
the Bible or other books from which she assigned passages to
memorize.

Outdoors I was given a wagon to play with and was per-
mitted to entertain myself as long as I didn't soil my clothing. Even if I was wearing denim overalls, I had to be careful
not to dirty them too much; Mrs. Walters was strict about
that. Dust was okay, but no more than dust, and definitely
not mud. If the weather had been rainy, I needed to be very
careful if I went outside. Mud was a transgression of major
proportions, even as a result of watering plants in the garden.
Most of my play was outdoors, where I collected and hauled
rocks to build castles and other structures.

Maybe to help occupy me, the Walters brought home a
dog and named him Waggs. He was a spaniel of some sort,
and while the Walters didn't interact with him and kept him
strictly outdoors, he became quite meaningful to me. The
Walters didn't enroll me in school, and because their house
was remote from other homes, I rarely had contact with
other kids. Waggs became my buddy. Each day I fed him
and cleaned up after him. As I watered the garden or made
up games outdoors, I kept up a running conversation with
Waggs.

The whip hanging in the kitchen came down from its spot
on the wall frequently after that first Christmas. Mostly Mr.
Walters did the beating, usually in the kitchen or my bedroom. In a fit of anger over something he or his wife said I'd
done wrong, he grabbed me and lashed me. If he was going
to thoroughly whip me, he stripped off all of my clothes and
stood me next to a wooden chair so that I faced the back of it.
He bent me over the chair so my arms reached down toward

the seat, and he bound my wrists to the legs where they met the seat. Then he beat me hard, often yelling as he did it. The pain was bad and made worse by his grunts and his words. "You little bastard! You ungrateful son of a bitch!" The horse-whip had wide leather thongs, so the lashes didn't draw blood, but they left me bruised red and purple and weak with pain. The whip handle was like a flexible club covered in woven leather, and when he hit me with that, it didn't break my skin either but also left bruises.

Many times after a beating Mr. Walters threw me out-side naked, to be left there overnight. I tried to curl up under anything that gave shelter. My pain, and at certain times of year the cold, made those nights long. Insects and bugs came buzzing and crawling and made it worse. Waggs provided some comfort.

Numerous reasons were cited for the beatings. I might not have made my bed correctly. Or I might have left some-thing lying out in my room that should have been put away. Or my crime might be loud, boisterous play or running about. Given poems and Bible verses to memorize, I was whipped for mistakes during recitation. Or God help me if I broke a plate while wiping dishes or if I allowed my sailor suit to get dirty. Failure to clean my plate at mealtime also brought a beating. Oftentimes punishment came if I didn't answer a question quickly enough.

I lived in constant dread and became scared to death to touch anything or do anything. I became a little automaton. I tried hard not to break any rules, but I was a little kid and made mistakes, especially at first, when I didn't understand all the ways I could anger the Walters.

The adults I'd known before this had been much different from the Walters. The Walters' behavior stunned me. Never did I believe I deserved the kind of punishment they dished out. I don't believe I experienced ill treatment of any kind

before I came to live with them, and I think this gave me a
certain confidence about what was fair and what was not.

From the very first, Mr. Walters warned me not to cry, not
while he was beating me or at any other time, or I would be
disciplined more. In short order I learned to bite my tongue
and not cry out. As time went by I became pretty tough.
Another important step in preparing me for life as a runaway.

During my early days with the Walters, I waited until
nighttime to cry alone in my room. I cried for home. Of
course, home no longer existed the way I had known it, but
that didn't matter. I could see it. It still lived in my mind. I
tried not to be noisy and draw attention to myself, but I cried
for the house by the river where I felt safe. Eventually though,
I stopped crying altogether.

Henry Walters did most of the punishing, but Eleanor
Walters was always in the background, like a spider spinning
her web. Many of the whippings delivered by Mr. Walters
were the result of Mrs. Walters making up things and then
reporting on me when her husband arrived home. If Mrs.
Walters misplaced or spilled something, she blamed it on
me. Almost worse than the whippings was the psychological terror that she perpetrated in advance of the beatings.
She reminded me all day long—or for several days during
the extended periods when Mr. Walters wasn't home—what
would happen when "Uncle Henry" got home. When he
returned, Mrs. Walters didn't say anything to her husband
in front of me, and that made it worse, because my insides
churned up as I waited for the blow to fall. At dinner I
couldn't eat, knowing what was coming, but not eating
brought the threat of even more punishment. If I was sent to
bed, I couldn't sleep, thinking about the various warnings.
That's when Mr. Walters often came looking for me for a
beating, when I was lying there in bed.

Sometimes Mrs. Walters didn't wait for her husband to punish me. She would make an accusation, order me to take off my pants, and tell me to lie across her lap for a beating.

I tried but could not find a way to soften Mrs. Walters or bring a smile. She rebuffed me if I put my arms around her or tried in other ways to placate her when she turned angry. Either she cussed me out or she told me to go to my room and not bother her. I persisted for a while in trying to express affection, not just to avoid beatings but because I was desperate for warmth and reassurance. I held out the slim hope that she would be gentle if I could just find a way to be good. In spite of the terror of living in that house, I wanted to feel that I belonged to someone and they cared about me. The Walters were all I had left in the world. They pointed that out to me often.

Over and over the Walters told me that I'd never amount to anything, that I possessed no skills of any kind. If they told me to do something, and I didn't do it precisely as they instructed, they said it meant I was dumb. They drummed that into me. They also said I had "bad blood." I didn't understand the phrase, but I knew it meant something was awfully wrong with me. I now know that a lot of Orphan Train kids were told the same. It meant we were worthless garbage born to low-life people. The Walters also told me I was ugly. "You're the ugliest kid in town," they'd say, "and it doesn't make any difference what town you're in. Just look at yourself." Hearing words like that day after day, year after year, you become convinced they're correct.

Deep down I've never lost the feeling the Walters were right. However, time and experience have given me a dueling perspective. I wonder why, if I was so blamed ugly and inept, the Walters eventually signed me up for tap-dancing lessons. Or had me memorize Bible verses and poetry and perform

recitations in front of their friends. You'd think they'd want
to hide me away and not have me show my face in front of
other people. Americans went to the movies in large numbers
back then to see child stars like Jackie Coogan and Freddie
Bartholomew and Shirley Temple, and it's been suggested to
me that the couple believed I could make money like those
kids did. The Walters' fortunes took a turn for the worse in
the Great Depression. Letting their help go was an early sign.
So was our move to a house that wasn't as nice. Still, as a
child, I took them at their word when they said I was worthless and stupid and ugly.

Strangely, my sister Marian showed up at the Walters' house
relatively early in my stay there.

I was six or seven when my appendix burst. This was
before antibiotics became available; a burst appendix was a
big deal and could be lethal. I was in the hospital for what
seemed like a long time, and when I returned to the Walters'
house, I was kept in bed to finish recovering.

It was then that Marian showed up in Gallup to live and
work at the Walters'. She was about twenty years old. The
addresses of children adopted off the Orphan Train were
sometimes supplied to their birth families, so Marian might
have corresponded with the couple. It could be they learned
my sister was an unmarried woman without much means
of support. The Walters may have sent for her thinking they
could get a nanny and built-in housekeeper while I was recu-
perating. At that point the cook and maid were gone.

Marian arrived at the Walters' while I was too young to
think of asking the right questions, such as how she came to
be there, how long she'd stay, or why she was there at all. All
I knew was that I was thrilled to see my sister and expected

her to stay with me forever. I did notice that Marian became extremely nervous after a while. She bit her fingernails a lot and cried often. The Walters must have treated her badly, too.

I was still in bed recovering from the appendectomy when Marian came to my room to ask a favor. She'd broken a bottle of perfume while cleaning the Walters' bedroom. Fearing Mrs. Walters' response, she asked me to take the blame. She figured I was just out of the hospital and nothing bad would happen to me. So I did it. I told Mrs. Walters that I got out of bed to walk around a little and knocked into the bottle by mistake. Shortly after she heard my confession, Mrs. Walters yanked me out of bed and threw me into a tub of ice water. The shock damn near killed me. Marian was so sorry. She sobbed and asked me to forgive her.

I didn't blame Marian for what happened. Instead, I felt a certain amount of pride in taking responsibility and protecting her. Besides, my sister couldn't have known what would be done to me. *I* hadn't guessed what would be done to me. We came from a home where a punishment like that was outside the realm of possibility.

During the period Marian lived in Gallup, she often hugged me and kept me by her side whenever possible. I liked to watch her sitting at a dressing table as she brushed her long, straight blonde hair. Then one day she disappeared without saying goodbye. I was still recovering from the appendectomy. Marian hadn't stayed long at all. The Walters refused to explain my sister's sudden departure.

Leaving couldn't have been Marian's choice. The Walters must have forced her to take off without a word. Like me, she must have seen the Walters as all-powerful. She must have heard about Mr. Walters' stature in town. She knew that the Orphan Train people had agreed to have the Walters be responsible for me, and she must have decided there was no way to protect me or get me away from them. By then the Walters may have adopted me, and Marian may have found she had no legal claim. I'm sure that's the case.

Losing Marian was awful. I never saw her again. One more blow in a series of blows. Each one made me tougher. Each one made me close off in a way to protect against the next one.

Now I understand that a lot of other kids who rode the Orphan Trains suffered the way I did. The Orphan Train organizers didn't understand the harm they did to us children. They meant well; they wanted to rescue children from life on the streets or in orphanages, but many times it went badly.

As I grew older, the Walters sent me on errands into town to fetch items from various stores, and those trips down the hill provided wonderful relief from what was going on at home.

For one thing, they provided glimpses of the way other people lived. On the sidewalks or in restaurant windows, I saw families enjoying each other's company. Adults smiled at each other and at their kids; people gave each other hugs. I told myself the same would happen to me someday.

Beyond that, Gallup was an interesting place to be.

One of the first things I learned during my trips downtown was not to go into the deep arroyo, or gulley, that split the town in two. Gallup is situated in a valley, and in those days houses sat on facing hills to either side of the downtown, with the business district mostly on one side of the arroyo. A couple of bridges spanned the arroyo to connect the residential area where we first lived with the commercial district on the other side. One bridge was for automobiles and pedestrians and the other for trains. Residents were warned not to walk into the arroyo, although in dry weather you could go down into the gulley among the tumbleweeds and come up

the other side for a quick shortcut from the residential area
to the commercial district. However, a couple of times a year
cloudbursts flooded the arroyo, drowning people who were
caught by surprise down in that gulch.

Two major transportation corridors ran through Gallup:
Route 66 traveled right across the city and was the major
east-west conduit for the nation, and then there was the
railroad. Route 66 linked towns and rural communities from
Chicago to Los Angeles, allowing farmers to bring their produce to market, but that's not to say it wasn't primitive. The
two-lane highway was paved where it ran through Gallup,
but rural stretches were still dirt at the time, which I discovered during escape attempts. Trains were a faster, more reli-
able, and comprehensive means of transport. Freight trains
ran frequently, and I counted as many as 120-car chains.
Looking to the east out of Gallup, you could see a train coming about ten miles away from the direction of Grants, New
Mexico. Trains rounded the distant hills to curve onto the
desert plain, and at first the smoke from the locomotive was
the only thing visible as a train crossed the tan and brown
expanse. I loved seeing the approaching trains. They meant
freedom to me, the freedom to come and go. That desert to
the east was bounded in places by red bluffs but was essentially flat and marked by sagebrush, ironweed, and mesquite.
Going the other way, west out of Gallup toward Winslow,
Arizona, by train or highway, you could see spectacular cliffs
light cream to tan in color reaching up from the desert floor,
with a plateau at the top.

Snow falls on Gallup in winter, but the heat is what
impressed me. That plus dust, dirt, and smoke. The city sits
to some extent in a basin, giving leave for the wind sweeping
down off the surrounding hills to stir up dust. Near to Gallup
in those days were the Gamerco coal mines, which employed
many of the Mexican people living in the area. The mines

plus the railroad terminal with its large yards and multiple tracks meant there was lots of smoke in the air. If I had time, I liked to watch coal-fired locomotives add freight cars on the network of switching tracks, building up long trains for journeys east and west. Meanwhile, passenger trains on their way through made long stops at the terminal so their passengers could dine at the Harvey House while engines replenished coal and water in the rail yards.

Smoke from all of these coal-burning trains, added to the dirt blowing down off the hills, plus the coal dust generated by the mines, couldn't have made downtown Gallup a particularly pleasant place to be at the time. Not so for me, especially when I had opportunities to speak with friendly locals. The one shoemaker in town, an Italian guy, always made me feel welcome in his shop when I dropped off shoes for repair. Also, I liked visiting Frank and Martenita Castello, a Castilian Spanish couple who I believe were my godparents.

Occasionally Mrs. Walters sent me to Frank and Martenita's house for one reason or another, and that was a real eye-opener because Martenita gave me cookies and hugged me. She was a real motherly type, and I loved spending time in her company. Also, my only contact with other children was at Frank and Martenita's. Once in a great while, I was allowed to visit the Castello house long enough to play with the kids, and it was from them that I heard what school was. The couple didn't seem to be friends of the Walters because I never saw them at the Walters' home. The Castellos may have been chosen as my godparents because they were Catholic. I'm guessing that the Walters came to know about Martenita because she worked as a domestic for an acquaintance of theirs.

Years later, on a return visit to Gallup with my wife, we stopped by the shoe repair to say hello. An old man now, the shopkeeper told us that Henry Walters had aspirations for higher political office when I was first taken in by the couple. The shoemaker was certain the Walters wanted to adopt a child so that they could look like a traditional family unit. That was the thinking in town, he said. It would make a nice story, the way the Walters had taken in a poor orphan and made him part of their family. He said that Mr. Walters' aspirations went nowhere, and he suggested that the couple lost interest in me at that point.

The shoemaker's version of events hit home. It definitely fit with my memories of childhood: In public I was always treated decently. Not warmly or kindly, but at least not violently. Listening to the old man's take on the Walters, I realized that the shoemaker had not just been friendly when I had visited his shop, he'd noticed me and thought about me. From what he said, other adults had, too. In a way, it made me feel better. As a child in Gallup I may have felt entirely alone, but there'd been adults who sensed the couple's attitude toward me and viewed my situation with sympathy.

Why didn't anyone step forward to help me? It was a different time and place. There was no such thing as Child Protective Services. In that small town, Mr. Walters was a social powerhouse. In addition to being the mayor, he belonged to various fraternal groups, including the Shriners and the Masons. A "little guy" like the shoemaker—especially a small business owner—would think twice before making any kind of accusation and thereby endangering his own livelihood.

During that same visit to Gallup some twenty or more years on, I learned from another local man that he'd heard long ago from someone that my sister had gone to South America, married, and died there. He couldn't tell me more than that. I didn't know how to begin to check out his story.

• • •

During my years in Gallup I found it an interesting place to be for another reason. My impression the first day I saw Gallup was correct: I'd arrived in Indian country. Gallup was the Indian capital of New Mexico, and Native American people and their culture fascinated me. Many tribes had reservations nearby, including Navajo and Hopi, and most days, Indians could be seen squatting on the sidewalks making their jewelry and selling it to tourists. Also, there were large annual public gatherings in Gallup that drew many different tribes.

On my travels back and forth from the Walters' house on errands, I stopped to watch the men pounding out silver for jewelry and polishing turquoise or the women weaving rugs with vegetable-dyed, hand-made wools that had been sheared off their own animals. The women did the weaving; the men sheared the wool and dyed it. I wasn't bold enough to try talking to Indians as they worked, and besides, I had the impression that few of them spoke English, but they seemed fine with letting me observe.

Indian men wore jeans with big turquoise belts. Navajo and Hopi women dressed in blue or purple blouses and skirts. Both men and women adorned themselves with turquoise and silver necklaces and bracelets. I think the more turquoise jewelry they possessed, the more status they had. Beaded headbands decorated the men's heads, and scarves covered the women's hair, which was piled up underneath, but a few women wore their hair in braids or long and loose. At ceremonials, you'd see men wearing headdresses, moccasins, and leather leggings with bells and feathers that jingled and swished as they danced. The only man who dressed differently was a Gallup medicine man: He dressed more severely in a blue jean shirt and pants, with a simple beaded headband his only decoration. He set up his bench on a downtown sidewalk and put out pots and bags of herbs to dispense remedies. White people as well as Native Americans bought from him.

Indian ceremonial grounds perched on a rise above the commercial side of town in a flat area encompassing two or three acres. Tribes gathered there once a year for ceremonials that lasted several days. Everybody in town attended, so I went with the Walters. Mr. Walters was an Indian agent, meaning that he was a federal representative who was supposed to look out for the welfare of Native Americans in his designated area—to see that they were fed, educated, and, if possible, employed. Agents were also supposed to keep a census on the Indians and be involved in development of the economic resources on their lands. As a result, Mr. Walters' attendance was definitely expected at the annual Indian gatherings. Bringing me on their outings to these events was an exception to the way the Walters usually treated me—a fortunate one, because it gave me an informal education about Indians and their ways.

At the annual gatherings we watched the rituals of the Hopi, Navajo, Zuni, Walapi, Havasupi, and others. Each tribe had its own dances and rituals. The Navajo and Hopi danced every night wearing their full regalia. Another attraction was Navajo sand paintings. You talk about marvelous skill and beautiful paintings. The Indian artists would take sand in their hands and let it trickle out to create patterns. There wasn't a vast array of colors, but the hues were utilized in ways that were intricate and artistic. They didn't add pigments to the sand to tint it; instead, Navajo artists sought out stones of different colors and ground them to create a palette in black, grey, white, rust red, brown, tan, and yellow ochre. Each sand pattern had a unique meaning. Every night the artists destroyed their paintings and every day created new ones. It seemed a shame to destroy these works of art, but the Navajos wanted to invoke different spirits with each day's pattern. As I took in these different forms of art and culture, I came to greatly admire the Indians.

Maybe ten thousand Indians showed up and camped outside town for the annual gatherings in Gallup. Others camped out on the sidewalks, and some passed out drunk there. The city fathers didn't complain because the gathering brought big business to town. For Gallup, the multi-tribe event was like the World's Fair. Adding to the festivities, cowboys showed up to hold rodeos.

Gradually life at the Walters' house got worse. Mr. Walters continued to be gone for days at a time, and when no one else was there except for me, something very strange happened with Mrs. Walters.

Strange is too mild a word. Evil is what she was.

Until very recently I haven't talked to anyone about this, not even to my wife of sixty-five years. What happened with Eleanor Walters so revolted me that I didn't want to speak of it. But, as hard as it is to talk about, I think what happened with her is an important part of my story. Mrs. Walters demanded that I pleasure her with my tongue. You can imagine how disgusting that was to a little boy. Mrs. Walters made me afraid of sex.

I don't think Mr. Walters ever knew what his wife was doing. If he did, he didn't let on. And I wasn't going to tell him, as scared of him as I was.

At first Mrs. Walters was subtle. She'd leave the bathroom door open when she was ready to bathe. From the tub, she'd call me to bring her this or that—another towel or a bar of soap that was out of her reach. Or she'd yell for me to come shut the window in the bathroom because there was too much of a breeze. I did as she said, but she'd shriek when I entered the bathroom as if I was an intruder. It did feel like I was at fault, like I was guilty of something. It seemed wrong to see an adult naked.

I didn't know what to do. Mrs. Walters had told me to help her, and I'd done what she'd asked. I tried to avert my eyes elsewhere in the bathroom, away from the tub to the sink or the toilet or the window or anywhere else but her. Still, it was impossible not to glance at Mrs. Walters after a while, because she kept me in the room with her, talking to me. I was frozen with fear but also curious, observing the differences between her adult female body and my childish one.

Then she'd say, "As long as you're here, wash my back." So my eyes landed on her body and I had to look. Mrs. Walters had grey hair, but without her clothes she looked like a younger woman. Sometimes she called me to the bathroom when she wasn't in the tub yet and was standing there totally naked. At the sight of her complete nakedness, I wanted more than ever to run from the room, but I knew I better not. Either choice, staying or going, could bring terrible repercussions.

Always I dreaded what might happen next. Would she turn the situation on me and accuse me unfairly the way she did at other times? What if she reported to Mr. Walters that I'd come bursting into the bathroom? That was a huge anxiety. Our time in the bathroom was made to seem even more dangerous when she warned me not to discuss this with anyone, or I would be in *a lot of trouble.*

After a number of experiences like this, Mrs. Walters told me to disrobe because I was going to bathe next. She waited until I was undressed to tell me to wash her back. Time went by and these episodes continued. Then she ordered me to wash her front. Then she took to ordering me into the tub with her.

After I sat down in the tub facing her, Mrs. Walters reached over to rub my penis with her fingers or a washcloth. She rubbed me over and over. If my penis became erect, she'd shriek, "Look at you! You're disgusting!" Now I understand that it was her intent to get me aroused, but then I didn't understand, I only felt evil and disgusting.

Finally Eleanor Walters came to the other thing, which so revulsed me that I will never forget it. The first time it happened, she was washing dishes in the kitchen. "Get over here, you little son of a bitch," she ordered. I may have been seven or eight. She lifted her skirt in front, put it right over me, and instructed me what to do with my tongue. I couldn't believe this was happening. I fought to get away, but she held me in place.

"Beg for it!" she said. "Let me hear you!"

I was sick. She had a strong grip and she had me trapped. The smell of her was intense. She didn't bathe more than once a week, and the area between her legs smelled bad.

I tried to get away, but she held my shoulders and repeated her demands. I screamed and cried. She slapped at me with one hand and held tight with the other. I did what she instructed. I will never forget the odor. "Beg for it!" she told me. "You little cuntlapper, beg for it." She didn't let go until I begged for it.

Then she released me from under her skirt. "You little son of a bitch," she said, "if you ever say anything about this to anybody, you'll get worse than this."

As time went by, Mrs. Walters made her demand of me again and again in various rooms of the house. This, more than anything, was why I tried to escape the Walters as often as I could. It's possible that I could have taken the whippings, but the sexual part was more than I could bear.

Were you wounded?

In a photo taken in Japan shortly after Emperor Hirohito's surrender, William stands in a doorway between two buddies, an arm slung over each. His slouchy, almost joking pose betrays confidence, even a certain cockiness. At the same time, William is still an awkward boy turning to man, his skinny frame and very long legs obvious beneath high-waisted pants.

The picture was taken on the Japanese home island of Kyushu shortly after William and other Marines landed in Nagasaki and then traveled to the city of Miyazaki on the same island. Their assignment was to receive and destroy weapons from returning enemy soldiers and to administer city affairs from the one nonresidential building spared by Allied bombers.

Fluent in Japanese, William was given translation work in Miyazaki. Daily he crafted communications to Miyazaki residents alongside a bright and attractive young woman named Sadako, who became a good friend, but there was also a second woman translator, Meiko, employed at their headquarters as an interpreter for one of the other officers.

Despite his new, almost brash self-assurance, William was unfailingly polite with the two women. In fact, this will be his approach with women for the rest of his life. It drew them to him immediately, this careful respectfulness, as well as an emerging adult handsomeness that he never recognized in himself.

Many of Miyazaki's women gained a certain impression of American men. It was hard not to. American soldiers had to be discouraged from visiting Miyazaki brothels. All week long Marines worked at the nearby racetrack taking weapons from the surrendering Kwantung Army returning from Manchuria, and as soon as they had a day of liberty, many headed straight for the local girls, whether experienced or innocent.

Several times William walked Meiko home from work. She may have agreed to let him do this because of his good manners at the office. Or maybe she didn't feel she could turn down his offer because he was a member of the occupying force that employed her and thanks to which she and her family were able to eat better than most others in devastated Japan.

Privately Meiko must have wondered why William didn't make any overtures.

One evening as they reached her house she paused, turned to twenty-year-old William, and asked, "Were you wounded in the war?"

It took a minute or two for Meiko's meaning to dawn on him.

The young woman had touched on what he never confided to anyone. Not the type of injury that she assumed, but something else from long ago. Sexual behavior was the furthest thing from his mind. He didn't feel attracted to her or to Sadako, with whom he spent far more time. William never felt sexual attraction to anyone. Not that he was aware. That kind of impulse was buried deep. It didn't have a snowball's chance in hell of stirring.

In William's ideal future he imagined marriage. He wanted to believe there could be love and affection, but beyond that, fear lurked.

CHAPTER THREE

The Runaway

I did commit a major crime repeatedly during the time I lived with the Walters: I ran away. To me this was not a criminal act—it was a survival tactic. The Walters' behavior went unchecked by anyone. It came down to me to protect myself.

Chances are the Walters told their friends and associates that I was incorrigible and ungrateful. News about my escapes had to be common knowledge since I ran away so much. Mrs. Miksch was consistently cold toward me when she occasionally came to the house and when we visited her home, and this had to be why. I tried my utmost to avoid the Walters' wrath, but good behavior didn't make any difference. Never did I talk back or get snippy with the couple; my goal was to try to be perfect and appear compliant. Sometimes they accused me of having a sullen look on my face, and I suppose that could be true. But if anger showed in my eyes, that was a slip on my part, because I knew the results if surliness was detected. However, I did run, and that was not a slip.

The first time I tried to run away, I wasn't more than six or seven. I was too young to understand that people wouldn't give a child as small as me a lift down the road. Jumping a train out of town wasn't easy for someone my size either. I made my first attempt when the Walters sent me to town to get something and I just kept going, figuring it would be an hour or more before the couple came looking for me. There was a wonderful feeling of exhilaration at getting away—plus fear about being caught.

In between escape attempts, I secretly mulled over what I'd like to do to Mr. and Mrs. Walters. I hated her more than I did him because she revolted me in so many ways. I pictured myself shooting them and every other form of retribution. There were guns in the house, but Mr. Walters never taught me anything about using them, so my revenge fantasies remained just that—daydreams that helped me feel a bit better.

My first few getaway attempts were over almost as soon as they began. People refused to help. After a few tries, I gave up for a while, maybe as long as a year, so for a short period an outsider might have viewed me as a dutiful boy in every possible way.

It may seem surprising, but leaving me on my own did not appear to worry the Walters. In the weeks after Marian's disappearance, being home alone became part of my training. I was instructed never to leave my room while the Walters were gone and definitely not to answer the front door. I was well aware of the punishment if I disobeyed.

The Walters home was relatively isolated, with neighboring houses distant from one another in the Gallup hills. The climb from downtown up to the Walters' house was long and steep, so the couple made the trip back and forth only by car. Repeating that route over and over on foot for errands helped me develop strong legs, another plus for a life on the road, but that didn't necessarily make it easier to flee if left alone. Success depended on knowing how long the Walters would be gone. There was no point in heading downhill if they could spot me as they drove up.

One disadvantage of the Walters' location—and a considerable one—was the distance from their house to the highway out of town or to the railroad. That's not to say I never tried running away during the day. If I was sent on multiple errands that might take a few hours and place me downtown, those few hours could give me a good head start, and I might try. Even in this, timing was everything. I was more likely to bolt on the spur of the moment if a freight train was about to leave Gallup just as I arrived downtown. Or, if I was in a lot of trouble and awaiting Mr. Walters' return home, I might risk discovery by taking the slower route and putting my thumb out as I walked along the highway out of town.

Near the Gallup rail station, I observed the way hobos jumped onto freights along the tracks a short distance from the depot, where there were fewer odds of being apprehended. They timed their boarding for when a train was still moving slowly. I looked and learned but was too small to hop a moving freight car by myself, which meant I had to scramble aboard while a train was stopped at the station. I slipped into an open boxcar or climbed up to ride the small platforms between cars. Nearly always I was caught in short order by a brakeman making his rounds. If a boxcar door was left ajar, a brakeman going from car to car would peer inside. During my early attempts, I didn't have the good sense to hide myself under packing materials left behind inside a car. If I perched on the small outside ledge at the end of a car I also remained clearly visible. Within a couple of years, however, I was smarter and bigger and could successfully travel by train as far away as Grants, New Mexico, and Winslow, Arizona, where I stayed for as much as a week or two doing small jobs for locals before someone discovered I was a runaway and sent me back to Gallup.

During longer escapes, I was able to get by earning food or a few cents by feeding chickens, hogs, and cows on ranches or farms—any chores within reason that a little kid could do. There were lots of odd jobs. Say they mowed a wheat field, I'd take a rake and gather up the residue. I learned that it was a time of shortages, and no one wanted to throw away food.

The majority of times during my earliest escapes, my youth and my solitude drew attention, so the police apprehended me and returned me to the Walters. Most children were in school, so I stood out as an obvious runaway in daylight hours whether in Gallup or elsewhere. Back then, the police didn't have any pity for kids on the run. Their attitude was, "If you'd manage to behave yourself, you wouldn't get into trouble with your folks." Policemen were never too gentle in their handling of me. The fact that Mr. Walters was a major player in town politics contributed to the attitude of Gallup's cops.

On occasions when I did successfully reach the highway out of Gallup without being stopped, I hoped my young age would garner sympathy from a stranger driving down the road. However, my early attempts were doomed to failure. Drivers asked, "What's a kid your age doing out here?" Some said the same thing as the police: Behave yourself, and you won't have trouble. Others didn't seem to mind that I was a runaway; they were sympathetic, or at least didn't reprimand me, but they didn't want to get in trouble with law enforcement by aiding and abetting a runaway.

A prostitute in Gallup picked me up during one of my flights. I was sitting on a curb downtown crying over a recent incident at the Walters', and she came out of the hotel or wherever it was she worked and inquired as to my condition. She was an older woman, maybe forty, and was very nice to me. We went to a restaurant and she bought me a meal. The only reason I knew this woman was a prostitute was I'd been told prostitutes were known to hang out in houses of ill repute next to the railroad tracks at that end of town. I may not have understood what a prostitute was, but I could tell from the

Walters' tone of voice that it wasn't good. After the restaurant, she took me upstairs to the floor where she worked. All the other women giggled because she had a little kid in tow. During our short time together the woman was considerate and protective, but she did in the end turn me over to the police. Like all the other adults who brought me to the police, she thought it was the correct thing to do. Still, she was one of only a few people who showed empathy toward me.

The prostitute's kindness was confusing. How could a "bad" person be so kind, and how could "good" people like the Walters be so mean? I may have been young, but the contrast in behavior was apparent. The Walters were the people who were supposed to take care of me and be decent to me, but they had turned my life upside down with their cruelty. Here was someone they said was sinful, and she seemed decent and caring. My bewilderment led me to question what *God-fearing* meant. That term was thrown around a lot back then, including by the police: "If you were any kind of God-fearing boy, you'd stay home and keep out of trouble." The term came to mean nothing to me. What mattered was people's actions and how they revealed themselves.

It's hard to believe that the word *God-fearing* held much meaning for the Walters. They didn't go to church often, but they made a big deal of it when they did attend. We had to be dressed to the nines, and the Walters had to greet the minister and all of the locals in attendance. "Here's William," they would say warmly to whomever. They made it clear I was an orphan they'd taken in. The other churchgoers would tell me, "You should be so grateful that you were taken in by these wonderful people."

In spite of whatever else I think about them, I have to say that the Walters showed a certain amount of respect for my religious background. They were not Catholics, but they had my godparents, the Castellos, take me at the age of eight to

the Catholic church in Gallup to have me baptized. I assume
this was because the Walters were informed by the Orphan
Train people that I was born Catholic and for some reason
not baptized shortly after my birth.

Each time I ran from the Walters, I learned something new.
Almost immediately I picked up an important lesson about
where not to go. One night I slipped away from the house,
made some good distance down the road, and spotted an
irrigation canal. The banks of the canal seemed a good place
to curl up and get some sleep. This was a huge mistake.
Mosquitoes descended in swarms to eat me alive. To this day
I can hear the sound of them, their whine turning into a roar. I
was bitten so many times I became swollen all over. I lay there
in misery asking myself if I wanted to return to the house
and take the beatings and Mrs. Walters' evil demands, or if I
wanted to be a feast for mosquitoes. I found my way back.

Soon I learned to never go through the center of towns,
where people might wonder about a young kid on his own. I
avoided eye contact with adults because this might make me
seem worried. If I was lucky enough to arrive in another town,
I tried to blend in with the community. My prepared story was
that I'd become stranded while away from home and needed
to get back to our farm, which was about ten or fifteen miles
outside town. If I was successful in making a jump down the
road, I used a similar story to look for a lift to the next place.
The tactic of shorter hops was safer than putting my thumb
out and asking for a ride to Winslow, a few hundred miles
away; at my tender age, that would identify me as a runaway.

If you saw the country around Gallup, you might wonder how I survived there on short hops. The landscape looks
like endless miles of flat desert covered with sage and rabbit

bush, but as you move through it, you discover the land is gently undulating. You can't see what's just up ahead until you get there. A building comes as a relief, or even a single tree. The wind is almost constant, a thin whistling sound. And yet I liked it. The blue sky came down to the horizon almost entirely around me. There was a feeling of serenity. Cows survived there, and so could I. On ranches that popped up here and there I found work.

As I hitched rides, avoiding molestation became a sixth sense. I'd say one out of nine or ten drivers made an overture. There was almost a routine. They'd start out talking friendly, and the next thing was a hand on my knee and "You know, you're a good-looking young fellow." Depending on how urgent the situation seemed, I'd say, "Oh, I forgot something. Why don't you let me out here," or a flat-out, "Let me out here!" I can say that I never had to fight anyone off. It usually wasn't overt at first, so I had time to get the picture and didn't have to outright accuse anyone. Most drivers acted as if they better approach the thing carefully, to see if you were willing, because they didn't want to be reported to the authorities.

Following each escape attempt, there was a beating and I was deprived of an evening meal or two. The Walters said that if I liked being outdoors so much, I could stay outside overnight. They also reminded me that they had taken me in when I had no one else in the world—that they had provided for me, and that I was ungrateful.

While being beaten, I always told myself there'd come a day when this would never happen again. That no one would hurt me anymore. That I would escape. I don't know who I thought I could run to, young as I was, but the idea of freedom was strong in me. It kept me going. On the one hand, I was the little boy who grabbed on to Mrs. Walters trying to placate her and make her like me, and on the other, something inside told me to run, run, run.

Without warning, one day we moved from the nice stucco house on the right side of the tracks to a home in a lesser neighborhood. The Depression may have hit the Walters hard enough to cause the move, but money never felt like a major problem in our daily lives because we continued to eat well, Mrs. Walters signed me up for dance lessons, and apart from not having hired help, life continued on as before.

The new house was situated on a dirt road in the hills on the other side of the valley. In the new location, instead of seeing distant homes and surrounding hills, we had a vantage point on mostly the industrial and commercial side of the city and Gallup's rail yards. To my eye the new location wasn't shabby, but it wasn't the "in" place to live, like the previous neighborhood. The lot was about a half-block in size and sharply inclined, with the wood-frame house built on a couple of levels. Unlike the Walters' other home, there were no sidewalks on the street and no landscaping in the yard apart from a hedge—only dirt, rocks, and weeds. Mrs. Walters liked to sit on the front porch in a chair swing where she could watch the street and the view below. If she was sitting on the porch swing, I could sit on the porch steps, neither of us talking.

A balcony jutted out from the second floor at the back of the house, and Waggs liked to rest underneath it to escape the weather day or night. On evenings that I was beaten and thrown naked outdoors, I joined him under the balcony, glad for his warmth in cold weather and for his company any time of year. Down at that level of the house was a cellar where food was stored, so if he and I were able to get inside the cellar to rest on the dirt floor in the hot season, it was a cool refuge for us.

The cellar had cement walls and wood beams that ran across the ceiling. The Walters stored potatoes and vegetables there, which kept a long time in the cold, dark space. Apple cider was also stashed in the cellar, and the unfiltered juice was allowed to ferment and turn to hard cider. On occasion I was allowed to drink cider in its nonalcoholic form; it tasted quite good. One of my chores was to retrieve items from the cellar, which was reached by going out the kitchen door and onto the balcony, then down a tall stairway to the ground and around the corner of the house—or by going out the front door and around the house and down the hill.

The lot was so steep that the posts supporting the back balcony were about twenty feet high. One night Mr. Walters drove home with a number of drinks under his belt. He rounded the driveway to park in a space down behind the house but went crashing right into the posts. The noise woke me. I jumped out of bed and scrambled outside to see what had happened. The posts had collapsed, leaving the balcony hanging at a crazy angle. Mr. Walters was staggering around looking knockdown drunk but was otherwise okay. My instinctive response was dread, thinking I might get blamed and whipped for this situation, like all the other things I hadn't done. It was a relief when I was able to return to bed and fall asleep without further incident.

In between attempts to flee, I continued to try for the best behavior possible. Increasingly I was given literature to memorize, usually with a deadline. This was a task I believed I did well, because I could commit material quickly to memory, but it seemed like the faster I learned the text, the shorter the next deadline, as if Mrs. Walters was trying to test the limits of my ability. And no matter what, there was criticism and punishment. "The Chambered Nautilus," Psalm 19—I absorbed these and repeated them back precisely, I thought. However, at times I mispronounced words, and more often I didn't recite with the proper emotion. The material was assigned without any briefing from Mrs. Walters. Walt Whitman's "O Captain! My Captain!" was a poem written in reaction to the death of President Lincoln, but I had no idea. During a visit to Mrs. Miksch, Mrs. Walters called on me to recite Whitman's poem, but I didn't display the appropriate sorrow and anguish. I finished and she said, "You stupid kid, you don't even understand what you're talking about!" It was true, I didn't.

A particular poem Mrs. Walters had me recite seemed to be about me. That one I comprehended. It had the feel of my life at the time:

The Preacher's Boy

I rickollect the little tad, back, years and years ago—
"The Preacher's Boy" that every one despised and hated so!
A meek-faced little feller, with white eyes and foxy hair,
And a look like he expected ser'ous trouble everywhere:
A sort o' fixed expression of suspicion in his glance;
His bare-feet always scratched with briers; and green stains on his pants;
Molasses-marks along his sleeves; his cap-rim turned behind—
And so it is "The Preacher's Boy" is brought again to mind!

My fancy even brings the sly marauder back so plain,
I see him jump our garden-fence and slip off down the lane;
And I seem to holler at him and git back the old reply:
"Oh, no: your peaches is too green fer such a worm as I!"
Fer he scorned his father's phrases—every holy one he had—
"As good a man," folks put it, "as that boy of his was bad!"
And again from their old buggy-shed, I hear the "rod unspared"—
Of course that never "spoiled the child" for which nobody cared!

If any neighbor ever found his gate without a latch,
Or rines around the edges of his watermelon-patch;
His pasture-bars left open; or his pump-spout chocked with clay,
He'd swear 'twas "that infernal Preacher's Boy," right away!
When strings was stretched acrost the street at night, and some one got
An everlastin' tumble, and his nose broke, like as not,
And laid it on "The Preacher's Boy"—no powers, low ner high,
Could ever quite substantiate that boy's alibi!

And did *nobody* like the boy?—Well, all the *pets* in town
Would eat out of his fingers; and canaries would come down
And leave their swingin' perches and their fish-bone jist to pick
The little warty knuckles that the dogs would leap to lick—
No little snarlin', snappin' fiste but what would leave his bone
To foller, ef *he* whistled, in that tantalizin' tone
That made the goods-box whittler blasphemeusly protest
"He couldn't tell, 'twixt dog and boy, which one was ornriest!"

'Twas such a little cur as this, onc't, when the crowd was thick
Along the streets, a drunken corner-loafer tried to kick,
When a sudden foot behind him tripped him up, and falling so
He "marked his man," and jerked his gun—drawed up and let 'er go!
And the crowd swarmed round the victim—holding close against his breast
The little dog unharmed, in arms that still, as they caressed,
Grew rigid in their last embrace, as with a smile of joy
He recognized the dog was saved. So died "The Preacher's Boy"!

When it appeared, before the Squire, that fatal pistolball
Was fired at "a dangerous beast," and not the boy at all,
And the facts set forth established,—it was like-befittin' then
To order out a possy of the "city councilmen"
To kill *the dog!* But, strange to tell, they searched the country round,
And never hide-ner-hair of that "said" dog was ever found!
And, somehow, *then* I sorto' thought—and half-way think, *to-day*—
The spirit of "The Preacher's Boy" had whistled him away.

> —James Whitcomb Riley,
> *The Works of James Whitcomb Riley,*
> Volume 5: *Rhymes of Childhood*

I doubt that Mrs. Walters and I understood the poem in the same way. As far as I could see, the boy in the poem was reviled unfairly. His facial expression was thought to be nasty, his clothing was never clean enough, he was seen as sly and untrustworthy. You're not told that the boy has done the hateful things he's accused of. People assume he's done them because that's just the way he is—that he's as bad as his preacher father is good. He and I were the kid that nobody cared about, except for the little dog. The dog understood that he was good and lovable. Just like me and Waggs. The poem talked about outward appearances. To the rest of the world, the Walters appeared to be the good ones, and I was the ingrate. The poet understood my plight, and this provided some comfort. I think I read this one with expression.

To me, the whole performance thing seemed like a kind of joke. If the occasional guest was due to arrive, the Walters sent me to my room to change into my white sailor suit and stay hidden until the right dramatic moment. Then, when they were ready, they called me out to perform. After the dance lessons started, I was told to dance for their guests as well as recite. This was mortifying because I was not very coordinated. My dancing embarrassed the Walters, too, because I was beaten for my missteps as well as faulty recitations.

When I was about eight or nine, Mr. Walters' term as mayor of Gallup ended and we moved again, this time to Winslow, Arizona. Of course they didn't explain the reason for our move. Why Winslow, I'll never know. The city was hotter than hell, flat as a board. The Walters often returned to Gallup by train, about a four-hour trip one way, I think, owing to the many stops along the route. Regular visits to Gallup might have been required by Mr. Walters' work as an Indian agent.

Mrs. Walters continued to take me for dance lessons in Gallup, which seems remarkable given my lack of talent, but then parking me at dance class gave her the advantage of time alone to visit Mrs. Miksch.

Winslow did possess one major attraction: a beautiful Fred Harvey luxury hotel and restaurant called La Posada, which I now know was the last of architect Mary Colter's masterpieces. The station looked like a magnificent Spanish hacienda and was intended to honor Winslow's status as headquarters for the Santa Fe Railway, the company that commissioned the Harvey hotels.

However, there was little in Winslow that I could enjoy. Again, the Walters didn't enroll me in school. A number of miles from town, a huge meteorite had long ago crashed into the desert, and, surprisingly, I was allowed to make my way out there to see the crater a couple of times. Since I had no information that could help me understand and appreciate the crater, it quickly lost its appeal. Back then, the huge bowl in the earth was not an established landmark, and I don't think there was even an access road. Today there's a visitor center and observation trails for Meteor Crater, and it's definitely worth seeing, a gargantuan depression about three-quarters of a mile from rim to rim and 550 feet deep.

The Walters' mistreatment of me let up a bit in Winslow. I had the freedom to wander in and near our new town, and while Mr. Walters still beat me, the whippings weren't constant like they'd been in Gallup. But when Mr. Walters was away, Mrs. Walters never let up on her sexual demands and her threats.

One good thing about Winslow was that I was able to have more contact with other children. We didn't become close friends, probably because I didn't attend school and seemed like an outsider. Still, a group of kids let me hang out with them at times. About five miles outside town was a place named Ruby Hill where two other boys and I went to collect the red stones that gave the hill its name. The stones we gathered were actually garnets, not rubies, but we liked to think we were collecting valuable gems. I also enjoyed hiking with the group to a reservoir created from an artesian well, although one night they sent me off to look for something and ran off, leaving me alone in the dark.

In Winslow there was an incident with a snake that gave me a different sort of glimpse into Mrs. Walters' character. We were both on the front porch of the Winslow house when I picked up what looked like a small, light beige, braided cord. It was a rattlesnake. I must have gasped when I realized what it was. In a cool voice, Mrs. Walters told me not to let go. Without another word, she went into the house. I did as she said. The little snake thrashed back and forth, but I had picked it up right near the head, which kept it from biting me, and when it twisted its tail up, I held it out from my body. I was shaking while I waited for Mrs. Walters to return, especially since baby rattlesnakes were supposed to be the most deadly. It seemed like forever before she reappeared with a shotgun. Mrs. Walters raised the gun at me and said, "When I tell you to let go, drop it." I held steady as best I could. She gave the order, I let go, and she blasted the rattler. She was a good shot. At that moment, and that moment only, I actually felt admiration for her. I guess you could say she was an example of a tough, western pioneer woman. She was capable of making a snap decision, handling danger, and disposing of a threat. What was also clear at that moment was her confidence about the control she had over me, believing that I wouldn't let go of that snake.

A confrontation in Winslow strengthened my resolve to break away. The boy who delivered our newspaper was a much bigger kid, about sixteen or seventeen to my eight or nine years, and he liked to torment me. If I stepped out into the front yard to take the paper from him, he liked to slap me with it or begin to hand over the paper and then snatch it back. Or, if he saw me coming, he might throw the paper to the opposite end of the yard to make me chase it. Finally, one day I threw a rock and hit him. He reported this to the Walters, and their response was to hold me so the fellow could beat me with his fists. During the pounding the Walters told me this would make a man out of me.

I had to take the blows, but I imagined a fairer fight, with me hitting back. Someday that's how it would be. From hanging out with other kids, I knew I was large for my age. I promised myself there'd come a time when I'd escape the Walters and be able to stick up for myself. A bigger, more powerful version of me would land lots of punches before another person inflicted damage.

It had taken a while for this resolve to develop. You get slapped around enough, and finally there's this transition where you decide you won't let it happen anymore once you're able. First I'd get away from the Walters, and, as soon as I was bigger and stronger, I'd never let anyone bully me again.

Meanwhile, in Winslow, an adult stepped forward to defend me. In the five years or so I spent with the Walters, this was the only time anyone interfered to protect me from the couple. It didn't go well for the man. Mr. Walters and I were both out in the yard while I was doing chores, either watering or trimming back a hedge. I did something that displeased Mr. Walters, and he began to smack me about the head. A neighbor in a nearby yard saw this and came over to intervene. Mr. Walters punched the man in the face and knocked him out. The man never tried to help me again.

It's not hard to guess what the neighbor was thinking after that. If he thought about reporting the incident to the police, he might have figured he'd get nowhere with it. I was the only witness; his claim would have been hard to prove. My fear of Mr. Walters had to be obvious, leading the neighbor to reckon I wouldn't dare back up his story. Or maybe it was enough for the man to have been knocked out cold, and that ended the matter.

The chip on your shoulder

He sensed in her a warmth, a sweetness. Her oval face at rest was serious, her dark eyes penetrating, but she liked to smile, and on the rare occasions when she had criticism to deliver, her tone was surprisingly gentle. At the same time, this short, dark-eyed girl could be strong and bold. The mere fact that she often left her protected neighborhood to pal around with the guys in William's neighborhood showed daring.

After high school each day, she worked in a factory that made sausage casings. The things she liked best about the job were that she got to wear oversized rubber boots, since the floors were hosed down constantly, and she got to buy buckets of beer from a nearby bar for the other factory workers. Underage kids could buy beer at bars in those times, no questions asked. She liked to tromp through the streets to the bar in her big boots. William sensed that the guys at the factory would have strangled you if you'd done anything to harm her.

It was such an odd thing about the girl that she loved that job. One more thing to endear her to him.

Sweetness combined with spunk. Just the right combination in a wife, as far as he was concerned, because events over his twenty-plus years had made him crave warmth and affection but also forced him to be tough and independent. Besides, he found her beautiful.

The question was, would she have him?

It was a long shot. They'd never kissed. They'd never even held hands.

The right moment arrived, catching him off guard. The opportunity thrust him past fear of rejection to action.

He asked if she was willing to marry him. He held his breath.

"Yes," she said, "but you'll have to get rid of that chip on your shoulder."

That chip had taken years to acquire and perfect. It was part of his armor, his defense against attack. You didn't wait for assault; you thwarted it in advance. The key to success in a dangerous world. He couldn't have survived without it.

For her, he would do it. She was going to be his everything.

CHAPTER FOUR

Boys Town

I was nine years old and sitting by the fireplace with Mr. Walters at our home in Winslow. I believe he'd been drinking. Mr. Walters asked me something, and, as had happened many times before, he decided that I didn't respond fast enough. Whatever he asked is long forgotten, but I recall what Mr. Walters said next: "I'll teach you to answer me." There was a horse quirt in his hand, and he smacked me across the face with it real fast. Without thinking, I grabbed a nearby fireplace poker and hit him over the head, knocking him out.

I don't know what possessed me to strike back. It could have been the slash of pain directly across my face. There was no sitting still for it. The beatings, okay. I lived in a tough world where a common child-rearing approach was spare the rod, spoil the child. But lashing me across the face was beyond the pale. In that instant, I was pushed to outright rage. I'd always thought Mr. Walters might kill me at some point. When the quirt lashed my face, my response was instinctive. You could say I got my macho, my whatever. I had never raised a hand to the man prior to this. At nine I may have been big for my age, but Mr. Walters was still a lot larger than I was. In spite of fantasies about revenge, one thing I had not dreamed of was hitting Mr. Walters with the fireplace poker.

I believed that someday I'd be able to stick up for myself, but not there, not then, not in that house against that large man and his terrifying wife. I looked at Mr. Walters on the floor and was scared witless at my unmitigated gall. Mrs. Walters came screaming and hollering, and I cowered back, saying nothing. Then Mr. Walters came to.

They didn't lay a hand on me, except to rush me to my bedroom. They locked me in, and I stayed there for a day or two until they could bring me before the local justice of the peace. Meals were left at my door, and I had to use a bedpan. I was scared to death. In the courtroom, I sat in a daze before the JP and heard him sentence me to a home for incorrigible boys. Mr. Walters then took me east by train. There were few words spoken. I imagined we were heading for a reform school and it would be a kind of prison.

In Omaha, Nebraska, we disembarked and rode a bus ten miles out the Lincoln Highway to Boys Town, which was run by Father Edward J. Flanagan. I had no idea what Boys Town was. The fact that it was so far out of town reinforced my idea that it was a prison—that and the fact I'd been sentenced there. In retrospect, my eighteen-month sentence seems strange, because I learned boys usually were sent to Boys Town to stay until they were adults and not for limited periods of time. My sentence had to have been specially arranged with Father Flanagan, possibly by the JP.

After we reached our destination, my fright began to ease up. I quickly learned that all kinds of boys were sent to Boys Town, not just those convicted of crimes or labeled too difficult to control by their families. Many boys were sent simply because they were homeless.

When I stepped away from Henry Walters that first night, I was sent directly to a dormitory, escorted by an older boy who told me not to worry, everything would be okay. Boys Town had boys called "cops and guides," and he was one of these. The next morning another guide took me on an orientation tour. From the outset he made it clear no one would hurt me. He said all the boys were treated with respect. This was quite a revelation.

My panic let up, but it took longer to feel entirely safe. Gradually I saw for myself how the boys were treated, and everybody was friendly and willing to help me in any way they could. There were no indications that the boys were ever beaten.

This complete reversal of reality confounded and thrilled me. I'd been right to believe my life would get better someday. This was the place I'd been running to, even though I hadn't known it existed.

New experiences came along one after the other. When I turned ten, it was the first time I could recall my birthday being celebrated. The fathers and nuns recognized birthdays at dinnertime by bringing you a piece of cake with a candle on it, and all of the boys sang "Happy Birthday." I was able to attend school for the first time, which I found exciting. I had to catch up with other boys my age, but I got ahead real fast, shifting from classroom to classroom as I learned. My performance in class was praised, which caught me by surprise, and no one made me feel bad about starting out in classes with the younger boys. Since the Walters had provided me with picture books about Greek myths and jigsaw puzzles of the U.S. and the world, I did arrive at Boys Town with some knowledge of geography and Greek mythology as well as some poetry and Bible verses, and that helped.

As much as I liked attending school at Boys Town, I didn't graduate from eighth grade or high school because I wasn't there long enough.

Boys Town was a relatively new institution. The property was a farm when Father Flanagan purchased the land in 1921, and by the time I arrived, about 1935, at least a few hundred boys lived there. Prior to founding Boys Town, Father Flanagan had created what he called The Workingmen's Hotel in Omaha, which took in older men who were homeless and provided them with shelter. That's where he got the idea for Boys Town. Start at the source, he figured, before boys grew to men in that condition. Today the Nebraska Boys Town is a huge place, a city practically, and there are other Boys Towns in multiple locations across the nation. Now they take in girls as well and even whole families.

There were only a few buildings when I arrived: a main building, two small residences for the staff, and a separate house for Father Flanagan well away from the village proper. During my stay they began construction on a new chapel thanks to money donated by Miss Mary Dowd of New York; it was a separate, Gothic-style building that was quite large and would become the most imposing building in the whole establishment.

Everything for the boys was encompassed in the main building, which had multiple floors. In the basement was a mess hall, the first floor housed offices, on the next several floors were classrooms, and on the top floor was a dormitory. The teachers were Irish Christian Brothers who wore robes that made them look like Catholic priests, but they were full-time, lay educators rather than priests. The Brothers were very good teachers and very strict. A small house provided separate living quarters for them, and another housed a laundry and the nuns who taught the lower grades at Boys Town and also did housekeeping. One of my duties was to work with a few of the nuns in the laundry.

A child did not have to be Catholic to live at Boys Town. Every denomination could be found there. Father Flanagan, being in his right mind, which not all priests were, did his best to provide services for whatever religions were represented, whether Jewish or Protestant.

When I came to live there, they were just beginning to construct separate apartment buildings for the boys. This building plan went into full swing after the release of the 1938 movie *Boys Town* starring Spencer Tracy and Mickey Rooney, which drew much attention and a lot of financial support for Father Flanagan's efforts. Before I left, I was able to live in one of the new residences. Each single-story brick building held four apartments accessible by a central hallway. The equivalent of a family lived in each apartment: an older boy, a middle-range youth, and a number of younger kids, with the older taking care of the younger. Some of the boys who lived there were actually young men—some as old as twenty-one or twenty-two—so there was quite a range of ages. It surprised me that boys like me who had never been to school before this could be designated as father figures for the family groupings. Father Flanagan was quite enlightened for his time.

Father Flanagan didn't want boys going outdoors in the severe Nebraska winters, so he arranged for construction of underground tunnels to connect the apartment buildings with the main building. This was another example of his unique thinking in that day and age.

I became close to Father Flanagan and even traveled with him at times when he performed Sunday services nearby or made other appearances locally. He was quite a guy—a good human being and an unusual adult. For instance, he and I were playing ping-pong one time when he was approached and interrupted by a businessman visiting from Omaha. Father Flanagan told the businessman he'd have to wait until our game was finished. "The kid comes first," he said.

A big, strong man, Father Flanagan had been a handball champ at college back in Ireland and was a boxing fan, but he didn't believe in corporal punishment and was usually a gentle soul. Still, he could be strict and had a temper. One chilly evening I was supposed to go somewhere with him, and when I showed up, he told me to go back and get a coat or a sweater. I disputed the point with him and got cuffed on the side of the head. That episode taught me to follow his instructions without question. Still, he immediately apologized for giving me that light blow and said he was sorry he let his temper get the best of him. Before this, no adult had ever apologized to me for anything. Father Flanagan's expression of regret made a huge impression.

On occasion I did see teachers at Boys Town smack boys on the back of the head for misbehavior, but that was the extent of physical punishment. To my knowledge, nothing worse happened to any of the boys under Father Flanagan's watch, although once I did see Father Flanagan slap a boy on the face. In all my time at Boys Town, it was the one time I saw Father Flanagan really angry. That morning at breakfast he entered the dining room and asked for a certain boy by name. The boy stood. Father Flanagan went to him, slapped his face, and gave him a severe tongue-lashing. This kid had been stealing money from some source at our home. However, he was not forced to leave Boys Town, because I did see him on later occasions.

Father Flanagan carefully thought out the operation of Boys Town, and again, his thinking was exceptional for that time. Overseeing our society of boys were a mayor, six councilmen, cops and guides, a prosecutor, a defense lawyer, and a postmaster—all of them boys. (Boys Town had its own postal number and post office.) If you disobeyed a rule, you came up before a court run by other boys with no adult interference. If charges were brought, you went to trial with a defense attorney representing you and a prosecutor in opposition. If you were found guilty, the punishments varied from mild

to strangely unique. For minor infractions, you had to do
without dessert for a number of days or be kept home from
a special event or activity. One of the most severe punishments involved attendance at our weekly movies, which we
boys loved. If you were found guilty of a serious crime, you
had to attend a movie but stand in front at the side of the
room with your back to the screen. Believe it or not, that was
quite a punishment—to hear the film but not see it while
you watched all the other boys enjoy themselves. There were
other punishments as well, none of them violent, but each of
them effective. People from Mars Candy came to Boys Town
and gave each kid a candy bar; anyone who misbehaved that
week had to forfeit that. The circus and carnivals also came
our way, and one time we were visited by a traveling exhibit of
the Crown of the Andes, an ornate gold crown made long ago
in South America that was covered with hundreds of emer-
alds and was then owned by an American businessman. If,
just prior to these events, you'd been found guilty by the boys'
court, you missed out on the fun.

The Boys Town policy about no corporal punishment
amazed me. It was hard to believe you could do something
wrong and not get a beating for it. I wasn't perfect by any
stretch of the imagination—now and then I ran off for a
quick trip to the nearby town with other boys or smoked a
cigarette—but never was I horsewhipped or tortured. And
the movie punishment or missing a carnival made me think
twice before engaging in more mischief.

Here's another consequence for bad behavior that took
me by surprise and seemed pretty clever. If you got into
a scrape with another kid, you didn't go before the court.
Instead the Brothers immediately scheduled a fight between
the two of you, but for this fight you wore gloves and fought
in a ring. If you were caught tangling with a smaller boy, he
could arrange for a substitute in the ring who was your size.

The two of you had to go three rounds of boxing wearing sixteen-ounce gloves, which were like big pillows so that no one got hurt but allowed you to get things out of your system. Afterward the two of you had to shake hands and were expected to put it behind you.

It did take a while to believe life could be this different and this good, but eventually I relaxed. At the entrance to Boys Town there's a statue of one boy carrying another and with it the quote "He ain't heavy, Father . . . he's m' brother." Father Flanagan liked to say, "There's no such thing as a bad boy." He believed in the importance of nurture versus nature. Or course, there have been boys who left Boys Town and afterward did bad things, but I think overall, Father Flanagan's philosophy was correct. If a boy doesn't have to grow up with violence and anger, it makes all the difference.

Father Flanagan believed boys who were academically challenged might do well with trades instead, so he had a wood shop and a dairy farm and eventually an auto shop, print shop, and other shops. If you found academics too difficult, he didn't insist that you attend school after a certain age. I think state law required children to attend through the end of grade school. However, all of the boys did some kind of work, even if they attended classes. You had your personal chores to do, keeping your room clean and that sort of thing, plus you were required to help in the dining room or kitchen or laundry. In the wood shop, all of us boys participated in making a beautiful desk for Father Flanagan. Thousands of pieces of wood were incorporated; each of us was shown how to inlay a portion so that when the desk was finished, we each could say we had a hand in it.

In the laundry I mangled the sheets, as they used to call it. A mangle was a machine as wide as a sheet, with a hot roller that pressed the sheet flat. Each time a sheet came through the roller, I grabbed one side of the sheet and a nun grabbed the other. We folded it and grabbed the next one to come our way.

In the film about Boys Town, Spencer Tracy handed out candy to little Pee Wee on a regular basis. I never saw Father Flanagan giving out candy, but the nuns did keep a dish of goodies for the boys in the laundry. Once we were done with our shifts, we got to choose a piece of candy or a baked good. My recollection is that the nuns were nice. All wore the traditional, heavy wool habits and kept their heads covered.

Athletics were important at Boys Town. Leading up to and during my time there, our football team stacked up fifty-three games without a defeat. The team had to travel quite extensively to get games against equally matched opponents. It was difficult to find agreeable opponents because Boys Town had a built-in advantage: Many of the boys had experienced a delay in their education, so that by the time they reached high school they were already in their early twenties and were far larger and more mature than the teams they faced.

At a little lake that froze over in winter, you could learn to play hockey and become part of the Boys Town high school team that competed at Ak-Sar-Ben Coliseum in Omaha. (Ak-Sar-Ben is Nebraska spelled backward.) I was young for the team but I was a good-sized kid, and I think they made me a member because skating came naturally and I had strong ankles from all the walking I'd done in Gallup and thereabouts—the errands to town and the runaway attempts. Boys Town provided almost every sport you could think of, including baseball and volleyball. I played volleyball, and we won almost every game thanks to a kid named Kurt Von Vorenkamp.

Rumor had it that Kurt had been a member of Hitler Youth. He was a big kid, about 220 or 230 pounds and six feet tall, and towered over everyone else. His German accent was strong, but his English was pretty good. Kurt may not have been a member of Hitler Youth in the old country, but he did present a tough-guy image, and at Boys Town he actually formed a Nazi youth group. We became friends, and I became a member of his group. I think I was drawn by Kurt's arrogance and apparent strength. In spite of his constant harangues on the subject of National Socialism and Aryan superiority, in retrospect I doubt Kurt knew much about it. Actually, one of Kurt's ears was deformed, which the Nazis might have considered a tragic flaw. He never harmed anyone—with one exception—and his group did nothing violent.

There's only one occasion when Kurt became physical with another boy. They got into some kind of altercation and began to fight. The remedy of three rounds in the ring wearing gloves was ordered, and because Kurt was such a big boy, one of the Christian Brothers replaced the other kid as his opponent. We saw then that Kurt was a fighting fool. He didn't know anything about boxing, and neither did Brother Bertram, but they started in, and Kurt walloped the man. I can still hear the sound of Kurt's glove making contact. It sounded like a wooden board smacking a side of beef. Good thing they only went three rounds. I bet Brother Bertram never wanted to challenge Kurt in the ring again, but then I don't think anyone needed to. I believe that was Kurt's one fight at Boys Town.

Later I realized that Kurt used the idea of superiority and Nazism to cover for his fears and insecurity, because he was not nearly as tough at heart as he let on. Years later, while I was serving in the Pacific during World War II, I ran across him. On a beach in the Marshall Islands, on Enewetak Atoll, I saw him, a Navy Corpsman, tending to the wounded. His deformed ear, which was unusually small, helped me spot him. I don't think Kurt was hard of hearing; the ear certainly didn't keep him from military service. He was caring for wounded soldiers gently, with no hint of that earlier thug. I didn't learn more about the man he'd become, because the scene on the beach was chaotic and we didn't have time to discuss our current situations or how we'd each arrived there.

During World War II, I saw Father Flanagan briefly as well. He traveled about the U.S. visiting his boys as they prepared to ship off to the European Theater and the South Pacific. I'm not sure whether I saw him while I was on the East Coast or had already been sent to California. Whatever the case, at our stop, he inquired among the troops if anyone had been to Boys Town, so I came up and introduced myself. He recognized me, saying, "Oh, my dear boy!" We talked for a few moments, and I told him how much I had liked being at Boys Town and that I wished I'd been able to stay. Father Flanagan asked what had happened to me after I left. He shook his head and said he was very sorry they hadn't been able to do more to keep me at Boys Town; my stay was court-ordered, and he couldn't do anything when it came to an end.

Kurt formed his Nazi group at Boys Town well before the war, in the early years of Hitler's rise to power, and we didn't know enough to associate terrible violence with Nazis. In spite of our tough-guy posturing, Kurt's group didn't violate the rules of the place in any overt way, but at the same time the kids at Boys Town were afraid of Kurt. I think I clicked with him because our thinking was similar: No one was going to pick on us. From him, I learned to talk tough for the first time. If another boy said or did something that offended me, I mouthed off, but I want to think this didn't happen often. It's likely that hard knocks brought Kurt to Boys Town, and like me, he had a deep-rooted fear of being victimized, no matter how safe Boys Town might seem. Maybe Kurt sought my friendship because of my fair hair and skin and

German-sounding birth name—VanSteenburgh—which I had learned by then from Marian.

Looking back on my friendship with Kurt, I think my experience at the hands of the newspaper delivery boy in Winslow played a role in making me gravitate to a much bigger boy. Here was a seemingly hardened, eighteen- or nineteen-year-old who welcomed my friendship and acted as if he was ready to defend me if need be. It was a very satisfying turnabout for ten- or eleven-year-old me.

Counseling would have been appropriate for Kurt and me and others, but Boys Town didn't provide it back then. Father Flanagan was doing all he could simply to feed us and clothe us and educate us with the slim funds on hand. Later, as their resources grew, Boys Town did offer that kind of help.

I had other close friends at Boys Town. Daniel Backrak was the polar opposite of Kurt: He was a nice kid who suffered from a severe physical deformity and was very meek. His back was twisted, making it impossible for him to stand up straight, forcing him to walk awkwardly. I became Daniel's protector in a way because I was bigger and stronger. I was also buddies with a boy named Crawford; he was black. As you might guess, neither was a member of Kurt's group because neither fit with that Aryan concept.

We were never told why other boys landed at Boys Town. You could choose to tell other kids why you'd been sent there, but no one would do it for you. I did learn that my friend Daniel had been beaten before arriving there, so it may have been beatings that crippled him. Like me, many boys ended up there because they'd committed crimes. If so, they might have families who still cared about them, and their families would visit, like Crawford's did. After Mr. Walters dropped me off, there was no contact with him or Mrs. Walters. While

I was relieved to be away from the abuse and was enjoying life
for the first time in a long time, I envied boys who received
letters or were visited by relatives. When I saw Crawford with
members of his family, I wished that I was the one having
those visits. Deep down, I felt alone.

Mostly, I stayed out of trouble at Boys Town. The worst sin
of my small group of friends was to sneak off to the nearby
town, Millard, a cross-country trek of one or two miles
across railroad tracks, to buy candy and cigarettes, which
we smoked or pretended to smoke. We weren't the only
ones to do this, but sneaking away was not something the
general populace of Boys Town did. I don't want to suggest
that we were the bad ones, only that we were among the
boldest. I had developed a certain independence during my
years trying to escape the Walters' home. If one of us boys
was able to raise a few cents from the many visitors to Boys
Town, we sneaked off on a Saturday or Sunday when there
was no school and then tried to sneak back in without getting caught. No fences or walls contained us, and no patrols
were set up to stop us from leaving or returning; it was just
that you were on your honor not to do so while you lived at
Boys Town. Getting caught during these forays was a matter
of chance: Someone in town might report you. If we were
caught, we'd have that movie punishment. I realize today that
the town councilmen, mayor, and merchants in Millard easily
recognized us as strangers and called Boys Town as soon as
they spotted us on their streets.

I came to know Father Flanagan while traveling with
him as an altar boy. My choice to become an altar boy had
nothing to do with a belief in religion; it had everything to do
with the goodies you got. Until the movie drew attention to
us, provisions at Boys Town were modest. For example, our

usual breakfast was oatmeal or some other porridge. I became an altar boy in search of a better breakfast. Every Sunday Father Flanagan served mass and visited with the residents of a home for the aged in a town about an hour away. I wasn't allowed to go every Sunday, but I did travel there with Father Flanagan every third Sunday. After we said mass, people at the home served us a breakfast of bacon and eggs and sweet rolls. Ironically, we referred to the old people's home as "the poor farm."

Tourists came by the hundreds to see Boys Town, but very few of us boys had contact with them, only the older ones who served as guides. The idea in encouraging visitors was to present the philosophy of Boys Town and inspire donations. Groups of people gathered at the main building, and a certain number, maybe twenty, were led by a guide to designated locations around the campus and farm as he filled them in on the operation of Boys Town. Only occasionally did the rest of us run into an outsider, and we didn't ever ask a visitor directly for money. It was more a case of us being stopped with an inquiry and then being handed a tip, which we were not supposed to accept. Those tips provided change for our trips to Millard.

The movie *Boys Town* was shot partly on location there toward the end of my stay, and I was selected to be an extra in the film, which was very exciting. The small role gave me a little insight into filmmaking and caused me to dream about a movie career. My part in the movie arrived when a dog ran up the road and a semi truck drove along and hit the animal. I ran to rescue the dog. I reached under the truck to haul him out, and Mickey Rooney took him from me. In the end my part was cut from the final version, but I was in some group scenes. Spencer Tracy won an Academy Award for his performance in the film and so did the screenwriters. During the shooting of the movie, I had a chance to talk with Spencer

Tracy and found him to be quite friendly, but Mickey Rooney seemed full of himself, with little time for any of us boys.

I had been sentenced to Boys Town for only eighteen months, but I didn't know this. If I'd heard the JP deliver my sentence back in Winslow, it must not have registered because I was terrified and in a daze when he handed out my sentence. Or maybe I heard what he said but chose to forget it because I came to love living at Boys Town.

On the day I was informed that it was time for me to leave, the news was horrifying. Mr. Walters appeared without warning and took me back to Winslow. I told myself that if Father Flanagan had understood what the Walters were like, he never would have let me go back. My departure was sprung on me at the last minute, meaning I had no time to protest to anyone in private. I was afraid to say anything negative about life in the Walters' home in front of Henry Walters.

Safety Domino 7th

By age fourteen William had become a wild child. Two years into life on the road, good manners weren't the question; his was a wildness of spirit. William came and went as he pleased—except when the cops picked him up for vagrancy and threw him in jail. Otherwise it was up to him to find work, food, and shelter. If a job wasn't to his liking, he could quit. If he felt threatened while hitching a ride or riding the rails, it fell to him to terminate the danger one way or the other.

So it came as a shock when suddenly William was contained against his will, not in jail but in another kind of prison. At least that's the way he saw it.

A railroad strike hit as he was traveling through a remote stretch of Texas. Suddenly his main form of transportation was gone. Vehicle traffic in the region was almost nonexistent. In the few farmhouses he found on foot, no one had work for him.

William hiked the roads for a couple of weeks without a meal. Never did he wander far from the railroad tracks, his lifeline. The pecan harvest was over, but a few nuts still hung here and there or lay scattered on the ground. Beyond the orchards he combed the fields for remnants of other crops but didn't find much. Three meals a day weren't necessary, but he couldn't put together the equivalent of one.

Finally trains thundered down the tracks again. He was saved. William caught a freight west riding atop a boxcar, speculating about the best places to jump down for work and food. In Tucson the train slowed to a halt so that his boxcar straddled a city intersection. Nearby a police car had also stopped. Time to make himself scarce. Before he could slide across the roof to reach the ladder to the ground, William passed out, landing on the street right in front of the cop.

He woke up in a hospital bed. Was jail next? How to flee? Nothing felt broken, but he could hardly move. The doctor's diagnosis: malnutrition. William had been skinny to begin with, but the lack of food had made him skeletal. Hospital staff took pity and treated him kindly; nurses brought trays of food and guided him to build back his strength. Okay, this was good, this was fine. Guaranteed meals, nice people, a roof over his head.

He was starting to feel more like himself when two men in suits came to visit. They asked about his background and why he hadn't been eating. By now William had become a practiced liar. Whenever questioned, he said whatever seemed necessary to keep from being sent back to the Walters. His stock story was that he was on his own because his father and mother were both dead and he had no relatives. Always he named a fictitious hometown in a state back East to keep people from checking with area law enforcement.

William's two interrogators didn't explain who they were, nor did hospital staff, and William was not bold enough to ask. After all, for much of his life, asking questions of adults had brought thrashings. At the end of the long questioning, the men seemed to accept that William was entirely on his own. Four or five days passed. The nurses continued to stuff him with food and to encourage long walks down hospital corridors. William was feeling a whole lot better when a nurse announced it was time to leave and he should get dressed. Fair enough, he was ready. But the same two men appeared and with no explanation led William out of the hospital and into a car.

They drove out of Tucson, not a word said. Were these cops? Were they hauling him to reform school?

The car seemed to be heading south toward the Mexican border. There was no explanation. Hours went by. His terror grew. He'd been kidnapped.

Saguaros, barrel cactus, and prickly pear gave way to pine forest and oak on the east and scrub grasslands to the west. In the distance were rocky hills and mountains. Then it was all grassland, the tufts of grama grass spreading to the horizon. During all of this, William had seen only one truck and one farmer in a wagon, back at the start of their trip. He continued to hold his tongue. Reticence to question was firmly rooted in his psyche with a number of other timid tendencies that might have been surprising to anyone who observed his outward independence.

Finally they stopped. Their destination: a large cattle ranch. The two suits turned William over to the foreman and told him this was where he'd be working.

William didn't speak up. There was no point. He was miles from nowhere.

As days went by, the ranch hands did not overwork or mistreat him. The food and lodging were decent. William wasn't paid, but that happened as often as not during his ramblings. A variety of tasks came his way, none of them harsh. The thing was, he had not sought out the job and didn't know where he was or how to get out of there. He'd lost control.

William's primary job was to look after a prize bull named Safety Domino 7th, the only name he remembers in connection with the ranch. A Hereford, Safety Domino turned out to be a gentle guy who was treated like royalty. William was instructed to polish his horns and hoofs, brush him thoroughly, and work powder into the white portions of his coat to make them look whiter.

Months went by. William's bosses noticed that his overalls and shirt were falling apart. A couple of ranch hands were ordered to take him into town for new clothing. At a general store in a town a couple of hours away, the men bought him new overalls and a shirt. Afterward the men decided to get drinks at the bar and told William to wait in the truck. The chance he had been waiting for. He fled, hid where he could observe the truck finally drive away, and lay low until nightfall. Then he set out down the road in the direction opposite to the one the truck had gone, putting as much distance as possible between himself and that ranch. No food, no money, no ride, but freedom.

CHAPTER FIVE

A Twelve-Year-Old on the Road and Rails

During our passage from Boys Town back to Arizona by train, Mr. Walters broke the silence with curt words only when necessary. Back in Winslow, Mrs. Walters also was not particularly glad to see me. However, the two of them told me I could turn over a new leaf and be a good boy now.

The couple no longer beat me. They'd seen the result of physical violence on their part. Also, Mrs. Walters didn't try anything sexual. Otherwise, life in their house continued like before—constant reprimands, no conversation, unfair punishment by other means. In short order, the Walters pulled a gag on me they'd done many times before: They promised to take me someplace special and canceled at the last minute, blaming the cancelation on bad behavior on my part. In times past it might have been a trip to the movies, but this time they promised a major, major treat: a vacation in Honolulu, where we'd travel by ship. I imagined this to be the trip of a lifetime, with the prospect of ocean travel especially interesting. The Walters went to the extreme of packing our suitcases, and then, right on the verge of departure, they canceled, saying that my behavior wiped out the possibility.

The Walters may have lost the money they were going to use for the trip or needed to abandon the plan for another reason. They chose to pin the cancelation on me, but I didn't for one minute believe I was at fault.

I ran away, this time successfully. By now I was about twelve and large for my age, which meant I had a better chance. I've never known whether I got away by my own choice or whether the Walters didn't want me back and didn't care whether the police reported seeing me.

While the Walters were asleep one night, I slipped out of the house and caught a freight to Gallup. In both Gallup and Winslow, I'd watched how hobos positioned themselves to hop onto freight cars after trains left the station and how they timed their jumps off before trains pulled into the depot, in both cases to avoid detection by railroad employees. Now I was big enough to try these strategies. Still, I was afraid that first time because I didn't know what lay ahead and because I knew what I was doing was risky.

I'd often traveled from Winslow to Gallup with Mrs. Walters by rail, so I felt more comfortable taking the train east. Also, that fit with my aim of going back to Boys Town. However, with the passage of miles I rethought my plan. The people at Boys Town might be compelled by law to return me to the Walters. I decided instead to head for southern Texas and Oklahoma because of the warm weather in those states and because I'd heard at Boys Town that jobs were easy to find there.

Each time I became too hungry to ride farther, I jumped off the train to look for work. This made me one of countless people on the move in the United States in 1937. The Great Depression began in 1929 with the stock market crash on Wall Street, but until I fled the Walters, the Depression hadn't affected me much. I soon saw its effects everywhere I went. There was a dismal look to the countryside, as if something grey had descended upon the earth and given everything a down-at-the-heels appearance. Homes were dilapidated. Rooftops with missing shingles remained that way. Paint that had faded or peeled was left to deteriorate badly. Many farms looked abandoned. Their fields were barren and their orchards half dead. As I moved from place to place, I found out that years of drought had led to widespread farm failures in Oklahoma and Texas in particular, but also parts of New Mexico, Colorado, and Kansas. The parched earth was blowing away in storms of dirt so bad that visibility was sometimes reduced to zero. People told me that thick, brown clouds of dirt had blown as far east as Washington, DC.

In cities, I saw people waiting in long lines for bread and soup handed out by churches and community groups. Except for one occasion, I didn't join them. I didn't want to beg. In rural areas, people were packing up their families and moving out, but not everyone, so I was able to earn food or a few dollars at remaining farms and in small towns here and there. Even so, plenty of times it became obvious that the people who briefly employed me didn't have enough food for themselves and were letting me work for food out of the kindness of their hearts.

The first night I fled Winslow, a hobo was also waiting to jump on a train, and he instructed me what *not* to do. For one thing, I was too short to get into boxcars from the ground. The roadbed kind of slopes down away from the track, and the car rides high above the track. To catch a ride on a boxcar, I needed to grab the ladder at the end of a car and climb up to the roof. At the top I could crawl onto the catway that ran the length of the roof and stay there until I arrived at my destination, then climb back down the ladder when it was time to jump off.

Later I saw there were places where the roadway levels out, so in those spots I could catch a boxcar with the hope of riding inside. There's actually a step or footrest below the car door opening and a railing on both sides, so I developed the technique of grabbing the railing and putting a foot up on the step and more or less launching myself from there into a boxcar.

With the help of other hobos, I also became adept at hopping off trains. We'd see a town coming, wait for the train to slow some, and look for a grassy area or slope where we could jump off without getting killed and could disappear into the brush. I was shown how to stand well back into a boxcar and get a running start going the same direction that the train was going, so it was almost like the train was standing still. I'd jump from a height of about four feet and hit the ground running or rolling.

At first I had no bedroll, no nothing. Sleeping outdoors or in open train cars, I froze. In short order I was either given a blanket or bought one, wrapped it around my waist, and tied a cord to hold it in place while traveling. Rough as it sounds, I wouldn't trade my days on the rails and on the road for anything now. It's an experience very few people have had.

As I hitched along highways and grabbed free rides on trains, I became educated in that kind of travel by talking to other hobos. Hobos generally were nice people. They were simply folks without jobs searching for work. If you walked two or three miles outside a town you'd find "hobo jungles." These were camps set up by transients beyond a town's jurisdiction so that people on the move like us wouldn't clash with local authorities. Small towns did not want us in their midst.

If possible, hobo encampments were situated near a stream or river in a wooded area that provided water and shelter of a sort. Kind of amazingly, it seems to me, when people moved on from hobo jungles, pots and pans were left behind for the next people to camp there, because hobos had to travel light. The hobo jungle was a society unto itself where people shared food, news, and know-how. Even though I was a boy living in the camps, I was expected to bring back my share of food or fuel. This might amount to a few eggs or a piece of meat or lumps of coal earned by chopping wood or weeding someone's front yard, but together we created a meal. The common attitude was not to beg for food. At times people offered us food, but we insisted we'd take it in exchange for work. I could usually count on getting one meal a day in a hobo jungle.

During the evenings in the camps, there was a feeling of ease that I'd never known in the Walters' house. It felt like an extended family almost—one that would soon break up. The older guys sat around the fire smoking and talking. In some of the homes and ranches where we worked, there were radios, so we shared updates on what FDR was doing to help people like ourselves. Sentiment about the president around the campfire was favorable but existed alongside personal despair because it was too late to save the hobos' own farms.

Information about jobs and food was delivered around the fire as news bulletins of a sort. A hobo couldn't return twice to the same house to swap work for food or lumps of coal; it was asking too much in hard times. If someone found a particularly congenial family, though, he advised the rest of us about the opportunity, but we had to be careful not to overdo it. Town folk with heart couldn't be hit continuously by a string of transients. They had only so much to give and only so many small jobs needing to be done, whether it was cutting firewood or repairing a fence. In addition to offering news, some hobos carried guitars—especially southerners, it seemed—and sang around the evening fire. The rest of us joined in, although I never had a voice, couldn't carry a tune. Didn't matter, I guess. No one laughed at me. Some people even danced to the music. A couple of guys might do an Irish jig, hopping around. Those were happy times, if we were far enough out of town that we didn't have to worry about calling attention to ourselves with music and laughter.

I was never abused in the camps. I didn't run into any crooks there either. On occasion I saw women and girls in hobo jungles, but they were in the minority, and I never saw a girl on her own. I did see husband and wife combinations out on the road looking for work and a better place to settle, and I saw families. As far as other boys my age, I rarely saw them traveling by themselves. Not all farmers uprooted by the Dust Bowl had the wherewithal to own a beat-up car or truck, so you'd see many a family trying to make it together to California by way of freight trains. This process was more difficult for them than for single people hopping trains. I saw parents lift their children onto a boxcar before boarding themselves as the train picked up speed. A time or two, I saw children jump back off to be caught by their father because he couldn't make it on board in time to join them.

The idea of hobo life didn't scare me. Not too much, anyway. In Gallup I'd become familiar with the hobo jungle outside town, which was quite a large camp owing to Gallup being a major railroad junction, with railroad lines heading off in multiple directions. I'd also had a taste of being alone on the road, walking east or west along Route 66 out of town, so I didn't fear solitude. What did worry me was being caught and sent back to the Walters, so I kept handy my stock story about my parents having died back East.

Hobos were good teachers. They'd advise about various dangers on the road and also give more general tips. Their news about work possibilities wasn't as important to me as other information. Word might get around that pickers were being hired in Indio, California, or Pocatello, Idaho, and everyone would take off for these places, but I chose not to travel long distances. Instead I usually looked for ranch or farm jobs in Oklahoma and Texas, sometimes straying into New Mexico and Arizona. The Deep South I stayed away from entirely. During the Dust Bowl, the huge exodus of families from Texas and Oklahoma meant those states had a smaller available labor force, so people like me could make up the gap in short-term work, but from what I heard, there was a large population of black people in the South who kept the farm labor market covered.

At first I was only able to get go-fer work because I lacked experience, but on many jobs I had a chance to learn important skills. Eventually I could operate and do maintenance as well as any adult on farm machinery: plows, farrows, balers, trackers, and hay rakes. I found that I could bluff my way into a job and learn on the fly and do pretty well that way. Farmers couldn't pay much, but they'd feed you and house you and, if you were lucky, give you maybe twenty-five or fifty cents a week for your efforts. The vast majority of times, though, I only got room and board.

As I hitchhiked and rode the rails, a varied landscape flew past. There was a vast difference between regions. Traveling the Texas Panhandle from Amarillo northeast to Ponca City, Oklahoma, I could see across a flat plain to the horizon. The land was mostly prairie dotted with tumbleweeds and scrub and few trees. The same from Amarillo going south to flat, hot, and dusty Lubbock. Like it says in a song I once heard, the only way you'd want to see the latter was in the rearview mirror of your car. Down around southern Texas, the land transformed to hills and forest, so I found the countryside around Austin, San Antonio, and Houston more beautiful than up north. Near Gallup the desert terrain turned hilly and stony with huge rock cliffs marked by caves. Portions of the Arizona desert gave way to forest. Most of the time I watched the changing scenery go by from railroad cars instead of from cars or trucks. With so many people having fled, traffic was nil along the roads.

It's hard to talk to people today about the way things were back in the 1930s. Most have no idea how different life was. In the South and Southwest it was more like pioneer days than modern times. If I walked along a road, I was just as likely to see a family pass by in a horse-drawn wagon as I was to see an automobile. However, I could walk for hours between towns and ranches without the possibility of seeing any kind of ride. Only on Route 66 could I expect to see relatively regular traffic flow.

In freight cars I learned to stand up to strangers. This was called "making your bones." If you were fortunate enough to grab a ride inside an empty boxcar, the best places to sit were in the two corners at the forward end of the car, away from the strong draft coming in the open door. At first, I let men bully me into giving up a corner because I was only a kid. But after a while, I found that I could fight back—usually not physically, but by standing my ground and projecting a willingness to fight. At Boys Town, I'd learned to talk tough, but that was always to other boys. Now I told off adult men and threatened worse. This worked well enough. It helped that I was growing taller. No one ever displaced me again from my position in a boxcar. Once or twice I actually landed a blow to protect my place in a corner, but usually I was able to warn men away.

I don't want to give the impression that I often needed to defend myself. Mostly we hobos were in the same position, wanting to travel safely and avoid trouble. In fact, if a bully confronted you—typically a guy who was drunk—you'd often get the backing of other hobos to warn him off.

My increasing toughness must have shown. On one occasion, a mother on her way to California with her daughter asked for my protection. In the hobo jungle outside Ponca City, Oklahoma, this lady approached to ask if she and her daughter, who was fourteen or fifteen, could join up with me. She was afraid for her girl in the midst of so many single men. Her husband had abandoned them, and the two of them had no experience on the road. They didn't have relatives in the area but did in California. The mother figured I was young enough at age thirteen or so not to be a threat to her daughter but big enough and tough enough to fend off other males. I don't think they would have had anything particularly to fear, but with a young girl, one never knows.

An important thing I could help them with was navigating rail yards. Train travel by hobos was not nearly as fast as travel by paying passengers and took some knowledge of how the rail yards worked. On a passenger train, you might take a day or two to go from point X to point Y. For us hobos, getting from X to Y might take a week or more. You had to wait and observe. For instance, aiming for the West Coast, you might catch a freight in Tulsa, Oklahoma, and arrive in Houston, Texas, at which point the train entered the yards to be broken up, with certain cars removed for a train traveling to Denver and others added to a freight train with a Dallas destination. You might be stuck in Houston waiting for the right train to take you in the correct direction. Finally you might catch a train to El Paso, Texas, only to see it taken apart again and redistributed to trains heading to a variety of other cities. Your third train might make several stops before reaching California, including Gallup and Williams and Kingman, Arizona, and any one of these stops could take a day or so. Wherever they had a "division," they ran the cars up humps constructed in rail yards to control the speed of the cars, and we'd say, "Oh, they're humpin' freight cars now." Railway crews pushed the cars up humps here and there as they rearranged them for travel in different directions. We hobos watched from a safe distance or hiding spot to see how divisions panned out. A train that reached the coast with 120 cars might have gained cars from 120 different cities. It was possible for a hobo to get really lucky and hop a single car that made the journey to the coast in a day or two as it met up with different trains, but there was no way of knowing at the outset which car to hop to make that speedy trip.

When the woman in Ponca asked for my help, it flattered my ego to find someone needing my assistance, so I offered little objection and flaunted my knowledge of riding the rails as I took the two under my wing. I got them to the West Coast in a week or so. The trip to California was a rare one for me. In Texas and Oklahoma hobos didn't experience deep prejudice; only in California did we feel that. Word was out: In California they hated hobos and called us "Okies" or "Arkies," no matter where we were from. The likelihood of making money in California was slim and none. Transient workers were told to remain at the ranches and farms in off-hours. Property owners wanted you to keep away from town, and they demanded that you buy supplies at their company stores, where the prices were much higher than in town and gobbled up any pay you might receive.

In addition to staying alongside the mother and daughter in hobo camps, I taught them how to board and leave a freight car, which cars to choose, and how to stay warm, if possible. By that time, my chances of getting inside a moving freight car were pretty good. If boxcars were empty, the brakemen left them open to air out. I'd leap up and get my chest on the floor of a car and pull myself in the rest of the way. It was a definite advantage over grabbing a ladder at the end of a boxcar, which forced me to climb to the roof for a more dangerous ride.

There were far riskier methods of catching a ride on railcars. Underneath the cars ran stabilizing rods, a support feature that extended the length of each car. While a train was stopped, some men inserted themselves up on the rods with arms and legs draped over each of the two parallel rods so that they could ride positioned between the car and the tracks. Riding the rods placed them just above the rails— awfully close to them—and they couldn't get off the train until it came to a halt. I couldn't understand how men dared to try it. It had to be awfully hard to hang on that way, and as close as they were to the railroad ties, if a rock on the track flew up at them, it could be deadly. Men rode the rods to evade the railroad police; they were able to drop off once the train stopped and get away much more quickly than those of us who rode above. Under the cars, you also couldn't be seen easily by watchmen. I only heard about the practice and never knew anyone who did it.

Another hazardous technique was to ride the blinds, which were the spaces between passenger cars. The blind was enclosed by accordion-shaped canvas that contained a small platform where you could stand when stepping from one car to another. But if you fell off that platform, you were grease. I never tried it.

For our journey I told the mother and daughter that we'd probably have the choice of coal cars, flatcars, and several types of boxcar. The prime car to jump was the boxcar because it provided overhead shelter and possible warmth. In many boxcars heavy sheets of craft paper lined the floor and walls, and you could roll yourself up in that material. Your body heat radiated into the heavy paper, and soon you felt pretty warm. Flatcars and coal cars, which were open to the elements, were the most uncomfortable rides. Flatcars had no sides at all. Coal cars had no roofs, and their sides were little more than half the height of boxcar walls and made of sheet metal supported by ribs to keep the metal taut. Steam locomotives pulled the trains, so if you rode in a flatcar or coal car, a stream of ash flew back at you from the engine, and you'd come off those cars blackened. Cinders among the ash could burn you or set fire to your clothing, with the worst burns coming if cinders landed in your eye along with the soot. To avoid ash and keep cinders from your eyes in open cars, you made sure to keep your back to the engine and ride as close as you could to the front or bulkhead of a coal car, right up against the wall.

Green-colored fruit cars were boxcars with thick insulation to keep the fruit cool, and the insulation in an empty fruit car provided a particularly warm ride in cold weather. Cattle cars were boxcars without solid walls; they had slats that let in cold and damp and needless to say were not the most sterile of locations. At times I rode in cattle cars, liking the fact they had straw on the floor that could be used as bedding—which wasn't too bad, as long as there hadn't been cattle standing in it yet.

I protected the mother and daughter against the worst hazards and managed to get them to California just fine, but on my own I wasn't always smart about staying away from danger. Looking back on it, I feel scared for the boy I was for a few reasons.

Memories of refrigerator cars terrify me most. These were boxcars that carried ice. At either end of each enclosed refrigerator car was a rectangular container for ice that reached from floor to ceiling. On top of the container was a lid that could open to the sky. Empty refrigerator cars rode along with their icebox lids open in varying degrees so they could dry out, with the lids aimed to avoid the stream of ash coming off the engine. Empty ice compartments made tempting containers in which to sleep. It wasn't hard to get in them because there was a ladder at both ends of the car leading up to the roof. It was just a matter of opening the lid and dropping down into the compartment. Getting out again was more difficult since the compartment sides were sheet metal; the only way out was to jump up and catch the opening to pull yourself out. At the station, however, if a refrigerator car was going to be put into use, the train pulled up alongside an icehouse built above the level of the cars. The engine pulled ahead just enough for each refrigerator car to pause under the icehouse; huge blocks of ice came sliding from the icehouse floor down a ramp into the waiting refrigerator car.

You did not want to be inside an ice compartment when a block of ice weighing five hundred pounds slammed down into it, the block making a perfect fit for the container. That, to be sure, was a danger, but you could guess at an approaching ice delivery and avoid being crushed by staying out of an icebox as the train slowed near a station. However, for warmth, I slept inside these containers, and I hate to think what would have happened if the lid had come down on a container while I slept. If the lid dropped shut, there was no way to open it from the inside. To make things worse, the container walls were thick, and no one would hear you yelling whether they were inside the car or out of it. You could be trapped in there for days, weeks, or months if the refrigerator car sat on a siding awaiting use. Also, I'm not certain, but it's possible you could die of asphyxiation with the lid down. There was a seal around the door lid that might have entirely kept out fresh air. Since the brakeman had to walk the top of the cars to open and lay back lids, he might spot bodies before the ice was released downward. I never ran into anyone who

actually witnessed a tragedy like that, I only heard apocry-
phal stories about it. The warnings were not enough to keep a
young, desperate fool from sleeping in an ice compartment.

Some train crews were considerate and friendly to travelers like me. Most were not. Men working for the railroad on
the trains and in the stations were fearful of losing their jobs,
and they did their level best to keep hobos off trains. During
the Depression, if you had a job like that, you weren't about to
lose it through dereliction of duty.

Railroad bulls policed the train stations and were known
for being mean. Them you didn't want to tangle with at all.
Their job was security, particularly keeping hobos off trains,
and they adhered to their job with a passion. By word of
mouth you'd learn about a railroad bull at a certain station.
Another hobo might say, "Don't even go there. Believe me,
that guy is not nice." The bulls could do practically anything
they wanted to you. Outside law had little to do with the
railroads; bulls were judge, jury, and executioner unto themselves. If hobos saw one coming, they scattered. You got
pretty cagey knowing who was a railroad bull and who wasn't,
but at first, being a kid, I wasn't up to that.

Early in my travels, in Victoria, Texas, I was caught on a
train by a railroad bull, one with a bad reputation. He only
gave me a severe boot in the behind, maybe because I was so
young, and said, "Don't let me catch you in this yard again."
A few months later I heard about a job on the other side of
Victoria from where I was in San Antonio, couldn't find a ride
on the road, and was desperate enough for work to chance
going through Victoria by train again. Sure enough, the same
railroad bull grabbed me. This time he handcuffed me around
a post, took a piece of water hose, and beat me to what felt
like a pulp on my back and legs. The beating didn't break the
skin through my clothing, it didn't leave open wounds, but he
sure gave me a bruising. He then hauled me by the scruff of

the neck to the edge of Victoria and told me to never let him see me again. Believe me, after that I would have gone around the world to avoid him. I could hardly move. I couldn't work and hung out in the nearby hobo jungle, where they took care of me until I was on my feet again.

Sometimes you heard about a hobo being killed by one of those bulls. If they so desired, they could do that. I never heard of hobos dying by jumping on and off trains, but I did hear of them getting killed by railroad bulls.

On occasion I ran into compassionate people working the trains. One night I rode a train from Winslow headed west toward Flagstaff in late autumn. It was bitter cold and snowing lightly, but I found my way onto a coal car. You can imagine what the wind and snow felt like while riding along in a big box with low sides and no roof. I was sure I was going to freeze to death. The train pulled off onto a siding in the middle of the night to let another train go by, so I decided to get out of the coal car to look for something warmer. In the pitch black, I ran right into the conductor.

"You were in that coal car?" he asked.

"Yes, sir."

"Man, you're going to freeze to death in there. Come with me." He took me back to the caboose.

The caboose was a home away from home for the conductors and brakemen, the last car on the train. You rarely see these anymore. They were always red and had a little dome on top with windows in it. From there, the conductor could see the full length of the train by looking straight ahead out of a window across the top of the cars or by looking out windows to either side. Bunk beds were built into the caboose, tables for doing paperwork, and a potbellied stove. While the engineer and fireman stayed up front in the locomotive, the conductor and two brakemen rode in the caboose. The conductor was like the captain of the team. The brakemen were responsible for the mechanics of the cars; at stops, they walked alongside the train making sure the wheels were greased and in proper working order. If the wheels didn't stay greased, they'd freeze up and drag, soon catching the train on fire. Also, brakemen kept an eye on the air hoses connecting from one car to the next, making sure the hoses were properly linked, because if the engineer wanted to throw on the brakes, he pulled on an air brake controlled by those hoses. The brakemen walked the length of the train at each stop making their inspections, but the conductor rarely left the caboose. It was there that he did all the paperwork, keeping the manifest for the freight cars.

I was extremely lucky that night when the kindhearted conductor discovered me, because normally he wouldn't have been walking around outside in the cold and dark. He had me ride the rest of the way in the caboose, warm and cozy. As we traveled along, he and the brakemen asked me about myself. I guess the conductor was sympathetic because he didn't see many boys my age trying to travel alone that way.

As I searched for work, I tried to stay near larger cities. Farmers tended to come there to purchase equipment and supplies at hardware stores, making them good places for job hunters to congregate. Also, smaller towns especially didn't want us around. To discourage us, all they had to do was enforce vagrancy laws: If you didn't have at least two dollars in your pocket, a sheriff could throw you in jail as a vagrant. In big cities, police had better things to do than enforce that law.

In the 1930s most small towns had justices of the peace elected or appointed by local citizens to dispense the law, even though many of them knew little about the law. If the police picked you up for vagrancy, they'd bring you before the JP. Or, say you actually had work, but there was a disagreement about payment. It might come time for a farmer to pay you, and instead he might call the police and have you thrown out of town. Or a farmer might promise to pay you ten cents a box for fruit you harvested but instead pay five cents. You could complain to local officials, but who was the JP going to believe—a local or a total stranger? In my experience, most employers were decent, but that kind of thing did happen to me two or three times.

If I didn't find work, I sometimes found eggs. Grocers paid a penny each for freshly laid eggs, no questions asked. Not that I'd steal. A farmer with fifty hens might have a few go wandering off his land. If I spotted a chicken on the loose, I watched where she laid her eggs and grabbed them after she strutted off. A grocer candled the eggs to check to make sure they were fresh. This meant he lit a candle and held it behind each egg to reveal a silhouette. If there was no lump sticking from the yolk, it had not yet begun to develop into a chick and was relatively new. Larger towns often had stores that sold only butter and eggs. In fact, you'd often find all kinds of specialty vendors in the cities: bread shops, bakeries for cakes and other sweets, meat markets, poultry markets, pork markets. Money went a long ways back then. A few cents from "found eggs" might buy me a cup of coffee and a sweet roll. For twenty-five cents I could get six pork chops and still have money left over. Not only did a Hershey bar cost just a penny, it was much larger in the 1930s.

I was twelve and still relatively new to hitchhiking when I had one of my more unusual experiences on the road. An act of unusual kindness. It was wintertime near Refugio, Texas, a small town between Victoria and Corpus Christi. I hitched into town, and in short order a cop in a car stopped me. Of course, I didn't have the necessary two dollars to avoid being called a vagrant. That amount may seem like a pittance today, but then it was a large amount to be carrying around, especially for someone like me. Most jobs tended to last no more than a week, and I considered myself lucky if I had twenty-five cents in my pocket.

The cop in Refugio took me down to the justice of the peace. The latter questioned me, and when I told him why I was there and that I didn't have any money, he gave me the maximum sentence of seventeen days. An odd number, but that's what it was. The policeman escorted me to the jail, which was a three-story building on the town square. He led me up to the third floor and put me by myself in a cell that was maybe ten by twenty. It had a wood-box potbellied stove, two bunks, and a barred window overlooking the square. Can't complain, I thought to myself. Warmth and a roof over my head. It was quite cold outside. I was in my cell about thirty minutes when the jailer came for me. Here we go, I thought, I'm going to get a beating. But he took me down to the square and across the way to the library, where he informed me that the justice of the peace said I could pick out three books. He handed me a pad and pencil and instructed me to write book reports on each for the JP. If I finished the books and wrote reports, the JP said I could have three more. I picked out books about Greek mythology and history, which I've been interested in all my life.

With twenty-four hours a day in the cell, I was able to read quite a bit, so I soon handed in my reports and picked out three more books. Meanwhile, I was fed three meals a day. The meals weren't luxurious, but in those days, living on the road, I was lucky to get one meal. Only while working on farms did I eat more. In jail they served me a lot of chili and stew and cornbread. Breakfast was usually oatmeal and toast and coffee. Lunch was a sandwich and maybe a sweet roll. I figured I was in good shape with this kind of eating.

From my cell, I could hear prisoners in two other cells. Men came and went from one but weren't kept there very long. The other cell contained a woman, and I heard talk that she was in for murder. She wasn't very pleasant; she cursed me a lot. I continued to have my cell to myself.

At the end of seventeen days, the jailer opened the cell door and said, "You're free to go." Enjoying the feeling of liberty, I didn't rush. I strolled down into the square, right into the cop. He made me turn out my pockets, and when I didn't have two dollars, he brought me back before the same justice of the peace. The cop said, "I found him without any money. He's an itinerant bum." The judge said, "Seventeen days." I said, "How can I get out of town if you keep locking me up?" The JP said, "Son, it's cold outside and you have nothing to eat, and I can't do anything about that. Here you get three meals a day and a little bit of an education. When it warms up, you're free to go." I said, "Bless you, Your Honor, you're a good guy."

Today you might see people on the road with backpacks, but in the thirties most of us hobos carried a bedroll made out of a blanket and maybe a piece of canvas that could be laid on the ground to keep dampness away. If we had more than a blanket, we tied cords around the roll and slung it across our backs slantwise. Inside the roll might be one change of clothes, if you were lucky.

In the southern Texas and Oklahoma farm country there were very few people about, with farms and ranches miles apart. A grove of trees or bushes provided hobo jungles both shelter and privacy of a sort. At a nearby stream or river it often felt safe to shed my clothes and bathe, then wash my clothes and spread them on bushes to dry in the sun. Privacy was rarely a problem.

Almost everyone you saw in a hobo jungle or riding the rails wore bib overalls. If you were lucky, a farmer gave you hand-me-downs, which you wore even if they were too big. That usually was the case for me. A time or two I saved enough money to buy new overalls in towns that had a Sears, Roebuck. They were cheap—maybe two or three dollars— and lasted forever. Denim at that time was so heavy that new overalls were stiff to the point you could hardly walk. You had to wash them at least once to make them wearable.

New shoes were too expensive. I didn't own any. I was always on the lookout for hand-me-downs, and as a result wore a lot of wrong sizes, either too tight or too large. If there was room, I put cardboard or linoleum in the bottom to make shoes last longer. Socks were out of the question; you were lucky enough to have shoes. The only time in my life I stole anything happened when I was walking down a residential street and spotted a pair of worn shoes sitting in a garage. At the time I wasn't barefoot but might as well have been. The soles of my shoes were worn through and so was the cardboard I'd replaced them with. There, in that open garage, sat a pair of used men's shoes. I'm not proud to say it, but I grabbed them. The stolen shoes didn't fit and put blisters on my feet; I ended up cutting out the parts that rubbed. I promised myself that I would never steal anything again. The theft haunts me to this day.

My determination to live as upright as possible was reinforced by the demands of hobo living. On the road I was always on the lookout for being entrapped and accused of malfeasance because there'd be no defense against accusations. I was always a stranger traveling through; locals would not believe my side of a story. It was crucial to stay away from any sort of crime.

Not that all hobos were pure in their motives. Once, hitchhiking into Dallas, I met up with another hitchhiker, an older man, maybe forty-five. We were both hungry and hoping to find work quickly. He asked if I'd ever done any house painting. When I said no, he said it was simple, I could do it easy, no problem. We could make a painting team and find jobs. In Dallas we'd get some paintbrushes and then solicit work. I thought he meant he had some money and we'd buy the brushes. Lo and behold, after we entered the store he let me know we were going to steal brushes. I told him, no way. Of course, he had in mind that he'd front for me while I stole the paintbrushes. We went our separate ways right then.

Following that, I tried and failed to find a job quickly in Dallas. This became the only time I stood in a breadline. I didn't like the feeling of taking charity and resolved not to take a handout again.

On farms I may not have been paid much or at all, and the hours may have been long, but the food made up for it. The farmer, other workers, and I woke to milk the cows at three in the morning. After that was finished, we returned to the farmhouse, where the farmer's wife served us steak and bacon and eggs and powdermilk biscuits. Those breakfast biscuits were out of this world. Gravy was poured over them. It was cholesterol up the ying yang, but we worked hard and probably burned it off. The farmer and the rest of us went out into the fields to labor until dusk, when we stopped for our second meal of the day, this time a big dinner. At lunchtime we might get a small snack, maybe one of those biscuits with homemade butter or honey.

Even though I was a kid, farmers assumed I could do the work, whether it was plowing a field or harrowing or whatever. Back then, boys raised on farms became adept at operating all kinds of farm machinery from an early age, and farmers expected their sons as well as their employees to take active roles in the operation of their farms. If hired, you were responsible for the way you treated the equipment as well as the way you did the field work.

The big moneymaker for workers in Texas at the time was cotton picking, but I wasn't any good at that. I think they paid a dollar seventy-five for picking a hundred pounds of cotton. I tried but just couldn't pick that much. To harvest the cotton, you carried a tow sack looped over your neck and shoulders so that it dragged behind you. This freed both hands to pick and stuff cotton into the bag's opening at your side. Women were the best cotton pickers, I think, because they tended to have slender fingers that could fit up inside the bolls with less injury. Sharp points rimmed the bolls, and it was necessary to slide your fingers inside the boll, or bloom, to reach the cotton ball and release it from the stem. Those sharp points jabbed your fingers over and over if you had thick fingers or no finesse. It was easy to get bloody. What's worse, the cotton balls were small, so it took a lot of them to make a pound. The women I saw, nearly always black, were fast and nimble doing this work. If you're hungry, you'll try anything, but I found I couldn't pick cotton fast enough or good enough. You were expected to pick clean, which meant removing cotton from the entire plant, not just harvesting the easy bolls on top. As a result, you had to stoop down over and over to pluck cotton from the sides and bottom of each plant. The black families had their little kids pick the bottoms and sides. It was hard work for all of them, out in the sun, bending over, pulling those sacks.

There was a worse job, and I tried that, too: picking broomcorn, the most agonizing work I ever had. But I'll get to that later. That was in Endee, New Mexico, near Santa Rosa, New Mexico, across the border from Amarillo, on the Texas Panhandle. I took that work for one reason: a girl named Ruby.

A series of ups and downs led me to Ruby and the broom-corn job, including an experience that still shocks and embarrasses me. In Leon Springs, about twenty miles outside San Antonio, Texas, I found a job delivering milk with a man who owned a dairy farm. I was thirteen or fourteen at the time. I rode with the farmer on his truck, and at each stop along our regular route, I ran inside the customer's house. In those days, milk products were delivered right into people's iceboxes. It was fine for me to go inside customers' homes; no one gave it a second thought. A bottle of whole milk couldn't be left outside on a doorstep in winter because cream would gather at the top of the bottle and freeze into a plug that pushed the cardboard cap off the bottle. In hot weather, milk would spoil if left outdoors for hours. We knew each customer's weekly order, and they left the back door unlocked. I stashed the milk in the icebox and picked up payment, which might be waiting on the kitchen table or on the back doorstep with the empties. If a family wanted something more than their standard delivery, they left a note in the empties along with their payment.

While we drove along making deliveries, I noticed that my employer brought up sex a lot, including asking about my experience. In that day, talking about sex freely was a no-no. You just didn't do it.

I was a complete novice about sex. Mrs. Walters' disturbing behavior made me not want to think about it at all. At Boys Town I'd overheard a few older boys discussing their imaginary sex lives, and whatever scant information I had by the age of thirteen or fourteen was acquired by listening to them. Certainly I knew little about how to approach a woman in that way.

In the short period I worked on this dairy farm, I also noticed that the farmer's wife seemed kind of different. She was a good-looking woman, maybe in her thirties, but she struck me as strange. Her demeanor was not like an employer. If she told me to do something, it wasn't an order, it was a request. She spoke to me in an unusually warm way, and her behavior made me a little afraid of her. I decided I didn't like her.

The dairyman and I drove about in the milk truck making our deliveries until one day, out of the blue, he said, "I don't want you to come on a delivery with me today, I want you to start working at the dairy. You can wash bottles, help with hand-bottling, and get orders ready for tomorrow's delivery." I didn't understand his instruction, because this seemed like a waste of labor; other workers already took care of those tasks. Nevertheless, I did what he said. After a few days of this, he returned from delivering milk, told me to come to the house, and said, "I'm going out in the pasture to see the cows for a while. I'll be gone for about an hour. While I'm gone, I want you to have sex with my wife."

His statement absolutely floored me. In my experience, decent people didn't say things like that or do things like that. The very thought of having sex with this woman scared me half to death. I argued with the man vehemently. I couldn't. I wouldn't. I didn't say it, but it felt like he was setting me up for a fall. The next step would be to report me to the police. He repeated his order and left for the pasture. I walked from the house to the dairy worrying and eyeballing his wife, wondering if she was in on the plan and what she expected me to do about it. For that hour I continued to do my work in the dairy and she did hers, and we crossed paths repeatedly, but I didn't get close to her, no no no. When her husband returned from the pasture, he asked if I'd done anything. He seemed extremely disappointed to find out I hadn't. This same routine went on for several days until it was time to be paid, and I got out of there.

· · ·

This was when the weeks-long railroad strike occurred. After traveling west, falling off the train in Tucson, and escaping from Safety Domino's ranch, I was determined to stay away from Tucson and avoid the risk of running into anyone who'd been instrumental in my forced employment. I headed east again and landed one of my best farm jobs ever.

I was hitchhiking with another guy near Amarillo. A farmer in a truck stopped alongside us to ask if we were looking for work. He said he was a minister but had forty acres in alfalfa that needed to be harvested. Did either of us know how to drive an International 15-30? I said I did. I'd heard this was the type of tractor most often used for farming. If the man had said he owned another model, I would have said I knew how to operate that as well. The minister asked my fellow hitchhiker, a man who'd told me he was trying to support his wife and kids back in Oklahoma, did he know how to operate a hay binder. The answer was yes. We reached the minister's spread in midafternoon, were shown to a small bunkhouse, and told we could start work the next day. Our employer needed to drive to Amarillo in the morning, so we'd be on our own at first.

Inside the bunkhouse, the other guy and I compared notes. I'd never operated an International 15-30, and he'd never operated a hay binder. We agreed that we had time to figure out the equipment in the morning before the minister returned. And that's what we did—we learned to operate the tractor and hay binder on the fly. We practiced, made a few starts and stops, and within a few days cut and baled the alfalfa on his entire farm. The minister handed us about a hundred dollars each. The size of our pay astonished us. For those times, the amount was astronomical. We felt like millionaires. Alfalfa wasn't that profitable a crop, so why he did it, I'll never know, unless he was moved by a spirit of true Christian brotherhood and charity.

Feeling flush, I decided to head for California to pick dates, mostly out of curiosity. I'd heard there were millions of date palms in Indio and they needed pickers. The fact that I had plenty of money in my pocket caused me not to worry about California's poor reputation for worker treatment. I'd never been to Indio and wouldn't mind learning a thing or two about dates. I didn't understand that the towering trees required special skill and bravery—and that they'd never let a kid like me do that work. My co-worker said he was taking his windfall back to his family in Oklahoma.

So I walked the road going west. Along came another farmer who asked if I was looking for work. No thanks, I said, I was looking for rides to California. The man offered to give me a lift to the other side of town, where I'd have a better chance of catching a longer ride. First, though, he had to pick up his daughter from school. Fine with me. I climbed into the bed of his truck. In those days, pick-up trucks didn't have second seating up front, so if you weren't driving you rode in back. At school we stopped to collect his daughter, Ruby, and when she sat down alongside me in the back of her father's truck, I decided that maybe I did want this job.

What exactly Ruby looked like has slipped away from me, but she was pretty. She may have been a little short, a little heavyset. In those days, a lot of farm girls were short and heavyset. Whatever the case, there was something about her that made me sit up and take notice. I may have been an innocent, and I may have been determined to stay out of trouble, but that doesn't mean I was immune to puppy love. The farmer stopped to let me off, but I asked him to tell me about the job. It was broomcorn. Feeling unusually honest, I told the man I'd never picked broomcorn, but he said it was easy. The pay was fifty cents a day plus room and board. I said I'd do it.

What I didn't know about broomcorn would make me sorry. Broomcorn, I learned, looks like any other kind of corn except it grows a bigger tassel at the top and doesn't produce corn kernels. The dried tassels can be used to make bristles for a broom. This variety of corn grows about eight feet tall, and during harvest you have to reach up over your head to almost that eight-foot height. You peel off a leaf, grab inside for the tassel, snap it off, and stuff it into the bag you're toting. Two parts of the process are agonizing: first, holding your arms over your head all day long to peel off leaves and grab tassels, and second, trying to avoid the saw tooth at the edge of each leaf that can easily cut you. I didn't quit at the end of the first day, but I did after a couple of days, my hands bloody and arms aching. Meanwhile, Ruby's father had hired another worker, a banjo-picking SOB from Arkansas who Ruby liked a lot. As a result, she had absolutely no interest in me. I can't tell you much about Ruby, but she did enthrall me, enough that I still know her name after more than seventy years. Ruby Johnson.

Escape from the Walters had given me a tremendous sense of relief and a heady sense of freedom. Every day away from them felt like an achievement. Over time, though, my solitude came to weigh on me. Loneliness became physical, a kind of ache in my stomach. I yearned to be part of a family or a group. But in order to survive, I had to keep moving. As crazy as it seems, there were moments I felt drawn back to Gallup. The Walters' house represented home and hearth; it was the known world. Out on the road there was the constant question of how to feed myself, where to find shelter, and how to avoid trouble with the law. And there were dangers.

At night, if there was no hobo camp and I had to sleep out in the open by myself, I had reasons to be afraid. In the desert you could lie down to sleep under clear skies, but somewhere else it could be raining, bringing a flash flood that would sweep through the desert and wash you away. If not that, then animals, insects, or dangerous people might get you while you slept. Also, the highway felt more menacing after dark. If a car or truck stopped for me at night, the urgency to move along quickly toward some kind of safe shelter made it feel like there was less time to judge what the driver was like before climbing in.

In daylight, one of the worst dangers was duststorms. They were awe-inspiring and terrifying. On the prairie, a storm first appeared as a dark wall of dirt in the far distance. Whirlwinds stirred up the dry soil so that the red-brown cloud seemed to take on a life of its own, rolling across the land.

In Oklahoma, outside of Ponca City, I was hit by the worst duststorm I ever saw. It was my practice never to stand still to thumb a ride; I always kept moving because rides could take hours to come along or not at all. That day there wasn't much of a breeze. As I walked along, all of a sudden a reddish brown wall appeared on the horizon. The dark band of color was maybe a half-mile or mile away, so I couldn't be sure what it was. In those wide-open spaces, mirages were common. I watched the wall of dust grow larger and larger. As it drew close, I couldn't see the top of the wall, and I couldn't see the bottom either because the dirt was all roiled up where it met the land. The opaque cloud began to seem like a mammoth wheel of dark rolling dust, like a Ferris wheel with the wheel rolling up and away from me. It was an odd thing to see. Awful and wrong. I picked up pace and ran to find shelter. There was nothing but a ditch, so I huddled down with my body curled up and my eyes, nose, and mouth covered. The thing is, a duststorm doesn't always pass by right away. It can take an hour, maybe two. That one seemed to take forever and may have lasted a couple of hours in my location. When it was gone, my eyes, mouth, and nose were filled with dirt, and reddish brown powder covered me from top to bottom. There was no water nearby, so I shook off the grime as best I could and kept going until I reached a farm. Farms and ranches in that part of the country all had hand-pumped wells, and no farmer would refuse you a drink or a washing-off.

Questions of survival and safety repeated themselves over and over. Today was the same as yesterday, and tomorrow would be the same as today. Always I had to move on, and always I felt removed from the people around me. If I saw children playing in a yard and a mother yelling for them to come in for dinner, I could hear the impatience in her voice, but I could also detect a note of love and understanding. I craved that kind of connection. During certain moments I imagined myself back with the Walters, but never long enough to lead me back to the misery of living with those two people.

Usually I told myself that my life on the road was a temporary thing. I always held the belief that things would get better. I don't know where that confidence came from, but it sustained me. Trusting in the future had gotten me through my time with the Walters and it helped me once I escaped.

Part of the answer, I suppose, is that life on the road expanded my education in a big way and helped me believe in myself some. I was learning skills necessary to feed myself, to find shelter, and to make at least a little income. I may have been twelve, thirteen, and fourteen, but I was not a kid in the normal sense of the word. Farmers never asked how old I was, they asked what I knew how to do. I was expected to do a man's day's work just because I could. It felt like I was on my way to becoming an adult who could make a decent life for himself. I believed that would happen. It had to.

My young age did make me different from other workers in one way: Ranchers and farmers didn't put me in the bunkhouse with the men until I was well into my teens. As a much younger runaway and then as a twelve- and thirteen-year-old, I was given a spare room in the house or a sleeping spot in a shed separate from everyone else. I appreciated the privacy. My employers wanted to protect me from molestation.

Only one time did I feel sorry for myself during those years. On a Christmas Day somewhere between Dallas and Houston, I was walking along the railroad tracks. There was a misty kind of rain, and I could see through windows of shacks I passed. Inside those little houses, even poor families were sitting down together to Christmas dinner. I thought to myself, here I am out here in this rain by myself with nothing to eat. But the day passed, and I got over it.

Happy family

William calls her Mother and she calls him Dad, not unlike many other couples of their generation once kids arrive. "Ask Mother about that." "Wait until Dad gets home." However, long after his wife died, William continued to refer to her as Mother or Mama or My Mama no matter whom he was talking to. Surrounding these terms were reverence and deep loss.

By the mid-1960s William and his wife have three teenage children. To all appearances they are an ideal family: hardworking parents who own a successful interior design shop in their small northern California town, mom and dad active in the community, kids doing fine at school, a dad who is handy at arts and crafts, a mother who is the instant confidante of every teenager who comes to the house.

Dorothea, the middle child, is popular at the high school. Her blonde good looks have been inherited from her father, and her warm personality very much resembles her mother's, although Dorothea is not as outgoing. In an attempt to overcome shyness, she decides to run for Citrus Fair queen, a contest that includes multiple appearances on the fairgrounds stage, including a talent competition.

She announces her plan to her family.

William's first response: "But Dorothea, you don't have any talent." She will remember this opinion decades later.

No matter. Her father hires a local actress to teach Dorothea a skit. She will dance a bit on stage wearing tails and top hat. William creates a stage set called "The Topper Club" and builds a nightclub backdrop that to Dorothea seems Hollywood in scope. She also remembers this long after.

William's teenage daughter wishes for a dad who praises her achievements, who smiles when she announces her latest accomplishment, and most of all, who expresses adoration of the person she is becoming. But he won't. Praise should be unnecessary. Boastfulness, he tells her, is wrong. Old voices linger in his head.

When asked by his sons and daughter why he doesn't say, "I love you," he says, "Look how I treat you. Doesn't that tell you I love you?" Out of fabric and wood he has crafted furniture for their bedrooms. At Christmas and Easter he creates elaborate decorations for their front yard and living room. He and their mother chaperone school dances and welcome their friends into their home. Happily he takes Dorothea and her brothers on driving trips around the country to ride San Francisco's cable cars and admire the view from the top of the Empire State Building. At Howard Johnson's, the three kids eat as much ice cream as they like and romp in the swimming pool. If a restaurant is all-you-can-eat, he doesn't complain as they try to eat the place clean. Still, his children want to hear the words. They watch other fathers express their love aloud, and they are hungry for the same from him.

Mother is, too. Sometimes she privately asks William about it. For him it's a question of a vault that can't be forced open. In his past, sweet words were not an option. Always she says she understands his problem. But does she?

It's hard for her to imagine the magnitude of his difficulty, not knowing the full extent to which William was injured. What his wife does know is that at times she must soothe him and soften his angry reactions to the rest of the world. He responds well to her gentle, quiet touch. In a way, she *is* his mother.

But William is a good man. Always he works hard to take care of his family. Mama does witness William's love. It's not like he's hardened. He brings her gifts; he slips cute notes into her sack lunches. If she or the kids are hurt in any way, he cries. Maybe the emotions that flow from her so readily have eased the way for him to reveal that much of his interior.

For a brief period as a teen, William witnessed firsthand how a large, happy family could express love without pronouncing it aloud. Their affection for one another came through in all kinds of gestures. Living with them, he basked in their general good humor and team spirit. To his surprise, this unrelated family let him be part of it. But years later, unlike the parents in that family, he is prone to outbursts. Nothing violent, but brief, volcanic eruptions of molten anger from places buried deep down. At those times, when one of William's kids misbehaves or says something that riles him, he lashes out verbally. His wife is quick to cover. "Oh, come on, Dad, you shouldn't be like that," she says. And later, out of William's earshot, to the offending child, "I know your father's words were harsh, but he didn't mean it, and you know he loves you."

And he does. He just can't manage the words. He may want to shake off the collar that tightened around his neck long ago, but it's too tight. It pinches. It still hurts.

CHAPTER SIX

Instant Family at the Reidhead-Harris Homestead

I was fired only once during my years on the road. This happened when I met up with a farmer building a silo for himself near Snowflake, Arizona, in the eastern portion of the state about midway between Utah and the Mexican border. I was still headed for California to pick dates but hitched another ride that sidetracked me.

What the farmer near Snowflake had in mind was not the classic, cylindrical silo but instead a rectangular silo constructed beneath the ground. To dig out the earth, he said we'd use a Johnson bar scraper, which was not a common farm tool. The scraper was exotic enough that I admitted to no experience, but the farmer was willing to give me instructions provided I did exactly as he told me.

We dug the hole for the silo about a hundred yards from the man's farmhouse, where he lived with his wife and kids. The Johnson bar scraper was pulled by a team of horses and shaped like a giant shovel. The farmer drove the horses and I kept pace behind, holding on to a rope attached to a bar curving up from the rear of the scraper. The rope dangled down from the bar and was used to create tension on the shovel-like scraper to keep it from emptying as it filled. It was important to adjust my hold on the rope to compensate for the increasing weight as the shovel filled and, very importantly, not to tie the rope around my wrist. If we hit a rock or other obstacle, the bar and rope could jerk up in the air and pull my arm out of its socket. With great care I followed the farmer's instructions, and we made good progress, dumping aside shovelful after shovelful. Finally a large, rectangular piece of land was scraped down to bedrock. The silo required another three or four feet of depth, but there was no scraping that rocky bottom.

Next we drilled holes in the rock at intervals down the length of the cleared site. There were no power drills like we have today, so we used a star drill, which needed to be beat on manually as we drilled. My employer then inserted dynamite in each hole. Dynamite came in a wooden box filled with sawdust that kept the dynamite from sweating in hot weather, the sweat being highly volatile nitroglycerin. Each stick was approximately one inch in diameter and six inches long, basically a cardboard tube packed with explosive. The farmer inserted a quarter-stick of dynamite into each hole and added black powder as a detonator. Then we ran a fuse out of each hole, tamped dirt in the hole, and connected the fuses from all of the sticks. We lit the fuse. Nothing happened. At that point, the man announced that he'd promised to go to town with his wife to do some shopping. He told me to stay away from our work in case it did ignite.

That was when I stopped following directions precisely. Being an enterprising young man and wanting to impress my employer, I waited what I thought was a reasonable length of time after he left and then returned to the job. I dug up the holes, put more dynamite in each, added more black powder, ran a nice new fuse connecting all of them, and lit it. This time the dynamite worked. Not only did it shoot bedrock into the air, the detonation blew out all the windows on the side of the man's house facing the future silo. If I hadn't been behind a tree, the explosion would have blown me up, too. Fortunately, the kids in the family were all at school.

With great apprehension, I waited for the husband and wife to return. I knew I'd done wrong and had to face the music. My intentions had been good, but being young and thinking I knew better than anyone else, I'd let my ego get the best of me. Of course, when the man returned home, he was furious. To his credit, he was also concerned that I might have been killed. He raked me over the coals for the destruction and the danger I'd caused and told me to get the hell out of there and not come back. It was going to be no small matter for him to replace those windows, since his farm was remote and glass was expensive. He did have a hole for a silo, though.

My tail down, I walked the road into Snowflake, where I had my first contact with Mormons. After spending some of my money on food and clothing, I decided I needed more work before heading to California.

Near Snowflake I found employment at a dairy, but the dairy owner and I ran into a religious conflict. He was a Mormon elder and insisted that I go to the Mormon Church, attend seminary (which was like Sunday school), and study The Book of Mormon. I went along with that for a very short time and then told him thanks but no thanks. Next a widow in town hired me. She was a great pie-maker and sold pies all around Snowflake and also made delicious cheese.

Like the dairyman before her, the widow required me to attend seminary. I went along with this because the woman was kindly and her baking and cheese-making were phenomenal. Everyone in the town was Mormon, and it became clear that if I wanted to work for them, none of them would stand for nonattendance at seminary. To my knowledge I was the only non-Mormon living in Snowflake. I studied The Book of Mormon but did so grudgingly and avoided seminary whenever I could, which meant I continued to be seen as an outsider. The town folk didn't give up proselytizing me, but at the same time, no one mistreated me because of my attitude. They welcomed me to a daylong town barbeque where the men roasted a whole calf on a spit and took turns mopping it with a sauce from a bucket. Bushels of corn were roasted in the pit below. The widow brought her pies to the party, and other women contributed salads of different kinds. In addition to the meal, there were three-legged races and bag races in a burlap bag. I'd never been part of anything like that before, and the rest of my life I've enjoyed recalling that celebration.

For several months I helped the widow with all of her tasks, but once her cheeses were made and set up, there wasn't much for me to do. I took to the road again. Leaving Snowflake I walked east and then south through forested mountain country to what today is the town of Alpine, Arizona, about six miles from the border with New Mexico. Alpine then wasn't really a town but only a post office designation for all the farms in the area. Like Snowflake, the area was settled by Mormons. Today Alpine is part of the Apache-Sitgreaves National Forest and draws visitors for hunting, fishing, and camping, but in those days it was pretty quiet, with a forestry station and not much else. Definitely no jobs. Walking the mountain roads, I turned back in a northwesterly direction aiming for the town of Heber, still planning to find my way to California.

Near evening time, two boys rode along on a mule and stopped to talk. They asked who I was and what I was doing there, and I learned they were brothers named Art and Glenn Reidhead. Art was fourteen like me, and Glenn was twelve. They were headed home for dinner and invited me to come with them. This took a great deal of persuading, because I was always ashamed to have anyone think I needed charity. I didn't like to accept anything unless I worked for it. But they insisted, and I went with them.

To get to their property, we left the road and traveled maybe a quarter-mile down a winding dirt lane, with me walking alongside them on their mule, whose name was Gyp. This was lumber country, where the few ranches and farms were carved out from forest. At the end of the lane, the woods opened to cleared land and a one-story house encircled by huge pine trees whose trunks were at least three feet in diameter. Beyond the tree-rimmed house, which was situated alongside a creek, lay farm fields. There were pens for pigs and corrals for horses and cows. The homestead was about 140 acres, with maybe 100 acres cleared. Fragrant pinyon pines grew wild in the nearby woods among other pines and firs.

Art and Glenn led me up to their house, which was startling in appearance. The structure was completely framed and had a shingled roof and double-hung glass windows but no exterior siding, only boards nailed to the framing. There was no front door. A back door led into the kitchen, but there wasn't even a small back porch or overhang to give quick shelter in rain or snow. Inside, the floors were pine boards, and the walls were other boards laid horizontally. It looked like the builders had run out of money. Six people lived there with no indoor toilet, no running water, and no electricity. A two-hole outhouse stood about a hundred yards away. More than anything, this was a simple pioneer home. There was a living room, kitchen, and three bedrooms.

Art and Glenn introduced me to their parents, Mr. and Mrs. Walt Harris. Art and Glenn's mother had been a Reidhead and married Mr. Harris after she was widowed. Between them they had ten kids, eight of them from previous marriages. Only four of the ten kids still lived at home in the main house. The youngest two were Kim, age five or six, and Nadine, eleven. A quarter-mile away, on an edge of the cleared acreage, the oldest Reidhead son, Delbert, had a small, rustic house for his family. Marvin Reidhead, who was in his twenties, also lived with his wife, Naomi, on the property in another home. I don't think Marvin and Naomi had been married long; when I arrived, she was pregnant with their first child. A little more distant, off the 140 acres, daughter Pearl Reidhead, a single woman, lived by herself on Smithers Hill. The oldest Reidhead daughter, Maureen, was a widow who lived farther away, but I didn't meet her, nor did I meet the two older Harris offspring because they also lived relatively far away.

From the start, Mrs. Harris seemed like the motherly type. A tall lady with a rounded figure, she smiled frequently. I soon saw that she rarely got on anybody's case about anything. Walt was more stern but was fair-minded. He was a grizzled kind of guy, shorter than his wife and maybe ten years older, which would place him near fifty. Although he didn't shave often, he kept the little bit of hair rimming his head trimmed short—by Mrs. Harris, who did the haircutting for everyone.

That first night I felt uncomfortable, being a stranger and taking their food. It did seem ample for the seven of us—lots of fresh fruits and vegetables and meat. They told me they killed and cured their own meat, both pork and beef. Their cash crops were corn and pinto beans. For family eating they had a vegetable patch and melon patch. Water from the nearby creek supplied the family garden, which was close to the house, but the water wasn't good enough quality for cooking, drinking, or bathing. For that they had to travel some distance and haul water back.

As we ate, the family tried to make me feel at home. They seemed different from most people, especially generous and welcoming. They asked me about myself, why I was hitchhiking, and why I was alone at my age, and their gentle approach made me feel I could speak honestly, so I told them that I had run away from a couple who took me in and mistreated me after my mother died. I didn't go into detail, and the family didn't press me. After dinner I made ready to leave, but Mr. and Mrs. Harris insisted that I remain there overnight. The next day the couple invited me to stay on and work on the farm with the other boys and be like part of the family. The more I got to know them, the more I believed that Mr. and Mrs. Harris made their invitation simply because they were good, kindly people.

The Reidhead-Harris family was Mormon but didn't make a point of it, and they never proselytized. They didn't appear to be religiously observant and didn't send their kids to seminary. However, we did ride regularly by wagon or by mule over to Alpine to attend dances at the combination schoolhouse and Mormon church.

It helped make up my mind about staying on when Mr. and Mrs. Harris said I could work with their boys. That would earn my keep, and I thought an extra hand for this family could be meaningful. They had plenty in certain ways—the food on the table, their good spirits—but they clearly didn't have much in others. In the outhouse, pages from the Sears, Roebuck catalogue were our toilet paper. Tools at the farm were primitive or old-fashioned. The only expensive piece of equipment was a separator with dozens of cone-shaped discs that separated cream from milk. That particular piece of equipment may have been purchased by catalogue from Sears, Roebuck.

My days had taken a surprising turn. It was fascinating to watch a close-knit family whose members obviously liked one another. They all got along, and they all were nice to me. Art particularly was insistent that I remain with them. He was more persuasive than anybody else.

It quickly became clear that Art and Glenn's mom was a good cook and a hell of a baker. Mrs. Harris churned her own butter, baked her own bread, and made her own ice cream. We kids helped out by taking turns at the churn and cranking the ice cream freezer.

Life at the Reidhead-Harris home was a revelation in another way. The family had much different ideas about personal modesty than most people I'd known. When we took baths once a week, we all eventually used the same tub, and it was no big deal for family members to see each other naked. I may have been naked with Mrs. Walters, but that was cloaked in secrecy and disgust. For bath time at the Reidhead-Harrises', a big galvanized washtub was set in the living room and filled with buckets of water heated on a woodstove. Water was a precious thing because it had to be carried from far away. Each of us stood in the tub out in the open to wash ourselves, and although no one hung around in the room while you bathed, if anyone needed to go into that room to get something, it was no big deal. Nobody thought anything about being naked in front of the others. The same thing happened when we undressed at bedtime. We didn't have pajamas; we slept in our underclothes. I wasn't accustomed to this openness and tried to keep myself covered and hidden, and they obliged me and kept their eyes away. I never quite got over being shy in front of the girls and Mrs. Harris, but no one made me feel bad about that.

Oddly enough, there was no rivalry between Art and me, even though we were the same age and I was suddenly sharing his parents. He wasn't bossy and didn't seem to resent me. Maybe that kind of generosity of spirit is why he eventually dedicated himself to religion; I learned decades later that he became a Mormon bishop.

Glenn was friendly but a little different. I wasn't as close to him as I was to Art. There was a bit of an edge to Glenn, and he was totally fearless. Even though he was a couple of years younger than I was, he liked to challenge me in a competitive way, daring me to do things he could do and I couldn't—like ride a horse standing up. In the course of working on farms and ranches, I'd learned to ride early on, but that didn't mean I could ride standing up on the back of a horse. I tried after Glenn challenged me but quickly slid down to straddle the horse when I realized I was going to fall.

I didn't feel singled out by Glenn for competition because he was that way with everyone. He simply was more adventurous and mischievous than his brothers and sisters. You never wanted to challenge *him*, because he'd try anything.

Water at the homestead was not easy to come by. For viable water, we had to haul our drinking, cooking, and bath water in a couple of barrels from a creek about a mile and a half away. About every third day we boys hitched up a mule to a flatbed, four-wheeled buggy to fetch water. Only one kid went on this errand if there was other work to be done. The buggy didn't have a seat, so you had to stand up to drive. At the distant creek you scooped up water in a pail to fill the barrels, and when they were full, you covered them with canvas for the return trip. Usually a lot of water spilled on the way home as it splashed through the covers. If it was warm weather and other work wasn't pressing, all of us boys did the errand and went swimming as well. We had fun and got our baths at the same time. Alongside the creek the family had hung one of those ropes you could swing on.

The Harrises had three mules and a horse. The horse was Belle and the mules were Jude, Gyp, and Nip. Belle and Nip were work animals only; Gyp and Jude could be ridden. Gyp was better for riding because she had a terrific gait, but she was treacherous. You never wanted to relax when you rode her. Gyp could feel through her flanks when you relaxed and would take the opportunity to throw you into the nearest barbed wire fence. Many was the time Gyp tossed me because I didn't keep my attention focused. She was also very clever. If you walked between her and Belle, she wouldn't kick you because she knew she'd get in trouble, so she kicked the horse, and Belle would kick you. Jude was a much sweeter animal but had a very poor gait. Mules have a backbone like a blade, whereas horses are more rounded on top. If you're riding a mule with a jolting gait, that sharp backbone hurts if you don't have a saddle, and the Harrises couldn't afford saddles. We did most of the plowing with Belle and Nip, who were useful only as plodding work animals. Mules are valuable on a farm because they're strong for their size; they can compete successfully against huge draft horses because of their power and determination.

One time I had a date to take a girl to the monthly dance at the local Mormon church/schoolhouse, which was maybe three or four miles away. I picked her up riding Gyp, and the girl got on behind me and put her arms around my waist. We were clipping along at a nice pace on our way to the dance when a rabbit ran in front of Gyp. All that mule needed was an excuse. She reared back and then came forward, throwing me over her head. It's a mystery how the girl stayed on, but she remained on Gyp as she came down on my back and fractured a rib. This ended the dance possibility for the evening. That Gyp was mean.

On the Harris farm we used a single-share plow, a curved plow that digs and turns over the soil in a single groove. It was pulled by two of the animals. After plowing, we broke up the clods of soil with a harrow. The Harris harrow was homemade, a frame constructed from two-by-fours and railroad spikes. Next we planted by hand, walking the rows. In the growing season, those were long days from sunrise to sunset.

Harvesting again was a homemade affair. The family had built a sled with a slanted front from which a sharpened sheet of metal pointed forward. Nip or Belle pulled the sled, and you sat on the sled as this knife ahead of you cut the cornstalks about six inches off the ground. The corn grown by the Harrises wasn't the type favored by people for their tables but was meant as feed for farm animals. As the corn was cut you grabbed armfuls of stalks, and each time your arms were full, you laid them off to the side in a bunch on the ground. When all the corn was cut, one person drove a wagon down the rows while others of us walked alongside the wagon to load it with the corn we'd laid out. In spite of my years using a variety of equipment on ranches and farms, I'd never seen anything like this setup before. The family's homemade techniques were all new to me.

The farmers in this region used a form of shared irrigation called acequias. Water came to us from far away, maybe even from the Colorado River. Neighboring farms worked out a schedule for the sequence of utilization, with water gates open and shut for each farm according to this plan. It was guesswork determining how long the water should flow in order to give a farm its proper share—the correct number of acre-feet of water. On the Harris homestead we boys were assigned to watch the flow and operate the gates. The family also employed channel irrigation for their family garden, but this came from the creek close to the house.

The Harris homestead was self-contained. We milked the cows and separated out cream to make our butter and cheese. Pigs were butchered and hung in a smokehouse. In addition to the supply of pork, chicken, and beef, there were tomatoes, sweet peppers, beets, peas, cucumber, lettuce, and squash from their garden, and just about every other type of vegetable you could name, and we ate it all. Mrs. Harris canned a lot of the summertime produce to enjoy in winter.

The colder months were busy, too. In late fall we spread canvas under the many pinyon trees on the property and banged on the trees with two-by-fours to knock off nuts. We collected the pine nuts in barrels, and all winter long we sat around the fireplace at night cracking the itty-bitty pine nuts with metal bars because we didn't have the small hammers typically used. The pine nut shell is ridged, and if you hit the ridge just right, the nut falls out cleanly. After we had enough shelled nuts to take to market, they were sold at towns like Winslow, Holbrook, and Phoenix—big cities where there was a market for them. Our winter nut cracking was part of a larger community effort. We didn't have a car or truck, and neither did many of our neighbors, so the shelled nuts were brought from local farms and carried to market by someone who did. You wouldn't believe how many nuts there could be. On a designated date in early spring, barrel after barrel of pine nuts arrived in the Harrises' yard from all around to collect for transport. The pinyon nuts brought in as much income as the corn crop, because pine nuts have always been pretty expensive.

The corn and pinto bean crops earned money for the family, and so did the pinyon nuts, but other sources of income were needed as well. In winter we cut posts for the highway department, which built and maintained barbed wire fences along the highways to keep cows from wandering onto the road. The cedar posts we sold them had to be six inches in diameter at the small end and six feet tall. That meant we could get one post from one tree—talk about environmental disaster. We chopped down a tree by hand and then chopped off all the branches. The family usually took on the job in snowy weather, so we worked in a couple of feet of snow. We were paid maybe fifteen cents a post for all that labor and all that destruction of trees. If we peeled off the bark, we earned another penny.

Gyp did the counting after we cut down cedar trees for posts. We took a team of mules to pick up the posts and were able to pile forty-two of them on the wagon. That was it for Gyp, not a post more. I know it sounds like I'm kidding, but we swore to this. One more post and Gyp wouldn't budge. We tested her again and again, but no go. Glenn, who was always the instigator of everything, decided to gather a bunch of twigs, put them under Gyp, and light them. "That'll move her," he said. She moved just far enough to place the wagon over the fire. We rushed to remove some of the posts from the load.

We kids didn't go to school. There was always work to do. Even if we weren't planting or cultivating or harvesting, we had to help with irrigation by opening and closing gates and standing around waiting for water to reach the crops. In summertime, if we weren't doing any of those tasks, we cut firewood.

The Harris farm was remote, and there was plenty of wildlife around. It fell to me to shoot a bobcat out in the yard that liked to go after the chickens, but I never did get it. I was supposed to shoot coyotes as well, because they got into the watermelons all the time and ate the heart out of them. I could sit two hundred yards away from coyotes, and they'd hear that small click of my .22 and be gone. I couldn't hit one to save my soul, although I don't think my heart was into killing them or any other animal. Still, hunting for the Reidhead-Harris family became a task of mine because I was the best shot.

I was no good at hitting bobcats or coyotes, but it turned out I had a natural talent with a rifle that came in handy bringing home food. The weapon I used had simple iron sights, and I believe I taught myself. Art claims that the pie-baking woman in Snowflake gave me the rifle. The iron sites were V-shaped, with a little ball at the end that you lined up in the crux of the V along with the animal you were hunting. This called for pure ability to point in the right direction and shoot. If we had no other meat to eat, it was my task to go hunting on the family's property and in the national forest all around. All we had was that .22, so I didn't hunt big game, mostly rabbits and squirrels. Nowadays I'm horrified at the thought of shooting a cottontail, but I was a kid then and we needed the food. I'd bring home two or three rabbits at most, and Mrs. Harris would make rabbit stew or fried rabbit, which was similar to fried chicken.

Mrs. Harris was the doctor in the family. Her cure-all for everything was horehound tea and poultices. Glenn had what she called "bad blood." Not the same kind I'd been accused of. He used to break out in boils—huge, oversized pimples on his arms and back. Doctors usually lanced boils and drained them, but his mother picked wild herbs to make a poultice and applied it over the boils. She also made him drink a ghastly horehound tea concocted from wild leaves that grew everywhere around the farm. That tea worked for the boils, and it appeared to be a cure for most everything else, too. No one ever died, either from ailments or that tea. I used to think to myself when I was sick, "Get over it so you won't have to drink the damn tea."

Mrs. Harris also made other remedies from herbs she picked in the wild—leaves that rid you of stomachache or diarrhea or whatever. She ministered to her neighbors in a variety of ways and was the midwife when her daughter-in-law Naomi gave birth. There were no doctors around.

I think it's accurate to say that I didn't often need a reprimand. Life at the Harrises' place felt idyllic. Their way of life was simple and good. We didn't need much outside entertainment. Mrs. Harris would cook up a mixture for ice cream, we'd take turns churning it, and all of us would sit around eating the delicious dessert while we talked and cracked pinyon nuts around the fire. We tossed quite a few of the nuts into our mouths as well.

For light at night, gas mantle lamps with kerosene provided warm illumination. The light given off seemed superior to electric. One lamp could light up an entire room. These were hand-carried lamps, and each had a central pipe in a glass casing. The pipe rose in a T, from which hung a couple of downspouts. On each downspout you hung two mantles, which were bags made of gauze fabric. At the base of the lamp, you pumped air up the pipe, and that created pressure to force gas up into the mantles. Once you got the air pressure up to draw fluid out of the pipe, you lit the mantles, and each glowing fabric mantle would give off light until it burnt up. You might need to get up and pump more air every so often, but a lamp could provide light all evening. The Harris family had four or five lamps they used throughout the house.

I looked forward to the evening once a month when we attended the local dance. This event was like old-time barn dances with western-style hoedown and caller, except it was held in the church/schoolhouse. Chairs lined the perimeter of the room, and local musicians serenaded us on fiddle and guitar. Adults and older kids danced while the younger ones ran around outside doing mischief. Older boys and girls sneaked off to kiss, but I didn't have any real girlfriends. Spring, summer, and fall we took ourselves to the dances, but not in winter when there was deep, deep snow. We lived at an elevation of maybe ten thousand feet, so those winters were quite cold.

For the first time since I was a young child, I felt part of a real family. I fell in easily with the Reidhead-Harrises. There was never an awkward moment, and they seemed to regard me as one of them. I never witnessed jealousy among the boys about what I got or they got, and we boys didn't quarrel much. The entire family treated me so good. For me, there'd never been anything like that—at least not that I could remember. Walt Harris acted as if I was one of his sons. If he told me something and I didn't do it, I got hollered at but never hit. They weren't a family that displayed obvious affection with hugging or caressing, but a feeling of contentment between the couple and between them and their kids was obvious, and I was lucky to be part of it. If Mrs. Harris made cinnamon rolls and they were warm out of the oven, she'd invite us all to come get some, and I could see that she took pleasure in doing that for us. It told me a lot.

If any of us kids misbehaved, we were given extra chores or extra work. You might have to do water duty for a week instead of taking turns with the others. Hauling water was not a chore we looked forward to because it was a tedious, rough ride on that buggy, and you had to drive in a way that kept you from spilling too much. Or, if you misbehaved, you might have to milk the cows or feed the hogs for a number of days in a row.

If you made a mistake in the course of your work, there was no punishment. You were simply expected to deal with the mistake. For example, one time I lost the plow with Belle and Nip attached and had to stay out until I recovered the animals. I'd been working the field all day, and when I was done, Naomi and Marvin invited me over to dinner at their home on the property. I thought I'd hitched the team outside their house, but after dinner I came out to find the animals and plow gone. They'd hung up the plow at the edge of the field and torn loose. I returned home to report to Mr. Harris what happened, and he said only, "Go look for them and don't come back until you have them." I grabbed Gyp, and it took me about three days. The animals wandered together here and there, and as I searched, people along the way told me what direction they last saw them headed. At night I slept under the stars, and I ate whatever the neighbors offered me as I went along. Near the town of Show Low, about ten miles from home, I caught up with the animals. They knew me, so it wasn't hard to round them up.

As homesteaders on their land, the Harrises were required by the government to make certain improvements to the property. Unfortunately they weren't able to finish the house and meet those requirements. Also, I believe they owed money on the land, either as part of the deal or because they had borrowed against it, I'm not sure. As hard as they worked, the family was hardly able to earn enough income to meet their obligations. It was difficult to grow a cash crop that paid much. Cutting posts for the highway department gave miniscule returns for the labor involved. Selling pine nuts didn't earn enough. One day I learned that the family was being forced to give up their home and move in with relatives in Utah.

The mood in our home turned dismal. Hours went by in silence. Family members had red-rimmed eyes; voices were hushed.

My spirits collapsed. Life with the Reidhead-Harris family felt perfect. Art, Glenn, Kim, Nadine, Pearl, Marvin, and

Delbert had become my brothers and sisters, their parents my parents. The love and contentment that marked their days had wrapped around me. Now that would have to end.

It was clear to me that I needed to leave the family. I set aside my feelings for their benefit and for mine. Survival had to be primary. It was necessary for me to think like that—me and all the other people facing dire straits in those days.

Mr. and Mrs. Harris didn't say I needed to leave. They encouraged me to stay with them. However, I wasn't really part of their family. My thinking was that I shouldn't increase their burden or their relatives'. Also, my chances would be better on my own. The family's future did not look promising. I thought about my earlier experiences with Mormons in Snowflake and was leery of going to Utah, where I'd probably be pressured into accepting the religion, so there was that, too. My view was relatively pragmatic. It was time to go my own way, and I had to accept it.

I'd lived with the Reidhead-Harris family about eighteen months, two years max. Now I was fifteen or sixteen. I came up with a plan. My old wanderlust kicked in. I'd visit a few different places starting with the West Coast. I was still curious about picking dates in Indio. After that I'd find my way back to Pennsylvania to look for my mother's grave and then go to New York because I wanted to see that enormous city.

I wonder about the other paths my life might have taken if I hadn't devised that plan. How could I know that going to New York would lead me to a young woman who eventually turned my life around in the best possible way?

The whole Reidhead-Harris family gathered to watch me go. Nadine cried. So did Mrs. Harris. They said again that I should stay with them, but I was convinced they had enough problems without having to take care of me. And I knew how to put on a strong face no matter what. Beyond which, I had earlier spent so much time being on my own that saying goodbye didn't affect me as badly as they thought. I may have even felt a little guilty because I was fearful of what life held for them, knowing they were in bad straits and that I might suffer as well if I stayed. In retrospect, I should have realized the Mormon community would come to their aid. Mormons stick together and take care of one another—it's their way. That last day, we said goodbye inside the house, and then I just stepped out the door and walked away.

It didn't occur to me to ask for the family's new address. I was young and socially inept. During my years on the road, I'd learned never to look back, only to move forward. Others had been friendly in the course of my travels, including Ruby Johnson's parents, but I didn't stay in touch with anybody. It would be sixty-four years before I got in touch with the Reidhead-Harrises, which I did with the help of my daughter.

Take this job and shove it

It was a wonderful job, the best William ever had, except maybe for his service in Japan for the Marine Corps after the war. At the end of William's work life, he enjoyed more than two decades at Macy's overseeing a dozen employees from his office on the executive floor of the landmark San Francisco store on Union Square as well as supervising home decorators in other northern California Macy's.

On all other jobs, William never thought the results good enough. Not even on fine, painstaking woodworking projects carried out in his well-equipped home workshop. However, in the Corps and at Macy's, as he gained acceptance from other people, ideas hammered into William about ugliness and stupidity loosened enough to allow feelings of value and worth.

And then one day, as he put it, he quit Macy's in a fit of pique.

In the Union Square store, a young woman who was floor manager of hard goods—furniture, bedding, etc.—was always late to work. She and William had gone out for coffee a few times and were friends, so she was in the habit of phoning him when running late to ask him to carry out a few tasks she was supposed to have accomplished at the start of her work-day. If display rooms needed to be rearranged or new items put on display for a sale, she asked him to have the warehouseman take care of those jobs. Officially William didn't have the authority to do that. He wasn't her boss, but she was essentially his employment equal, and the warehouse guys knew William and did as he asked.

One morning the young woman was late to work but didn't call William. A sale in her department had been scheduled for that day, and early customers swarmed her floor asking for help from the lone salesman. Overwhelmed and desperate, the salesman called William to ask for help. There was nothing William could do because he didn't have the authority to bring on extra workers. Then a second salesman scheduled to arrive on that floor in the afternoon happened to show up at the store early. As soon as William got wind of the second salesman's presence in the building, William located the guy, informed him that his department was swamped, and told him to punch in early because his help was needed.

William described what happened next: "When my so-called friend, the floor manager, finally arrived for work, she saw the second man on her floor well before his afternoon clock-in time and became furious. She summoned me and threw a tantrum right there on the floor. How dare I usurp her authority! What did I think I was doing? Ranting and raving, she told me that I had no right to stick my nose into her business. I said to her, 'You have some nerve. The next time you're late in the morning, don't call me. As far as I'm concerned, you can take the whole damn place and shove it where the sun don't shine.'"

So he quit.

William was still the boy who had decided that no one would ever give him crap or take advantage of him again.

CHAPTER SEVEN

Newsboys' Home

It was late autumn and awful cold when I left the Reidhead-Harrises. Southern California seemed like an especially good idea. I hit the road again, going from job to job on my way there. This was when the conductor saved my life by taking me into the caboose—and one more time that I didn't actually make it to California. I left the comfort of the caboose and headed for the nearest hobo jungle, where I heard through the grapevine about work back in the other direction, in Oklahoma and Texas. In those states I was able to earn a little bit of money and decided it was time to go north and east to find my mother's grave.

Marian had told me about my hometown. A name like Susquehanna stuck easily in my mind, even at age six or seven. I had so little to hold me to the past. Marian had also reminded me of my real last name, and I knew her last name was Cokely. What little information I could trust about my family came from her.

In the East, trains were not my first choice of transportation. In the cold of winter, travel was far warmer when you rode in automobiles or truck cabs, and the closer to the East Coast I came, the more roads I found, so hitching became easier. Still, one night a driver left me off in Roanoke, Virginia, in the middle of a snowstorm. I wasn't dressed for the weather and had no money for a room, so I went to the police station in the hope they'd give me a cell for the night. Sometimes in small towns police would let you do this. I can still see the globe atop the post in front of the Roanoke station: POLICE written in black letters across the illuminated white glass. At the front desk the desk sergeant listened to my story but didn't say much. Next thing I knew, he called a police car and instructed the cop to come collect me and drop me off outside city limits.

The cop deposited me alongside the road on a country highway with forest all around. It was late at night and the road was deserted. Now it seemed certain I could freeze to death, so I hiked back to Roanoke. At the police station I picked up a rock and hurled it at the POLICE globe, shattering it. No one came out, so I went in and reported my crime to the sergeant. He called another car and told the cop to take me far enough away so that I couldn't walk back. Fortunately, there wasn't much night left. I found a relatively sheltered spot in the woods, gathered brush around me, and huddled there until daybreak.

The icy weather didn't last long and the days became milder for a spell. More rides came my way, and finally I arrived in Susquehanna County, Pennsylvania. At the courthouse in Montrose, the county seat, I explained my situation, gave my family name, and asked if they could tell me where my mother was buried. The people at the courthouse were able to tell me where the cemetery was located in Susquehanna Depot but nothing else. They had no record of my mother's death or of my birth. A woman behind the counter said the courthouse had earlier burned down and many of the records with it, and whatever records did remain from the 1920s were in Harrisburg. She wasn't hopeful that the Harrisburg courthouse had anything that could help me.

The sheriff stood nearby as I talked with the woman. He said that after I was done at the cemetery, I should come to his house for dinner with his family and spend the night.

Meanwhile, the woman had thought of something. "I bet I can tell you who would know about your mother. She's a friendly old soul who seemed to know everybody in Susquehanna in those times." I was directed to a house on the outskirts of Susquehanna Depot. I don't know if I caught this woman on a bad day or she'd become cranky in her old age, but when I explained who I was and what I wanted to know, she said, "I hate to tell you this, but your mother was a lady of ill repute," and shut the door in my face. Not a word more than that. This was not a pleasant thing to hear. I knew I hadn't spent my early years in a house of prostitution. What the old lady said couldn't be true.

At the cemetery I found the section dating from my mother's time. It was overgrown and unkempt. I was unable to locate a grave marker for a woman with the last name VanSteenburgh or any name close to that. I decided not to travel to the Harrisburg courthouse on the slim chance of learning something about my family. The old lady's pronouncement rattled me. I tried to wipe it out of my mind.

It was a long walk to the sheriff's house outside Susquehanna Depot. His family lived on a classic sort of Pennsylvania farm, with a well-maintained house and barn and some horses, but it was not a working farm like those I'd seen out West. In the front yard his two children were playing hide-and-seek with neighbor children. One of the sheriff's kids was a girl about the same age as me, maybe a little older. I explained about the sheriff's invitation, said I'd traveled up north from Texas, and they invited me to play until dinner was ready. The sheriff's daughter and I ran off to the barn, where she followed me into a hiding spot in the hay. While we waited there hoping not to be found, she whispered, "Don't you want to kiss me?" I'd never kissed a girl. I gave her a small peck on the cheek, and she asked, "Is that all they taught you in Texas?"

My fears about anything related to sex held strong. Not to mention that I was a stranger in town. The girl's father being sheriff and all, a kiss seemed an especially bad idea. I made sure his daughter didn't trap me again. At dinner I avoided her eyes and didn't talk to her. Early the next morning I slipped away before anyone knew I was gone.

I was ready to hitch to New York, the biggest city in the world. The tallest building on earth, the Empire State Building, had been completed a short time before, and I wanted to see that. I wanted to feel what it was like to walk down the streets of an enormous city. I figured there must be all kinds of jobs I could get there.

A truck driver brought me into New York City through the Lincoln Tunnel. He dropped me around 110th Street far up into Manhattan. Right away I saw a policeman, a beat cop, and went up to him. I asked if there was anyplace where a boy like me could stay that didn't cost a lot of money. Here's one more reason that I think providence sometimes steps in and helps you: It was my great good fortune that he knew of the Newsboys' Home downtown. He said it was a nice clean place that provided room and board for boys about twelve years old to eighteen or nineteen. They let you stay there without paying until you got a job. If you didn't have money, you waited on tables and cleaned bedrooms to earn your keep, and when you got a job, you paid Newsboys' part of your earnings if you wanted to stay on.

I used to wonder who had made Newsboys' possible. In the course of working on this book, I found out: Charles Loring Brace, the same man who created the Orphan Trains. Fifteen or sixteen years old on the streets of New York, I had no idea that the same person who was instrumental in sending me toward a nightmare in Gallup was also the one who made it possible to find safe refuge in 1940 or '41.

The cop told me to look for Newsboys' at the corner of Duane and New Chambers Streets about a block from Third Avenue. Four or five blocks away, the foot of the Brooklyn Bridge emptied into New York City. City Hall was right nearby.

It bowled me over that I had to walk about a hundred blocks to get there. I couldn't believe there was anyplace so big it would be necessary to walk a hundred blocks to get from one point to another. Houston and Dallas were the only large cities I'd seen, and they weren't all that big in those days. Within minutes New York confounded me. The policeman gave me good directions, though.

At New Chambers Street I stared up at a building seven stories high. It looked a lot like a hotel. In the lobby were couches and chairs arranged about, and I could see a dining room beyond. The place seemed meticulously clean. Boys sat in the lobby and walked through looking comfortable enough with the situation. Behind the front desk was a tall Russian guy with stooped posture who ran the place. Later I decided he resembled the mad Russian bartender played by Leonid Kinskey in the movie *Casablanca*. His behavior made him seem like a wild Russian, and he was very emotional in a good way, gushing with warm feeling. When I told him why I was there, he said in a thick accent, "You came to the right place!" He laid out the rules and said I could wait tables in the Newsboys' dining room until I found a job elsewhere. I was required to begin my job search immediately.

On the way to my room assignment on one of the upper
floors, he filled me in about life at Newsboys'. Unless you
arrived with a buddy, you were given a single room. We
received fresh linens once a week and were expected to keep
our rooms clean and neat. Each boy's room was inspected
periodically. He informed me about the hours breakfast,
lunch, and dinner were served. Except if you were working
elsewhere at a job, you were expected to appear on time in
the dining room for each meal.

We walked down a well-lit hallway, and he opened the
door on a room that contained a bed, nightstand, and private
bathroom. It was nothing fancy, but it looked fine. More than
fine. The fire escape landing right outside ran the length of
the building, accessible to all of the rooms on my floor. I figured the fire escape would prove to be handy since there was
a ten o'clock curfew. I wasn't used to being restrained in my
movements because of my years on the road.

You could say I had become relatively rough around the
edges by the age of fifteen or sixteen. Apart from living with
the Reidhead-Harrises, I was used to setting my own rules.
I'd grown tall and wiry and strong enough from manual labor
to feel I could stand up to serious threats. Yes, I'd had to be
respectful of the law and of employers, but if the law wasn't
around, I could take care of myself if need be. Given all that,
my after-curfew activities were pretty tame. From time to
time I left the building late at night to go down the road to
buy a pickle or a potato knish from all-night delis. There was
a good old cop, a beat cop, who walked the neighborhood
regularly swinging his billy club. He had a special way of
handling his club, which was maybe eighteen inches long:
As he walked along, he repeatedly tossed his billy club down
at the sidewalk, it bounced up in the air, and he grabbed it
on the first bounce. He caught me out once. I was running
from Newsboys' when he threw his club, hit me in the calf,

and dumped me. Then he walked over, gave me a hand up, and told me to get back in the building because it was after curfew.

Mostly I was cooperative with the requirements at Newsboys'. The place was remarkable, and I respected that. It offered a homeless boy like myself a room of his own, fresh sheets and towels once a week, and food, all in a setting that felt like a nice hotel. It strikes me now that in places like this, where large populations of needy strangers are housed under one roof, you can have a lot of tension and chaos, but at Newsboys' the atmosphere was both easygoing and controlled. Also, the meals turned out to be quite good, based on what I knew about food at the time. I'm sure it wasn't gourmet, but then neither was I.

In New York, I took a multitude of small jobs. It turned out that employment in New York at the start of the 1940s, like everywhere else, was still pretty hard to come by and often short-lived. One thing was evident, though: If you worked in New York City, you didn't have to worry about getting paid, unless you didn't live up to your employer's expectations. A boss who didn't pay you had to fear the authorities. In fact, I could have reported to someone at Newsboys' that I hadn't been paid at the end of a week, and they would have stepped in on my behalf. In New York City, employers didn't pull fast ones on strangers nearly as often as people did in small towns, where law enforcement automatically took the side of locals.

There was a flip side to this coin. People who lived in New York's various neighborhoods—Greenwich Village or Harlem or Little Italy or the Jewish, Polish, and Irish districts—were very provincial in the way they regarded strangers. There was a lot of suspicion toward outsiders in those enclaves. You didn't walk through those neighborhoods unless you had business there, because everyone there knew one another, and if the residents spotted you, they'd look at you askance. Outside those enclaves, however, big-city ways took over.

Many New Yorkers assumed that residents of Newsboys' were criminals or future criminals since we were a collection of formerly homeless youngsters, but to my knowledge, in the year and a half I lived there, none of us got into trouble with the police. The youngest guys were mostly about my age, and a number were older. Quite a few were preparing to transition from civilian life into the military, because the U.S. entered World War II during that time.

While I didn't know of bad kids at Newsboys', there were oddballs living there for sure, and I do seem to attract oddballs. In fact, I attracted two of the oddest ones you'd ever want to see. One fellow who became my friend was a tall, lanky Canadian kid named Pye. That was his first name. He wore a partial uniform of the Royal Canadian Air Force—the pants and shirt but not the coat or cap. Pye talked constantly about the Royal Canadian Air Force as if he was enlisted in it, but his dream was to join the British RAF. Even before the U.S. entered the war, the military was very much on our minds because the English were already fighting the Germans.

My other unusual buddy was Riggs, which was his last name. He had a good voice and could tap-dance like you wouldn't believe. At the time, Riggs was the only black kid living at Newsboys'. In my experience it was unusual for a homeless boy to be so good at singing and dancing, and I think Riggs was self-taught. The third member of our group, whose name is lost to me, was a guy who could play the guitar.

I should mention that Riggs was accepted as a member of our group. It didn't matter that he was black. We had Jewish friends, too, as well as Polish. I know those days were supposed to be pretty bad in terms of racism and ethnic prejudice. Maybe in our small world it was different because we guys at Newsboys' had been with all kinds of people growing up.

All three of my new friends were about my age. In our free hours, the four of us hung out in front of Newsboys' on the sidewalk, with the one guy playing the guitar, Riggs dancing, Pye singing, and me listening and watching because I couldn't sing or dance. It was a great way to attract girls, between the singing and dancing. They passed by on their way to a nearby deli, the Tribune Theater, or City Hall Park, where they liked to hang out with their girlfriends. Newsboys' was situated in the heart of things in Lower Manhattan, close to Little Italy, Wall Street, the main commercial district, Greenwich Village, and a lot of other popular destinations.

A Polish girl named Susan liked to stroll by Newsboys', and she became my first real girlfriend. She was a little bit cross-eyed but not bad looking except for that eye, and she was very friendly and seemed nice. Susan had quite a reputation, but I didn't know that at first.

Susan lived in Little Italy, where there were actually quite a few Polish people residing at the time. She didn't seem to have the same strict parental supervision and restrictions about spending time with boys that the other girls did, so we made friends right away. It was just her and me, I thought, girlfriend and boyfriend. She indicated that we could be intimate, but I didn't go for it; I was very shy. The most we did was hold hands, go to the movies, and kiss. However, many other guys had done more than kiss and bragged about it, so eventually I found out about Susan's reputation. My friends told me she was known as "the town pump," which came as a shock and caused me to back away. From the vantage point of years, my reaction to Susan—and the other boys' reaction—seems childish and stupid, but that's the way things were back then. In today's world, it seems that few people would give her interest in sex and her forward behavior a second thought. Eventually I dated two other Polish girls from that neighborhood, but those two girls were entirely different from Susan and very circumspect in their approach to boys.

I laid eyes on the first girl I ever loved while returning from a date with Susan. I was escorting Susan back to her family's apartment in Little Italy when I saw another young woman walk out of Susan's building. She was beautiful and petite with a tiny waist and nice legs. Her dark, shoulder-length hair was thick and glossy and fell in waves around her oval face. Later I learned her name was Lucretia. Lucretia's beauty affected me in a powerful way because she was different. Her dark hair and olive skin made her seem exotic. Her tiny stature made her seem delicate. I was tall and blond and in my travels had mostly been acquainted with people who had fair skin and Anglo features.

On that first sighting, Lucretia didn't smile at me. She recognized that I was an outsider in Little Italy, and she may have taken an especially dim view of me because I was with fast Susan.

Each time Lucretia walked by Newsboys' with her two girlfriends, I watched her. The three of them were very much alike with their olive complexions and dark brown hair. As the days went by, I found myself hoping that Lucretia would walk by Newsboys' again with Pat and Jean, the Gallo sisters. They often stopped to watch the dancing and singing or to talk with us boys. Although Lucretia stopped with the other two, she wasn't nearly as friendly. Her parents had forbidden her to hang out with the guys at Newsboys', and beyond that she wasn't supposed to spend time with any boys.

Many things in our neighborhood drew visitors or caused people to stop right at our building. Near the front door,

against the outside wall of Newsboys', a man had built a news-
stand where you could buy candy, newspapers, magazines,
and cigarettes. From behind the counter at his small stand, he
sold us two cigarettes for a penny. We called those loose cigarettes "loosies." In between Newsboys' and City Hall, at New
Chambers and Third Avenue, there was a popular little Jewish
deli with a barrel full of big fat dill pickles, each one maybe
a nickel. Nearby we also had a Nedick's diner, part of a chain
famous for hot dogs, orange juice, and a ten-cent breakfast.
For ten cents at Nedick's you got a cup of coffee, two donuts,
and a glass of OJ.

On Third close to Newsboys' was a Horn & Hardart
Automat, one of a chain of restaurants made famous by Cary
Grant in the movie *That Touch of Mink*. At the automat you
could get a meal for a dollar or less. First thing when you
entered Horn & Hardart, you asked for change to insert in the
many food dispensers. Meat dishes, salads, vegetables, and
puddings were visible in rows of small glass-fronted compartments built into the automat's walls. You made your choice by
inserting coins into a slot in a compartment and then turning
a knob to open the glass door to retrieve your food. Girls
stood behind the banks of compartments constantly restock-
ing them. In the movie, when Cary Grant buys a piece of pie,
Audrey Meadows reaches through the little glass door and
slaps his face.

I noticed that Lucretia's favorite restaurant was Chock
full o' Nuts, which was started by a Russian immigrant named
William Black and may have been the first fast food restaurant in America. His lunch counters offered a cup of coffee
and a sandwich for a nickel. Their featured sandwich was
cream cheese and chopped nuts on dark raisin bread. The
sandwiches were made in New Jersey by employees using
tongs, so they were advertised as "untouched by human
hands," promising excellent hygiene as a major selling point.

At first I watched Lucretia from a distance. She and Pat and Jean stopped to chat in front of Newsboys' or caught our eye as they went off to the movies, and after a while we four boys went with them, always as a group, never as couples. A movie house close by was owned by a former prostitute named Maisie. She was the sweetest, most kindhearted lady, and she worked the ticket booth, maybe even the projector. If you were a kid with no money, she'd let you in anyway. Lucretia reported that her mother called Maisie's theater "the Scratch House" because you got fleas there. Another choice was the Tribune Theater on Nassau Street, a much nicer, fancier movie theater, but it was expensive for me, so going to that palace had to be a special occasion. Two or three sets of curtains hid the screen, creating a feeling of drama as they opened one after the other. A ramp led to the upper level, a mezzanine. At either of these movie houses on a Saturday afternoon we'd see cartoons and Pathé News before the feature, which might be a movie like *The Perils of Pauline*. A rooster used to crow to introduce the Pathé News, just like you'd see the MGM lion roar or the RKO tower shoot sparks to herald the feature film.

Lucretia and her friends said they always felt safe walking through their neighborhood and into ours near City Hall Park. This was because the Mafia had their headquarters on Mulberry Street in the heart of Manhattan's Little Italy, where Carlo Gambino (AKA "The Executioner") headed up his crime family. You had to walk by Mafia headquarters to get to all the good Italian food and shopping that Lucretia loved. Counter to what you might think, awareness of the Mafia was a positive aspect of the three girls' growing up in New York City. The Mafia looked out for Italian children. In fact, everyone in the neighborhood knew and looked out for the kids. Lucretia's and Jean and Pat's fathers were not in the Mafia, but they didn't have to be in order to know their kids were protected. No child who lived in Little Italy ever had to worry about walking on any street, whether they were Italian or not. The Italian Mafia would defend them to the death, the same as they would take someone else's life in an instant. The fact that everyone, Mafia or not, knew one another made many things easier. As little kids, Lucretia, Jean, and Pat could safely be sent down the street to the store for groceries, for example; the proprietor knew them and felt fine about giving them the items on their list, knowing that their mothers would pay for them later.

Lucretia's father worked for Pat and Jean Gallo's father, so the two families had a close relationship. In a way, the Gallos were a strange tribe. As I understood it, their mother did nothing but sit by the window crocheting and crying over her babies who'd died—crocheting and crying and having more children. Pat and Jean became largely responsible for mothering the younger kids and cooking and taking care of the house. Their hours away from home had to be a welcome break.

Another place we went with Pat, Jean, and Lucretia was the steps of the Fraunces Tavern, the historic landmark where George Washington gave a farewell speech to his officers at the end of the Revolutionary War. A brick building at the corner of Pearl and Broad Streets in the heart of the Financial District, it served as a meeting hall. We never went in, but we liked to meet on the steps. As far as we could tell, mostly big shots gathered there. One night when we were on the steps singing and dancing, this gentleman walked up and tried the door. Lucretia told him, "Oh sir, this place is closed." I admired her boldness. The man said, "I know, I own it." He laughed and didn't ask us to move but simply turned around and left. Maybe he'd seen our small gang and worried we might try to get in.

That evening was the first time I noticed how standoffish Lucretia was from the rest of us. She was bold in certain ways, like talking to that stranger, but careful in others. Pat and Jean were very forthcoming, joining in our singing and dancing and even holding hands with one or another of us boys as we walked along. Lucretia hung back and didn't sing or dance or hold hands. Although we boys held hands with Jean and Pat as if we were boyfriends and girlfriends, our gatherings were very innocent, and no one separated out as a couple. Lucretia was friendly enough but let us know that we weren't nearly her boyfriends. I didn't know this at first, but a big reason for her aloofness was that she had three brothers who were always around, and she was terrified that they would see her with us.

For recreation our group also liked to board the Third Avenue el and ride all the way to the Bronx or Coney Island, traveling high above the city, enjoying the view as we looked down. A nickel covered the entire round trip if you didn't get off and go downstairs. We never had money to spend on the rides at Coney Island, but we sometimes walked up and down the boardwalk.

Much later I learned that Jeannie Gallo had a crush on me during our Newsboys' days. This apparently was what held our group together, although I was oblivious. Jeannie encouraged the girls to hang out at Newsboys' so that she could spend time with me, and when I heard about it, the idea caught me off guard. I could swear I'd never even held hands with Jeannie.

Early on, Lucretia made it clear she didn't like me too well. A time or two she'd seen me at my worst. In those days, if somebody crossed me, I beat him up. For example, one evening another fellow from Newsboys' joined us for a walk down to 14th Street to the fruit market, where I purchased peaches or grapes for the group. The new fellow monopolized Lucretia. He walked with her and stayed with her. I didn't say anything about it at the time, but when we split up for the night, I waited until I got him alone and gave him a pretty good beating, telling him that Lucretia was my girl, which of course she wasn't. Lucretia found out and didn't mind telling me she didn't like me or what I'd done. My position was that I had taken the girls down there, I had purchased the fruit, so what right did this guy have to muscle in? I didn't say I was jealous of Lucretia paying attention to him, but that had to be obvious. I think I even wanted to believe that Lucretia was trying to make me jealous by walking and talking with the guy in a test of my affection.

It may sound perverse, but news of the beating "enhanced" my reputation at Newsboys'. At least, that's the way I saw it. It caused the other boys to treat me with greater respect. On another occasion, a newcomer claimed my usual seat in the dining room. We argued about it and took our dispute outside. We didn't want to endanger our residence at Newsboys' by continuing the argument indoors, so we stepped out of the building and around the corner. We exchanged words nose to nose. Finally he said, "Go ahead and hit me." I did. He was shocked and said, "Hey! What did you do that for?" His reaction surprised me. I was used to backing up my words. That particular boy and I actually became friends afterward.

I hate to say it now, but in those days in many ways I was a disagreeable person. When my friends and I walked down the sidewalk, I refused to give way to people coming from the opposite direction and made them swerve around us. I recognize now what a belligerent attitude I had. With that attitude and my wiry build, I don't think anyone at Newsboys' wanted to challenge me on anything. Though I didn't see it this way, it could be said that I took offense easily. If you said something about me that I thought was insulting or unfair, I'd let you know in word or in deed. My friends looked on but didn't join in.

Anytime someone outside our group came along and talked to the girls, I became hostile. A great irony was that I got into it with Lucretia's brother Angelo, not knowing he was her brother. I also didn't know that he was one of the most peaceful individuals you'd want to know. As a boy, his eyes had been injured and he was legally blind, and this made him meek and mild and afraid of a lot of things. Our group was hanging out by Newsboys' when Angelo walked past and said something as innocent as "Hey, Lucretia, what are you doing?" I came out swinging. Fortunately for Angelo, there were a couple of guys from the neighborhood ready to take me on right then. The scuffle blew over with no one getting hurt, but it solidified my reputation as a jerk. Lucretia turned to me, furious, and said, "That's my brother! Angelo wouldn't hurt a fly, and you're going to pick on him?"

A day came when Pat and Jean told us they were moving from Little Italy to Brooklyn. They said they would miss us. Now, I thought, it's now or never, before the sisters actually disappeared from view. Without them, Lucretia might never come by Newsboys' again. I got up my courage and asked Lucretia to go out with me. She turned me down. This should have come as no surprise.

After a while, finding work in New York became easier because so many men were being drafted. By 1939 it looked like the conflict in Europe was going to pose a serious threat to the United States. Our battleships in Pearl Harbor hadn't been attacked yet, but by the spring of 1940 our country was mobilizing in a number of ways for possible war. This included spending $1.3 billion to modernize and double the size of the U.S. Navy fleet. The president appointed a secretary of war, and by fall of that same year Congress approved our country's first peacetime draft.

All American men between the ages of twenty-one and thirty-five were required to register. More than a million were drafted for a year's service, and hundreds of thousands of reservists were called to active duty. Congress extended the draft about a year later, in October 1941.

Soon "Help Wanted" signs hung in windows all over New York City. Employment opportunities were usually temporary because most employers promised to hold jobs for soldiers until they returned home. Short term or long term, it didn't matter to me that much. Thoughts of a career didn't enter into it. My goal was simple: Earn enough money to survive.

One of my first New York jobs besides waiting tables at Newsboys' was as a printer's devil at a shop that turned out posters, leaflets, and flyers. Yep, that's what they called me. I soon decided that the printer's devil does the dirtiest job on earth. At the end of my first day, I was covered with black ink. To produce printed material in those days, you had to form text by melting lead and casting type from the melted metal. One of my tasks was to melt the lead and pour it into casts to form individual letters. After the type cooled, I broke off the letters to store them in alphabetized compartments. It was essential that I sort type accurately because a typesetter knew without looking where to reach his hand for letters. He set the small type along wooden rows resembling shelves. Wooden slats held together the words formed in each row of type. Once he had the words lined up, the typesetter pounded the type into place with a large block to level it.

In the next stage of printing, each page of metal type was inked. I did the inking by smearing it on with a rag. In the final step, a worker inserted sheets of paper into a machine press and pushed the paper down against the inked page—a tricky job, because you had to grab the sheet away after it was pressed by the machine and before the machine came down on the next sheet. I tried that once and nearly lost my hands.

After a certain number of printings, ink clogged the letters, and the type needed to be cleaned. For example, the O's filled and become solid black discs. I wiped off the metal type with woolen rags using a cleaning solution that had a strong, not unpleasant odor—it was an ink distiller, maybe ketone. During the cleaning process I became coated with ink.

Soon it came to my attention that the printers in these print shops were mostly alcoholic. In the place where I worked the people were hateful and miserable. Printer's devil was a dirty, unappreciated job. The bosses didn't hesitate to rap you hard upside the head if you didn't move fast enough. At the end of each day, I cleaned myself with the same solution that I used on the metal type, but my skin never came entirely clean. I quit after three or four weeks, but it took a while for the remaining black to wear off.

At the wharves I found employment first as a ship's chandler and then as a cable splicer for a shop I believe had a contract with the Navy, but a job in the movies lured me from cable-making. As part of the war effort, a movie company located in Midtown came to Newsboys' to recruit boys for Navy films. These were educational movies for the troops; for example, they explained why and how to avoid venereal disease. Other films showed new recruits the training ahead of them—running, swimming, diving, and all the exercises they'd be subject to at boot camp. At Newsboys' the movie studio looked for athletic-looking young men they could film in swimsuits or shorts so they'd look like Mr. America.

Auditions were held right in the Newsboys' lobby with everyone watching. It was kind of like a meat market. Fifteen or twenty of us tried out by putting on swimsuits and flexing our muscles or lifting things to show our physical strength. Four men sat in the lobby instructing us what to do, ordering us to pick up a chair with one hand, things like that. They also had us wrestle one another. In the end, five of us were chosen and asked to sign contracts. They gave us subway fare and directions to the location for filming.

We were paid in half-hour increments, ten dollars per half-hour of actual filming, which was very good money. At the studio in Midtown Manhattan, we found that quite a few other young men had been hired as well. They divided us into groups, with some boys used for boxing, others for swimming scenes, and so forth. First thing, we went to makeup. In those earlier days of moviemaking, makeup was laid on thick and you had to wear lipstick and rouge, which we found uncomfortably weird. We were told this was the only way our features would show up on film. Those of us who needed haircuts were given haircuts. The filmmakers did their best to make us look healthy, happy, and strong.

It didn't occur to me that there was an irony in having formerly homeless kids serve as models for the ideal American young man. After all, I did feel happy, healthy, and strong. At this point in my life, it seemed like I'd arrived. I had a roof over my head, three meals a day, and opportunities to get work, plus I could afford new clothes and shoes. The whole geography and atmosphere surrounding me had changed. The most profound difference was the fact of a secure home. I had a base from which to search for jobs instead of needing to wander from place to place. A job might not last long, but there were many opportunities for work, and at the end of a day, if I didn't find a job, I could return to my room and have dinner at Newsboys' instead of needing to move on to the next farm or town.

The five of us from Newsboys' were able to do most of the things the film people asked, whether swimming or running or wrestling or boxing. After makeup, we were sent to a waiting room until they called us. An indoor swimming pool was located at the studio. With direction from various people we dove and swam while another man filmed us. The makeup was such that it didn't come off in the water. This was the most fun job I ever had. It was just pure fun—and a chance to show off. Although we were shown wrestling and boxing, we weren't really doing that. The director posed us to look as if we were boxing or wrestling, but we didn't have to fight.

Young men who looked emaciated and sickly also showed up at the studio. They were supposed to portray what happened if you got venereal disease, malaria, dengue fever, or elephantiasis. In the service, recruits were required to take quinine or Atabrine to protect against malaria, but the latter turned you yellow, including your eyeballs. And I mean yellow. Quinine was in short supply because the Germans had taken the Netherlands; Dutch plantations in Java produced almost all of the world's supply of bark that quinine comes from. Eventually the Japanese captured the Philippines and Indonesia, which were the two other important sources of quinine. As a result, servicemen were required to take Atabrine instead. Some soldiers only pretended to take it because they wanted to avoid turning yellow, so enlisted men needed to be shown what the risks were.

The movie people said they were pleased with our work. The job lasted about five weeks during which we made maybe three films; then they closed up shop. I never saw the movies we were in, but when I was a new recruit in the service, we were shown similar educational films.

Now I was back "on my uppers," which means I didn't have work. Acting jobs were fun, but I don't think any of us expected more of the same. I had no idea that at age sixteen I'd soon walk into a fantastic opportunity. For a while I washed dishes in restaurants and then landed a job down on Broad Street in Manhattan in a hardware store. It was one of those old stores you saw at the time, a shop in the basement of a tall building. The usual clientele were maintenance men and janitors who needed supplies for their work in the tall buildings and skyscrapers around us. It was a small shop, it took only a short time to learn the merchandise, and after all the manual labor I'd done, the job seemed like a breeze. One customer, a Mr. Spadavecchia, came in frequently and began to single me out for help. I'd worked there four or five months when he asked, "Would you like a better job?" I was always on the lookout for that. He handed me his card, which said ITT, International Telephone and Telegraph, nearby on Broad Street. I was to take his card to the employment office at that address and say that he asked me to come in. Mr. Spadavecchia was an engineer, and I think he headed ITT's general machine shop. His card in hand, I walked into the best job of my life up to that point.

At the time, ITT scientists were working on something called "pulse time modulation," which apparently meant the regulation of time between successive electric pulses. I didn't have the foggiest idea what that meant and wasn't bold enough to ask. Nevertheless, I got a job in a secret laboratory at ITT, ensconced in a cagelike room with wire mesh walls. All I was told was that the work was pulse time modulation and that I was not to reveal anything about it because it was an industrial secret. Other employees approached the window in the mesh to speak to me. In the cage with me were gold, silver, platinum, and iridium in sheet, wire, and bar form. Scientists working on the project approached my window and might say, "I need two centimeters of a five-centimeter rod of gold." They filled out request chits; I located the materials. Using micrometers and very fine scales to measure and weigh, I provided them with the precious metals. I recorded in a book what I was giving out, and the scientists had to sign for it. At the end of the day I was searched before leaving the building.

The feeling of responsibility and the precision of the work appealed to me. The cost of materials made it essential that I be exact in my measurements, and from the scientists' viewpoint, it was also important to be precise. I'd never had a job before that required me to use my mind in a significant way and where I had that much responsibility. Not to mention, the work was neat and orderly, and my clothes stayed clean. On top of that, the scientists were patient and treated me well. It was an all-around wonderful employment opportunity for someone with my poor talents. I was paid way more than what I'd been paid for anything else: thirty-five dollars a week. It was also a nine-to-five job with weekends off. I was able to move out of Newsboys' and rent a studio apartment at 77th and Broadway for fifteen dollars a month.

A photograph from that time documents what I thought of as the new me. I'm wearing a wool overcoat and a hat and new shoes. The coat hangs open to show a three-piece suit, shirt, and tie. These were my going-out clothes, my tripping-the-light-fantastic clothes, purchased from Bond Clothiers under the Camel cigarette billboard on 42nd Street. The Camel sign blew smoke rings into the air above Times Square. I was quite the dude. For the first time in my life, I'd bought my own shoes and nice clothes, purchased with money from what I considered my first real job. I hadn't worn new shoes since childhood. For years I'd worn only overalls, and here I was, outfitted from a top men's clothing store that offered custom tailoring. My new pose was carried to an extreme: I bought a pipe and affected to be a pipe smoker.

The pipe was a stretch because on ranches and farms where I worked as a boy, there was no such thing as buying even ready-made cigarettes. We all smoked Bull Durham, which consisted of small flakes of tobacco almost like a powder and came in a cotton drawstring bag with papers attached. The only thing you didn't get with your purchase was matches. We rolled our own cigarettes using Bull Durham—unless you were really elegant and bought Bugler tobacco, which came in a can. We had a standing joke about Bull Durham: One guy says to the other, "Did you know that Bull Durham is half horse shit?" The other guy says, "Damn, I'm glad about that. I thought it was all horse shit." I doubt that I saw a real cigarette until I got to New York, where I was able to buy two for a penny at the stand outside Newsboys'. None of us boys could afford a full pack.

I would give up all forms of smoking about the time I went into the service. While in the Marines I became a boxer and came to consider myself an athlete, and serious athletes, I figured, didn't smoke.

In December 1941, Mr. Spadavecchia asked me to his house out on Long Island for Christmas dinner. To me the house looked like a mansion, although now I might not think so. That evening I met my boss's daughter. My new clothes must have caught her eye, because she made it clear she was attracted to me. I wasn't interested in her for a number of reasons. For one, she was way above me socially. At the dinner, attended by fifteen or sixteen people, many of them close to me in age, I was well aware that I didn't match the others in social graces or education. I didn't know proper manners in greeting others or carrying on conversation. I didn't know what fork to use. In movies of the time I'd seen people living elegantly, but until that evening I'd never seen this way of life in person. The discussion around the table made it clear that I had the least schooling of anyone present, by far.

From the day we met, in spite of my inadequacies, the boss's daughter drove me nuts with her interest. By this I mean she wouldn't leave me alone, which seemed like a really bad idea for both of us. I made the mistake of letting her know my address, and she showed up at my apartment every weekend. She wanted to go out, she wanted to do this, she wanted to do that. Talk about a kiss on a first date, she didn't hesitate. She asked if I had a girlfriend, so I tried to put her off by saying I had a girl, thinking wistfully of Lucretia.

The boss's daughter asked, "Do you bang her much?"

"HELL, NO!" The question blindsided me. I never would have expected talk like that from a girl. Not even Susan, who had a reputation, ever said crude things. That had been fine with me, because talk of sex scared me. I didn't like to think about sex, at least not in any way I admitted to myself, given my past at the Walters'.

"What are you, backward?" she asked.

I guessed I was backward.

This girl showed a fearlessness that may have come from an awareness of where she fit into society. But I began to think that sex was all certain girls—like Susan, the sheriff's daughter in Pennsylvania, and the boss's daughter—ever thought about. It also made me think that loose girls were the only kind of girl I could get. Mention of my travels may have led girls to think I was experienced in all ways, but I was a virgin. And I still had my antennas up, the instinct to avoid danger as the stranger in town. It would be a long time before I relaxed enough for physical intimacy.

Mr. Spadavecchia's daughter made me increasingly nervous. I was half afraid of her, and her interest made me feel self-conscious. I went out with her a few times, not knowing how to refuse her. While it didn't seem wise to date the boss's daughter, I also worried that she might complain to her father if I didn't. On one of our dates she bowled me over further by talking about getting married when we were of age. To make matters worse, the Spadavecchias invited me to their home several times. I tried to avoid their daughter by not letting her know when I was going to be home.

In spite of what I told the boss's daughter, once I moved out of Newsboys', I didn't see Lucretia anymore. Pat and Jean were in Brooklyn, Pye and Riggs were going to leave Newsboys', and our old group was breaking up. I'd be leaving town soon, too.

The lieutenant

William refused to speak of combat except in indirect terms. In the Pacific, most of his buddies died. Much about the experience was too painful to talk about. However, one memory haunted him in particular, and this he described.

In the Pacific, they were all scared, Marines or not. There was no way you could be in combat and not be scared. You didn't discuss it, and if you knew what was good for you, you didn't dwell on it. William never gave a thought to the fact that he could be killed. He wouldn't allow himself. It was a matter of self-preservation. Confidence and focus kept you safe. Going ashore with a small team onto Japanese-held islands was terrifying, but you had to manage to act fearless while frightened. Think about death and you might waver.

This policy tied in with another important survival skill learned well before boot camp: Whatever has gone wrong, put on a strong face and hold your ground. If you lose a comrade, cry later and do it in private.

Together these approaches help explain why the story of a certain lieutenant still pained William into his ninety-first year and why it seemed to have hit harder than all the other terrible things he witnessed during the war. The name of the lieutenant is omitted here because the man's family may not have been told the true story of how he died.

William admired the lieutenant. All the guys in his unit did.

A first lieutenant, he was the commanding officer of William's small, specialized Marine unit that carried out intelligence work in the islands.

Talk among the men was that he was a wealthy young man who had led a privileged life. They speculated that he'd been a boxer in college because something had toughened him up; he seemed unfazed by hand-to-hand fighting or guns and knives. The lieutenant liked to read, in particular poetry and other literary works, and he had a very refined, almost feminine appearance. The latter wasn't an issue, according to William: "Today there might have been talk that the lieutenant was gay, but back then, when he likely would have been ostracized for that, it didn't occur to us. You can't imagine the pride our outfit had in him when he came up against another officer known as Jungle Jim."

Jungle Jim liked to go into the tropical rainforest carrying pistols and knives on his belt along with his first aid kit and hand grenades. His hairy chest showed through his unbuttoned shirt, his voice rasped with annoyance, and he was the personification of the macho Marine. He played it to the hilt.

One evening Jungle Jim came to the lieutenant's tent on Saipan. William and some of the other men were hanging out there. Jungle Jim asked their lieutenant to go for a drink. He said no, he was reading.

The men watched to see what would happen next.

Jungle Jim landed a hard kick against the bunk the lieutenant was lying on.

The lieutenant got off the bunk and beat the pulp out of the man.

"We were the proudest guys in the Marine Corps," said William. "Our lieutenant had taken Jungle Jim to the cleaners."

There was a term for the type of officer that their lieutenant was. When inducted into the Corps, he was a "ninety-day wonder," meaning he had obtained a reserve officer commission by completing a three-month officer candidate school rather than gaining gritty, firsthand experience by working his way up through the ranks. This made the respect he had won from his men all the more impressive.

And that's why the following came as a terrible shock.

At the final turning of the war during the taking of Okinawa, William and his unit were positioned on a ship near that island. They had become part of a massive Allied maritime force that, until this moment in history, had been previously unimaginable in size. Still, the Japanese were putting up a good fight from the air. All around William's ship there was death in the water. Machine gun fire and bombs rained down, and kamikazes chose their final targets and dove from the sky. One of those planes dropped three bombs on William's ship and then crashed into it, hitting the bridge and lodging deep below. William and other survivors jumped overboard.

William and a number of the men around him were rescued from the water by an American AKA (attack cargo ship) that sent an LCVP (landing craft, vehicle, personnel) their way. An LCVP was a flat-bottomed boat about ten feet by twenty with shoulder-height railings. Once on board, William stood next to the first lieutenant at the railing looking out at the ocean, the two of them not saying anything. All of a sudden, without a word, the lieutenant pulled out his .45 and shot himself in the head. His body slumped down next to William in the boat.

It is this vision that stayed with William always.

"Seeing the lieutenant kill himself was more intense than seeing someone cut down alongside you while you're running up the beach. During an invasion you know that something like that can happen at any moment. This was entirely different, more horrifying in a way, because it happened in a quiet moment when I was feeling relief and figured the lieutenant was, too."

To the end of his life, William wondered what he might have done. Maybe he could have reached out a hand, grabbed the lieutenant's arm, and knocked the gun out of his hand. Or not—the shooting happened so quickly. Still, he reviewed the scenario again and again. It was an indelible image. How did it happen? How did the officer break down that way? William shook his head at the potential of that man and all that was wasted. And at the waste of war in general.

William tried to explain the lieutenant's suicide to himself. The young man had come from a life of ease and maybe up until then hadn't faced a situation anything like the one off Okinawa, where he was absolutely powerless. The attack from the kamikaze and the complete sense of helplessness they experienced did something to the lieutenant: the machine gun attack first, then bombs whistling on their way down, then the plane headed right into them. They had been unable to fight back. It was a sensation of total defenselessness and probably one of the most terrorizing feelings you can experience. The floating bodies, the wrecked ships, the continuing barrage all around them in the waters off Okinawa converged to assault the lieutenant as particularly severe trauma.

And what of William's own trauma? Not just at that moment but for the weeks and months leading up to it. He let slip a glimpse when he said that seeing his lieutenant shoot himself was far worse than seeing other soldiers cut down while they ran alongside him on a beach. Each time American forces invaded an island in the chain where William's small unit had carried out reconnaissance, William and his eighteen buddies joined in the battle. Dorothea once asked her father what it was like to fight in the war, and the response was swift and furious. He began to tremble; his eyes glazed over and grew moist. "I don't want to talk about it! Don't ever ask me again!" Seeing the effect, she wouldn't dream of it.

Wartime horror added to childhood horror. Until the 1980s, no one called the result of terrifying ordeals "post-traumatic stress disorder." Now we know that PTSD is associated with actual physical and chemical changes in the brain. Certain forms of therapy can sometimes alleviate the effects, but William never had any kind of treatment for his accumulated traumas.

In speaking of the lieutenant, William concluded his story with a quote he once heard: "War is a vast space of boredom interrupted by short spans of utter fear."

So what was it that bothered William most about the young man's unexpected death? That the first lieutenant was not able to put on a tough face and push past feelings of helplessness and horror? Or was it that his commanding officer gave no warning? William might have saved him if only the lieutenant had let down his mask and expressed those feelings— which would have been counter to the policy with which William conducted his own life: toughness at all costs. And which meant that the people closest to William did not completely know him.

CHAPTER EIGHT

Becoming a Marine

In 1942, when I was sixteen years old and still employed at ITT, I enlisted in the Marine Corps. I wasn't the required enlistment age, but I heard that if your body was warm, the military would take you. Friends at Newsboys' were leaving for the war, and this spurred me to enlist, but there was also the idea of adventure in going off to foreign lands. On top of that, I owed my country. I appreciated what it had done for me. After all, I was now on my feet and doing fine, and it was reassuring to know that ITT promised to hire me back when I returned from the war. I lied and said I was seventeen and enlisted in the Corps because they had a reputation for being the best of the best.

Before the Marines took you, you had to fit a certain profile. The Army was more careful about the age thing, but the Marines didn't question that too much. They were an elite organization, though. You had to be an upstanding individual. They turned down many who applied and rejected many who went to boot camp but no further. Applicants were tested for endurance and strength. You couldn't have been in prison or a drunkard. The Corps looked at your general deportment and demanded a clean police record. I'd been in small-town jails for vagrancy out West, but I don't think small towns kept records like that and, if they did keep them, didn't share them.

In my childhood I'd been the outsider, the kid with "bad blood." At Newsboys' my days were happier and far more secure, but I'd been aware that other people looked down at us, that we were outsiders. The job at ITT was too new to change that deep-down view of myself. As a Marine, I figured, I could put on a sharp uniform, stand straight, and be equal to the people around me. I would get respect from strangers. With America gone to war, the public showed a special respect for enlisted men. At movie houses during that time, they often turned up the house lights and asked all members of the Army, Navy, and Marine Corps to stand so everyone could applaud them. Only one man in the audience might be a Marine, because there weren't many then. I noticed that people applauded the loudest for Marines, which made me enamored of the Corps. The Marine uniforms captivated me as well; they were colorful and especially classy. The high collar attached by globe and anchors contributed to this effect. In the early days of the Corps, these high collars were made of leather, and that's why Marines came to be known as Leathernecks. Sometimes theater managers invited soldiers up on stage to ask where they were from, what their homes were like, whether they had girlfriends. The crowds seemed to love that.

If you were accepted into the Marines, they set a date for you to report to the nearest railroad depot and gave you a railroad pass and food chit. I was told to report to Parris Island, South Carolina. Walking across Grand Central Station to meet my train to Beaufort, South Carolina, I met another fellow about my age walking in the same direction, also carrying a bundle and also still in civilian clothes. We compared notes. His name was Robert Waggle, and believe it or not, like me, he was originally from Pennsylvania. We rode the train together and became acquainted. In Beaufort, we met up with other recruits arriving on trains from all over the East Coast. (Everyone east of the Mississippi came to Parris Island; everyone west of the Mississippi went to Camp Pendleton, near San Diego.) The Corps grabbed thirty-six of us at a time for the five-mile bus trip to the base, and Waggle and I were put in the same group, the beginning of a pattern that would last for a while because our last names began with W. From then on, we always wound up grouped together in boot camp for various exercises.

Upon our arrival at Parris, our drill instructor immediately gave us a taste of life there. "How did I get such stupid people?" he yelled. He got right in our faces. "Everyone else got smart guys!" On and on he went. We were told to place our feet inside the footprints painted on the ground, and when he saw that some of us weren't doing that precisely he called us maggots and the lowest of the low. That wasn't really the way our DI was—he turned out to be a guy we admired and liked—but at first we wanted to kill him. We'd arrived at night worn out from the bus and train rides and were kind of beaten down already, so it was rough to have someone talk to us that way. But I'd had so much of this in earlier times that it didn't really affect me. The DI's tirades were just more of the same old same old.

Right off the bat when I arrived at Parris Island, I was booted in the behind by a legend in the Marine Corps. One of the very first things they made us recruits do was strip and take a shower with a lot of other men. In my shyness at being naked in front of other people, I didn't move fast enough. I was only down to my skivvies when a master sergeant supervising the activity saw my slowness and kicked me hard in the rear to hurry me up. I found out later he was Lou Diamond, known as "Mr. Leatherneck," who by then was in his early fifties and serving in his second world war. His voice boomed so loudly that some men called him "the human air-raid warning system."

South Carolina's Parris Island was a mosquito-infested swamp. Surviving boot camp there gave you a certain cachet among Marines. Guys who managed to succeed at Parris Island were seen as the toughest of the tough. Camp Pendleton Marines in California were considered candy-assed by comparison. They lived in brick barracks and walked along paved streets. At Parris Island, everything was sand. There was no asphalt, or at least it was scant. All of our parading was done slogging across sand. Swampland was all around us, but we didn't see alligators much because they were as afraid of us as we were of them.

Our modest wooden barracks had wooden floors, and for both punishment and training purposes, we recruits were required to holystone the decks (floors). The practice came from the old days of sailing ships, when sailors were forced to clean decks that way. We used a stone that weighed about sixteen pounds and was shaped somewhat like a cinderblock. You inserted a wooden broomlike pole into a hole at the top of the stone and scrubbed the deck with the stone. The process was more like sanding or polishing than sweeping. Boy, that was hard work. Afterward we used a broom to sweep away the resulting wood grains and dust. Really, it wasn't necessary to holystone. The assignment was intended to aggravate you more than anything else and to teach obedience to orders no matter what they were.

As part of our training, we learned nautical terms to prepare for life on ships. We were never to use civilian vocabulary when there was a nautical term that could be used instead. Our beds were to be called "bunks." Corridors or aisles were "gangways." Steps and stairways became "ladders."

Walls in our barracks were "bulkheads," and the doors were "hatches."

A few weeks into boot camp, my DI, Sergeant White, asked why I didn't get mail. I said I was an orphan. "*Poor Marine*," he said. He was sarcastic, but in short order I had a deluge of mail. Sergeant White arranged for groups like the Knights of Columbus and other organizations across the country to ask their members to write to me. "And I want to see you answer each and every letter," he told me. I received so many letters from strangers that it was hard to answer them all. I made my answers short: "Thank you for taking the time to contact me. I appreciate it. Sincerely, William Walters." The DI stopped contacting those groups and stopped bugging me about writing back when he saw how much time it took for me to answer.

When you enlisted, you weren't called a Marine, you were a "recruit." They called us every name in the book in addition to that, including some I won't repeat. The tamer names were "boots" or "maggots" or "pogey bait." In China before World War II, Marines were issued candy like Baby Ruths and Tootsie Rolls as part of their ration supplements. Sugar and other assorted sweets were rare in China, so the troops found candy useful for barter with locals. To Marines, the Chinese word for prostitute sounded like "pogey," and as a result, Marines in China called candy "pogey bait." In boot camp, if they called us "pogey bait," they were saying we were candy-assed. Drill instructors yelled this right in your face, close up, eyeball to eyeball, bad breath and all. They were even allowed to hit you, although they didn't do it a lot. They wouldn't haul off and slug you, but they gave you a jab to get you in line if you weren't in formation, or they stomped on your foot or kicked you in the butt. They can't strike you anymore.

The name-calling and rough treatment had to be understood in the context of our training. Our officers wanted to be sure we recruits were tough. In certain situations at boot camp, though, you might be treated well. On the rifle range, for example, the DI and rifle coach saw I was good and gave me encouragement. Thanks to my days in Arizona, I knew how to shoot, so I knew what I was doing when we got to the rifle range. There was a feeling of camaraderie as the DI and rifle coach gave me tips. I found out that DI's placed bets on their guys on the range, and they especially wanted to see their guy excel. You learned not to take advantage; when you got back with the platoon, you had to react to the DI with the same respect as any other guy in the platoon.

The Corps constantly hammered into us that, if we made it through boot camp, we'd have a reputation to uphold as the best of the best. Until then, they told us we were the lowest scum of the earth. The Marines are the oldest organized military unit in the United States, dating back to 1775, and do have a time-honored tradition of dignity and service to maintain. Walk proud, they told us, walk high. Above all, revere God, country, and Corps. By the time we emerged from boot camp, those ideas were ingrained. I believed them and lived them, and I think everyone there with me loved the Corps and loved being a Marine. Once a Marine, always a Marine. You are never an ex- or former Marine.

By the end of boot camp I believed I would finally have something to be proud of. The day they hung the Marine Corps emblem on me, that day would be *it*. For all of us, I think, the day we were made United States Marines would be the proudest day of our young lives.

Everything in boot camp was right up my alley: shooting, fighting, feats of strength and agility. To train us in fighting, they had us do an exercise where we formed a circle and picked out the littlest guy and biggest guy. Gloves were put on the two, and they had to box in the ring. We took turns fighting the winners, and sooner or later you might get pitted against someone about your own size. In the process, the Corps wanted little guys to see that they could have the same ability to withstand punishment as the larger guys.

We also fought using pugil sticks, which were poles with padding on either end. The movements were like fencing in a way, with lots of dodging. Pugil sticks are fairly heavy and difficult to wield, so if you get hit with one, it'll knock you down. I was pretty good at that, too, and so was Waggle. Pugil fighting is more the ability to take punishment and stay on your feet rather than move with grace or skill.

Waggle and I were often pitted against each other at pugil sticks and at boxing. He was the same height as me but bulkier. At the beginning of my enlistment, I weighed about 135 pounds, but I gained some heft on workouts and Marine chow. Waggle and I got to the point where we didn't much care for each other. It was hard to be good friends when we were always doing our best to clobber each other. Right after boot camp we went in different directions.

The Corps encouraged recruits to develop strategic think-ing. One day in our barracks Sergeant White said, "We're going to play six rows of corn. I'm going to yell 'Fall out,' and I don't care how you get there, but when I look up I want to see six rows of corn lined up outside. There should be two sec-tions of corn, each with three rows and with a little space in between the sections. I want to see you in your normal order in that formation."

The sergeant yelled and we ran outside. He shook his head and said not fast enough, do it again. We did this sev-eral times. Finally we figured out where we were making our mistake. There were around sixty of us, and we were all going for the door at the same time, which caused a jam at the door. We decided to run out by rows, keeping ourselves in correct formation before we got there. Sergeant White wanted to see strategic thinking on our part, which would be important for us in the field. He saw our improvement and said, "You guys are too clever for me. We need to make the game more interesting. We'll put all the locker boxes in the aisle." Each recruit had a box maybe four feet by two by two that was kept under his bed. So we shoved our locker boxes out in the center aisle between our bunks, and now he yelled, "Fall out!" We tried to rush outside and form six rows of corn without breaking our necks. It didn't go well. Somebody said, "Instead of jumping over boxes and tripping, why don't we stand on the boxes, and when he yells, 'Fall out!' we'll run out the way we did before." When he saw us do this, Sergeant White said, "You guys are way too clever for me. We've got to make this more challenging." He locked the door. We appointed one guy to unlock and open the door before we rushed out. Again we had outfoxed the DI, and he decided we'd had enough. Exercises like these were tiring and at times may have seemed stupid, but in a way they were fun.

We recruits had a lot to learn. An important lesson was how to stack rifles the correct way so they could stand on their own in groups of three. A big sin for a Marine was to drop your rifle. A mortal sin. You must protect your rifle at all times. If it fell to the ground, sand or dirt could get inside, and the rifle wasn't likely to fire properly after that. Hooks at the top of our rifles, about six inches below the muzzle, made it possible to link three rifles together in a kind of tripod.

If a recruit allowed a stack of rifles to fall over because they weren't hooked up properly, he could be made to sleep alongside all three rifles with their bolts open. If the bolt was open during normal use and you hit the trigger, it slammed forward and could cut off your finger. Your finger wasn't the big fear when you had to sleep with three rifles; it was where the bolt was positioned while you lay on the bed. It faced delicate, essential body parts between your legs. You didn't ever want to drop your rifle.

Marines had the reputation of being the finest shots in the world with the Springfield '03 rifle, which was a marvelous gun. (The '03 stands for 1903.) It was a bolt-action rifle. Shortly after we entered boot camp, the M1 Garand, later known as the M1, came out, and we learned to use it as well. The M1 was a handheld, gas-operated, semi-automatic weapon shot from the shoulder.

At the time I was a recruit, it took seven weeks to go through boot camp and graduate. As we worked our way through, things did get easier, and the DI treated us with increasing respect. At graduation our officers congratulated us and finally told us we were Marines. I ate up all of that. Usually you graduate boot camp as a private, but I came out as a noncommissioned officer (NCO). My DI had told the powers that be that I could perform. I was stunned. It was the first time in my life that I stepped ahead of anyone. It meant graduating with a red stripe on my pants, an honor I felt extremely proud of. If you weren't a CO entering the Corps from Annapolis or The Citadel, usually you had to work your way up through the ranks to become an officer.

The respect commanded by being a Marine brought a tremendous change for me. Earning this distinction gave me a sense of dignity. It brings tears to my eyes thinking about it. Public acknowledgement and respect were not what I was used to. I came to see service in the Marine Corps as my life's career.

Before I was to report to Camp Lejeune in North Carolina for infantry training school, the Corps gave us new graduates ten-day furloughs along with free railroad tickets and stipends. I chose to return to New York to find Lucretia and ask her out again. There was no way she'd turn down a Marine in uniform going off to war.

My first day back in New York, I looked around my old neighborhood and at the Tribune Theater spotted Lucretia and a couple of her girlfriends heading toward seats in the balcony. I ran upstairs, said hello, and asked Lucretia out for a date. It was then that she politely spelled out for me why she would never, ever want to spend time with me.

Earlier Lucretia had made it clear that she wasn't my girlfriend and didn't want to be, but now she went into detail as to why she didn't like me. She said she didn't want to hurt my feelings, but she might as well let me know. She thought I had an inflated opinion of myself. She wasn't used to my rough and tough ways and couldn't accept them. Her brothers weren't like that, they were gentle people, and she didn't know anyone else with an attitude like mine.

Her words hit hard. My new status as a Marine made no difference to her. There was truth in what Lucretia was saying about me, but I didn't think my attitude was necessarily a drawback. She and I came from two different worlds. In the world where I had lived, if you sensed a threat you didn't hesitate, you acted on it. It had been necessary to establish my level with strangers, to let them know I wouldn't allow myself to be picked on. I held to the promise I made to myself as a child: No one would bully me again. But I also knew that Lucretia was right. Now I always hit first, whether I had a good reason or not. In Lucretia's world you didn't hit at all.

Lucretia was not the most beautiful girl I'd ever seen. She was not the Spadavecchia girl or the actress I would soon meet. But she was the most beautiful to me. And she was a kind soul; even her criticism was stated in a gentle way. Her refusal of me was devastating. During the days we had palled around with our friends, I'd wanted to believe she might feel the same for me as I felt for her. Now I realized she'd only been going along with the group. Looking back, I understood that she'd always hung back and even appeared to like another guy more than she did me—that guy who went to the fruit market with us and talked and walked with her so easily.

I found a seat elsewhere in the theater. The lights went down, but I didn't see what was on the screen. That day they didn't call men in uniform to the stage at the Tribune, which was a relief, because right then I didn't want to be seen or asked if I had a girlfriend. I had lost all hope.

That was the start of my ten days in New York City. The Hotel Astor, where I stayed, was moderately nice and centrally located on Time Square, close to movie theaters and play-houses, so I found distractions. Times Square was an exciting place at the time, with lots of young people out on the street.

Pye and Riggs were gone, so I amused myself by hanging out in Times Square on my own and going to movies. In those days, live shows often preceded the films. At one screening I saw Frank Sinatra perform. He was a skinny kid who hadn't hit it big yet, but even at that point in his career, the girls screamed when he came out on stage. At another movie, at the Paramount or Loew's State, I was invited up on the stage. I was the only Marine, so the MC interviewed only me. He asked where my home was, and I said New York. He asked if I had a girlfriend, and I said yes, but she wasn't able to come today. I knew that everyone would be surprised to hear that a Marine didn't have a girl. You'd be surprised how scarce Marines were then.

My furlough was almost over when I met a girl in Times Square. It was an easy place to meet young women. As I walked around in my uniform, I could detect a girl's inter-est and would stop to chat. If we hit it off, I invited her to a movie or dinner. On the ninth day of my furlough I met a good-looking brunette who liked Marines and was fun to talk to, so we went to dinner and the theater. I think this girl lived in Queens. She talked me into staying in New York an extra day, and I'm surprised I did, because I was so proud to be a Marine and had never disobeyed the rules. Either she really impressed me, or I was desperate for female attention, because I met her again the next day, ignoring the need to get on the train to Camp Lejeune. I think we went to see a movie at Radio City or the Paramount.

The next day I boarded the train to New River, North Carolina, to report to Camp Lejeune's infantry training school. Talk about the gods of fortune shining down on you. At the depot where I was supposed to catch the bus to Camp Lejeune, a Marine sergeant pulled up in a car and asked if I was headed to Camp Lejeune. "Hop in," he said, "I'll take you there." The friendly sergeant offered me a bottle of white lightning he'd gotten off a bootlegger in New River and talked me into taking a drink. It like to killed me. I never drank, and the stuff hit like 100-proof. He said I could crawl into the back seat and go to sleep. We arrived at Camp Lejeune around midnight or later, and he showed his pass to the sentry. The sentry pointed at me in back and asked, "What about him?" The sergeant said, "He's with me," and the sentry let me pass without checking my papers. When we were inside the gate, I asked where I should go. The sergeant said it was too late to check in and pointed out some empty barracks. "Sleep there and report tomorrow morning," he said.

The next morning when headquarters opened, the guy there looked at my papers and said, "Where the hell have you been?" I pointed to the barracks. He said, "You stupid son of a bitch, you spent two days there?" I nodded. He told me where to report. I didn't get court-martialed or anything, and that was the only time I ever did anything to warrant it. Of course, for a time, everyone thought I was the stupidest Marine ever to come down the pike. It took a while to live down my stupidity, but that was a lot better than a court-martial.

◆ ◆ ◆

I'd been assigned to Camp Lejeune's infantry training school to receive special language training. Back at Parris Island, boot camp graduates had been given a test that I couldn't make hide nor hair of. The test results were tallied within a day or two, and I was called in by placement officers and asked what I wanted to do in the Corps. Marine Air Wing, I said. They asked what I thought about Scouts and Snipers. I hadn't heard of Scouts and Snipers, but that didn't sound like the kind of service I wanted to do. I said I wasn't interested. The placement officers asked for my second choice. Tank Corps. Again they asked what I thought about Scouts and Snipers. Not interested. They didn't offer a reason why I should be interested in Scouts and Snipers, but the Corps often didn't explain its reasoning. I was surprised even to be given a choice. I guess they hoped I'd choose what they wanted me to do. So, well, if I couldn't do Tank Corps, they asked me, what was my third choice? Infantry. They put me in Scouts and Snipers.

Maybe the Corps placed me in Scouts and Snipers because the placement test showed I was quick at absorbing new information, which would be important in learning a foreign language. Also, they knew I was a damn good shot.

Six months at Camp Lejeune's language school had me speaking Japanese fluently. My memories of those classes are positive ones. Our teacher, who was connected in some way to the Library of Congress, set aside one hour each day when we could study history instead of language, and he made me an everlasting lover of history.

During those months at New River, I never left the base. There were weekends off or partial-duty weekends, but I stuck around and relaxed on base if I didn't have guard duty or KP. New River was not like Parris Island; it was a well-developed camp with all kinds of facilities, including restaurants, bars, pool tables, and ping-pong tables. I was pretty good at ping-pong and entered tournaments. During off-hours I read whenever I could, trying to educate myself, mostly history in addition to our textbooks.

I also boxed on base in Friday night smokers. Boxing interested me purely for the money; I know I didn't like getting my head beat in. Later, in Japan after the war, I volunteered for the Marine boxing squad, so I guess by then I did come to enjoy boxing. At Camp Lejeune, if you boxed in a Friday night smoker and won, you got twenty-five dollars, and if you lost, fifteen dollars, and both you and your opponent were given the rest of the weekend off. Our pay came from a collection taken among the guys who gathered to watch.

At my next stop after Camp Lejeune, which was Camp Pendleton in California, I continued to enter boxing matches, but there were no matches while I served in the Pacific. Even if we took an island, we had to be vigilant every night because Japanese could still be present. They were known to dig themselves holes or hide out in caves and come out at night.

With language school completed, I attended Scouts and Snipers school, also at Camp Lejeune. It wasn't until I got to Camp Pendleton in California that I learned I wouldn't be a sniper. The Corps was not great at telling you anything. You received your orders, you arrived at your destination, and then you found out.

Each day at Scouts and Snipers training we ran out to our training grounds, which included a forested area where we practiced climbing pine trees modified to resemble coconut palms. Most of the branches had been cut off the pines; the Corps taught us how to make our way up them so we'd be able to climb palms in the Pacific islands to get vantage points on the enemy. It was pretty tricky work getting up those trees. Your tendency was to hug the trunk and wrap yourself as close around as you could. Instead, what you have to do is keep your knees as far away from the trunk as you can and angle your feet inward with your boot spikes entering the bark. On a tree like that, as soon as you get scared, you tend to grab with your knees, which then causes you to slide down, which is called "skinning out" and is very painful. In addition, you've got to hold your arms straight out from you so that you can go hand over hand up the tree. That's really the only way we could get up a tall tree with no branches. At Camp Lejeune we shed most of our equipment before climbing the trees but still had to carry our guns, helmets, ammunition, and grenades.

For Scouts and Snipers we practiced a different kind of shooting from what we'd learned in boot camp. In boot camp at first we used the Springfield '03 and then the M1 to fire at targets 100, 200, 300, and 400 yards away, and we shot from different positions: standing, lying on our stomachs, kneeling, and sitting. At Camp Lejeune, they switched us back to the '03 because of its greater accuracy, and they positioned us much farther away from the target, having us shoot from a distance of 1000 yards. We were required to hit a target the size of a pie plate from more than half a mile away. None of us wore glasses; we needed to have superior vision.

At the same time, they taught us to string wire for field-operated telephones, and some of us were trained as radio operators for the field. In actual combat, stringing wire became one of the most dangerous things you could do. If the Japanese found the wire, they'd cut it and lie back waiting for you to come repair it.

At Camp Lejeune I saw my first female Marines. Nowadays they have women Marines in all fields of duty, but back then there were no such opportunities. Women

were allowed to join the Corps beginning in 1918 but were
restricted to clerical duties and discharged in 1919. Shortly
after I enlisted, opportunities opened again for women in the
Marine Corps. In 1943 the Women Marine Corps Reserve
was created, and that year saw the first women enlisted as
Marines for duties apart from clerical and the first female
commissioned officer. As far as I know, no women went overseas for the Corps during the war, but they were instrumental
in the war effort back home. Women recruits were assigned
many different functions, including radio operator, parachute
rigger, photographer, driver, aerial gunner instructor, control
tower operator, cook, auto mechanic, telegraph operator, and
post exchange manager. I think they were prepared to mobi-
lize if needed.

The mere presence of women in the Corps was a hard pill
for us Marines to swallow, and I'm sorry to say that we had deri-
sive terms for enlisted females. Marine women recruits were
officially called the Women's Reserve (WR), but they didn't have
an acronym, so we gave them one. Navy women were WAVES
(Women Accepted for Voluntary Emergency Service), Army
women were WACs (Women's Army Corps), civilian women
pilots employed by the Army Air Force were WASPs (Women
Airforce Service Pilots), and women in the Corps we called
BAMs, or Broad-Assed Marines. Women Marines trained separately, so we didn't usually see or interact with them.

However, at Camp Lejeune, during training for Scouts
and Snipers, we did glimpse the new women recruits as we
pushed and pulled machine gun carts on our way to field
exercises. The carts were designed to bear fifty-caliber
machine guns, but we used them to haul radios, telephone
equipment, electric line, and climbing gear. Two men
pulled the cart using a handle in front and two pushed from
behind. We were expected to pull and push the carts in a
five-mile dogtrot to our training location while we carried

ninety-five-pound packs on our backs and wore rifles and helmets. We were new Marines, felt tough, and were proud of it.

On one of those runs, we passed by the women's barracks
as they were doing side-straddle hops, the Marine term for
jumping jacks. This can be a very demanding exercise when
you do the hops correctly and execute a lot of them. As we
passed by, all of us guys started hooting and hollering at the
sight of women recruits. The women's instructors, who were
also women, never said a word. At the end of the day, when
we returned exhausted to our barracks, we were told to fall
out immediately after chow wearing full packs and rifles and
run all the way back to the women's barracks. At their barracks, the women were called out to watch us do side-straddle
hops so *they* could heckle *us*. This cured us of ever behaving
that way again. I can see it to this day: the women hooting
at us and what fools we must have seemed. Of course the
women loved it. In their newly won service, they had to take a
lot of abuse. Certainly *they* were tough. They weren't allowed
in combat, but it was a beginning.

While I waited to be shipped out from New River to Camp
Pendleton in California, I wrote a note to the Walters. I was
grasping for a feeling of belonging to someone, for a feeling
of family. The knowledge that I'd soon go off to war made me
desperate for that, I guess. I longed for connection the way a
beaten dog is drawn to its owner. I told the Walters that I was
being sent overseas for extra-hazardous duty and asked if I
could see them before I left. Our troop train was going to pass
through Winslow, and I thought they might come out to meet
me or possibly come to Camp Pendleton.

I recall word for word the note I received back: Sir—Your
note received. Contents noted. Sorry request cannot be
granted. Eleanor L. Walters.

The Walters did me a favor by not granting my wish. Within a few years I would be embraced by a far better family.

On the way to California with other Marines I rode on a civilian train to which a couple of troop cars were added. Early in the journey our train stopped in Georgia or Alabama so that my car straddled an intersection. At the edge of the intersection a beautiful brunette waited with other pedestrians for the train to go by. She caught my eye, waved hello, and asked for my name, rank, and serial number. She'd write to me, she said. She was true to her word. Her first letter arrived at Camp Pendleton, beginning a correspondence that continued after I reached the Pacific islands. It felt good to receive news from back in the States and to read friendly words, even if they came from someone I didn't know. She and I talked about her aspirations as an actress and what her days were like, but I couldn't tell her much about what I was doing.

On trains going cross-country, soldiers often flirted with young women who came out to wish them well. However, an episode like that could go another way for a soldier. A story circulated about a train that paused in downtown Dallas, where secretaries leaned out from windows in office buildings to watch the soldiers go by. One Marine, spotting a pretty girl up above, yelled for her to drop her name and address to him. The small piece of paper floated back and forth on its way down, taking forever to reach the ground. He ran out of the train to catch it, and while the paper floated on the air making its slow trip to him, the train began to pull away. He didn't make it back to the train in time and as a result was court-martialed.

You'd be surprised how many stories we heard about relationships formed while soldiers traveled by train through towns on our way west. Locals rushed to see trains coming through, bringing goodies and sandwiches that they handed through train windows as they wished soldiers well. During the war, rail lines moved military personnel alongside civilians. Stations were often full of people who checked train schedules and came out to see us. We deeply appreciated this outpouring of public sentiment. The population seemed far more cohesive in our country back then. No one said they hated the troops or the war. Everyone tried to do good by us soldiers.

At Camp Pendleton I underwent six weeks of combat conditioning and learned I'd be part of a Marine unit assigned to carry out special reconnaissance in the Pacific. Our nineteen-man JASCO (Joint Assault Signals Company) unit was formed at Camp Pendleton. We were going to slip onto Pacific islands as scouts but not snipers. We were attached to the Second Marines, Second Battalion, Second Division.

Combat conditioning for the Pacific was extremely rugged and physically demanding and had a psychological element as well. We jogged up and down hills all day long and simulated beach landings so that we'd know what to do on enemy shores. Live ammunition whizzed over our heads and bombs detonated nearby as we made our way across the sand. The Corps wanted us to get used to the sound and fury of war. I reconsidered the idea that Marines who trained at Camp Pendleton were candy asses.

The extreme nature of our conditioning seems strange in retrospect, because we ended up spending months on ships where we had an extended opportunity to get out of shape. Some ships had space and provisions for exercise, but most were too crowded. To accomplish an island invasion, military leaders devised a battle plan that organized a bevy of all kinds of troops—tanks, artillery, etc.—from all sorts of military units stationed in different locations. While you waited to meet up with other ships, yours could circle around in the

Pacific for months, especially if you were the first ones in position. Finally, on a designated D-Day, we all headed for the target island in a very complex operation—a logistical nightmare, it seemed.

Lucretia's friend Jeannie Gallo wrote to me at Camp Pendleton to say that Lucretia was getting married. This was a ruse on Jeannie's part, but I didn't realize it, not knowing that Lucretia's parents would have considered her way too young at age seventeen to get married. Writing with this piece of misinformation may have been Jeannie's way of finding out whether anything was going on between me and Lucretia. If I flew off the handle at the news, Jeannie would have uncovered a relationship or devotion on my part. Or, maybe Jeannie was just trying to discourage me from thinking about Lucretia ever again.

Jeannie's plan backfired. In spite of my continued feelings for Lucretia, there was absolutely nothing going on between us, so I wrote from Pendleton to congratulate Lucretia on her marriage. She immediately wrote back to say she wasn't marrying anybody. She asked where I got that idea, but I didn't tell her because it could have caused a rift between her and Jeannie. In this way, a correspondence began with Lucretia that continued after I shipped overseas.

Lucretia knew I was an orphan and probably continued writing because she felt sorry for me. Her mother regularly sent packages to two of Lucretia's brothers in the service— one in Seabees and the other in the Army—and when Lucretia told her mother about hearing from me, she and her mama began to send me packages as well. Their boxes contained salami and bread and other things you couldn't get in the service. Lucretia's father made wine, so her mother hollowed out a big loaf of Italian bread and stuck in a bottle of wine for me. I became the most popular person in camp and later in the Pacific when one of those wine-filled loaves arrived.

It tells you a lot about the resources of the United States during the Second World War that American troops were able to receive timely packages from home. Our country had enough fuel and transportation to allow family and friends to send cakes, cookies, and candies to soldiers in spite of the fact they were halfway across the world in the Pacific or European Theaters. The Germans weren't even able to provide adequate transportation to other countries to supply gasoline to fuel their tanks.

In her letters Lucretia asked if there was anything else I wanted, so I said I'd like to catch up on my education by reading books. She asked for preferences, and I told her history and nonfiction bestsellers. Until Lucretia and her mother sent me packages, I was unique in the camp because I was the only one *not* receiving parcels. Their packages from New York meant more than food, drink, and books to me; they gave me the feeling of support from a caring family.

Stubborn streak

The Marine Corps gave William an opportunity to become a manager, first of himself and then of other people. Dropped amidst the enemy on a Pacific island, he and other members of their small unit dispersed to carry out assigned tasks, the Corps trusting each man to work on his own and handle all threats that crossed his path. Later, in vanquished Japan, William oversaw certain civic affairs in the city of Miyazaki. Self-reliance, decision-making, and organization were skills that developed easily from a childhood spent figuring out how to survive. After he left the Corps, William's job as a farm manager and a brief stint self-employed further encouraged an independent spirit.

That's why later, when William, his wife, and three children fell on hard times and moved to California in search of work, he found it impossible to bend to a rigid mold.

It was the 1950s and the U.S. postwar economy was booming. A Ford factory in Long Beach, California, held promise; news came that they were hiring. William and his family moved from New Mexico to a rental house in Long Beach. The address was on Easy Avenue, which did not turn out to be prophetic.

Ford gave William his first experience working among a team of people in a union shop, and there lay the problem. Ford manufactured Lincolns in those days, and his assignment was to install Lincoln convertible tops on their frames. The first thing he didn't understand was that he was supposed to attach the canvas only on his side of the car. His supervisor had neglected to explain this. When William reached to spread canvas across the entire frame, the guy working on the other side of the Lincoln threw his hammer at him. It missed, but William got the point. Okay, share the task; he could do that.

The next lesson was more difficult: Slow down. Until this time, he'd mostly held jobs where speed was an advantage as long as you did the work accurately. On the one job that had called for adherence to union standards, he had labored with only one other man in a relatively relaxed environment. Well into William's second day at Ford, he found himself four cars ahead of the other men. It was suddenly quiet. William looked up from a convertible top to find that everyone else had stopped working. The other men sat down and refused to move until the lead man dealt with William.

"You're making everyone else look bad," said the man. "You're going too fast. Back off."

At lunch, no one sat with William. Comments tossed his way included "scab" and "union buster." That was not his intent. And yet . . . he didn't change. Couldn't change. There was something in him. Not just independence, but strength of will. The two were linked. Early on, they'd preserved him.

He resumed work. This time he finished his side of the car, stopped, and waited for his co-worker to finish his side. The other men complained. Get in the rhythm of things, they said; don't speed up and halt. William was still making them look bad.

To become eligible for union membership, you needed to be employed at Ford for thirty days. William's bosses took note of his co-workers' anger. After several days installing convertible tops, William was shifted to another location. He was a good worker, said the bosses; all William needed to do was match the pace.

William had a wife and three young kids to feed. He'd do it.

His new assignment, laboring among a different group of men, was to install the Lincoln convertible's rear window. This was a flexible piece of plastic with canvas rings that tacked on to the canvas cover. Again, the other men said he went too fast.

There was something wrong with this system. Or maybe with him, because he did need the work. Always before, he'd taken whatever job came his way. But maybe he wasn't cut out for assembly line work. If faster seemed better to him, he wanted to work faster. He wanted to make his own choices, to use his brains and ability.

Within a day or so, the bosses took William off the rear window job and put him on door locks. Okay, he told himself, don't be pigheaded.

But word had gotten out. The fellow who was supposed to teach William how to install door locks said, "You seem to be so smart at everything, figure it out yourself." William couldn't and was fired.

It came as a relief. He told his wife so. He promised to find other work, and he did. He always did. Whatever went wrong with a job, she knew he'd find another. As far as his wife was concerned, the jobs often did not match his intellect or ability, and often he was too set in his ways, but he would not give up. This she respected. The very stubbornness that got William into trouble also saved him time and again. It was the essence of him: When it came to survival, he would not give up.

CHAPTER NINE

Slipping onto Japanese-held Islands

It was only after our training finished at Camp Pendleton and we began to board a ship bound for the Pacific that fear hit me like a ton of bricks. Up to that moment, pride in the Marines and a sense of accomplishment had carried me forward. Then, in a flash, I saw the truth of what was ahead. This is it. I'm off to war.

I don't want to talk much about my experience in the thick of duty with JASCO carrying out our mission in the Pacific. Our little outfit was close-knit, and by the end of the war, all but two of us were dead. We weren't a brave bunch of guys, we didn't do anything heroic, but in our situation, it was easy to get yourself killed. I lost nearly every friend I had in the war. Whenever you talk about war, it sounds like you're claiming heroism, but you weren't heroic, you were scared to death. Anyone who says they weren't scared during fighting is lying through their teeth. You do what you've been trained to do, and afterward you want to get out and try to forget about it.

Eventually the Marine Corps created a number of JASCO units to assist with air, artillery, and naval gunfire aimed at Pacific islands held by the Japanese. My impression was that we were the first, created on a trial basis to assess if the JASCO idea was workable. Our unit consisted of only nineteen men. We were part of the Second Marine Division but at the same time stood as an individual group that operated under its own officers and protocol. When I found out about my assignment to JASCO, I was happy to know I wasn't going to be a sniper. There's a certain pride in being a very good shot, but that doesn't mean you want to kill people.

JASCO was a new approach to combat in the Pacific. The slaughter of U.S. forces trying to land on the islands led to its creation. The plan was formulated by the military well before our unit was created, because our unit was quickly put into action after a massacre of U.S. forces in the Gilbert Islands at Tarawa Atoll. The very next campaign, the Corps gave us the go-ahead. In fact, we were already overseas when Tarawa happened.

The U.S. was attacking Pacific islands that lay in chains leading toward Japan and that were controlled by Japan. General MacArthur and his Army troops traveled up the inside chains, the ones closer to the Asian mainland and Japan: Indonesia, New Guinea, Malaysia, and eventually the Philippines. In those days, the Marine Corps was part of the Navy, so our commanders were usually admirals. However, MacArthur commanded the entire Pacific. We called him Emperor MacArthur.

Under Admiral Nimitz, the Marines' job was to take the outer islands, including the Solomons, Marshalls, Gilberts, and Marianas. Each of these island groupings contained many smaller islands. After the Marianas came Iwo Jima.

U.S. strategy was *not* to take every island in these long chains but instead to leapfrog the Japanese, looking for islands large enough to establish airstrips where we could land, refuel, and fly on to the next target island. We leapfrogged the Japanese for a few reasons. This way the Japanese couldn't guess which islands we were going to target and which ones to reinforce and make bastions of. As a result, they had to use their resources to reinforce all the islands they held. By making selective attacks, the U.S. could cause Japanese forces on each island to die on the vine as they were cut off from the rest of their vine. Also, by not attacking each island, we avoided losing more of our men than we had to.

The U.S. took the first islands in these chains with little or no fighting required. Marines landed unopposed on Guadalcanal in 1942 and secured the airfield the Japanese were building there, but unfortunately the Japanese reinforced the island from the other side, and after the Marines landed, they struggled in a long, drawn-out land battle for six months until finally achieving victory.

Marines may have landed unopposed on Guadalcanal, but on the next island group it was a different story. In November 1943, the Japanese were ready and waiting for U.S. forces to land on Tarawa Atoll. There they slaughtered about a thousand Marines and injured another two thousand or more of our men when our troops landed in the lagoon at the Tarawa island of Betio. We didn't know about Tarawa's treacherous reefs and discovered that our boats could only deliver men two hundred to three hundred yards away from the beach. U.S. soldiers had to wade to shore in chest-high water holding their rifles over their heads while the Japanese shot them like sitting ducks. The Japanese lost thousands of men as well, but they taught the U.S. a tragic lesson about landing vulnerable forces on an island without advance knowledge of the tides, the nature of the reefs, and placement on the island of Japanese men and weapons. In those days there were no satellites to provide pictures of Japanese emplacements, and our limited aerial photography couldn't nearly reveal what was hidden in dense tropical vegetation. Also, the Japanese were very clever at camouflaging pillboxes and bunkers.

What the U.S. needed was advance, firsthand information on Japanese-controlled islands. Our newly created JASCO unit was assigned the task of providing detailed reconnaissance before other troops landed so that the nature of the shoreline was known and the U.S. could first carry out naval and air strikes. The men in JASCO slipped quietly onto these islands to convey information back to our ships and planes. Our unit always traveled as a group, all of us landing on a single island and then dividing up to perform separate functions.

At Pendleton, our unit had received special training day and night in shore/beach assaults. In our unit I'd been surprised to find Robert Waggle, the guy who was my frequent sparring partner during boot camp. Our trainers made sure that the nineteen of us in JASCO could operate a rubber boat and launch it from a submarine to go ashore, that we knew how to gather information on Japanese activity and what to do if confronted by the enemy. As a team, we had to land quietly and safely on an island and do our best to map out the island undetected in order to radio commands to the bombers and battleships waiting for instruction. You can see why our work was so hazardous. After JASCO surveyed the terrain and determined where the Japanese had installations, we radioed the information, marked the beach to facilitate landing, and hid out in the jungle, keeping as far away from bunkers and pillboxes as we could, which was a trick on small islands.

The men in JASCO performed three distinct functions once we landed on a Japanese-held island: air/ground liaison, shore/beach, and naval gunfire. I was assigned to the naval gunfire group. The air/ground men directed attacks by bombers on island targets. Naval gunfire had the same goal as air/

ground except we directed gunfire from battleships to targets.
Shore/beach put out stakes on the beach to indicate where
incoming U.S. troops should land. There was a difference
between the commands for bombers and those for battleships
because bombs and naval shells have different capabilities.
The Japanese had built bunkers on all of these islands and
surrounded them with coconut logs to protect them from
fire. Artillery or naval gunfire from battleships could hit the
logs, but coconut logs absorbed the shock with little damage. However, bombs dropped from the air could blow the
logs and the bunkers to hell. Meanwhile, naval gunfire was
effective at destroying cement pillboxes constructed by the
Japanese as machine gun nests and as housing for their heavy
artillery. Five-thousand-pound shells hurtling from our battleships traveled along flat trajectories and came in at a hell of
a rate, easily taking out cement pillboxes.

JASCO usually set up within three days of slipping
ashore. I had a map of the island overlaid by a cellophane
grid and could radio a battleship to say something like, "I
want a salvo on A3." Onboard ship they had the same map
and grid. In response they'd send a three-gun salvo: one
aimed five hundred yards long of the cement pillbox, one
aimed five hundred yards short, and one directly on. This
gave them a good chance of hitting. I'd inspect the damage
to see if the strikes were successful. If not, I radioed back to
specify that our guns needed to adjust aim by more or less
so they could hit again. After enemy targets were struck
successfully, we in JASCO were informed when H-hour was,
meaning the hour when the landing operation was to begin.
Usually that was early in the morning, around six. We hun-
kered down to wait for the other Marines to come ashore,
and after they did, we joined in the battle, fighting alongside
the Second Marines, Second Division, during each island
invasion. Until they landed, our unit remained as invisible as

possible, not wanting to tip off the Japanese to our presence.
To my knowledge, our JASCO unit was entirely successful
at this and made no enemy engagements that would have
ruined the element of surprise.

Once an island was taken, the men in our unit became
radio operators and telephone installation operators who
laid landlines. Eventually, JASCO units that landed on much
larger islands, especially those where the Japanese were
hidden in caves and tunnels that couldn't be easily scouted,
became entirely radio communications units and no longer
operated the way our early unit had.

The JASCO assignment was risky business but had its advantages. We didn't have to do any of the menial tasks that other
soldiers did. We didn't have to do guard duty or KP, we slept
past reveille, we had our own quiet little camp on the island of
Saipan in the Mariana Islands, and we received extra pay.

After missions, the men in JASCO always returned to
Saipan as home base. The Seabees built us a tent city on
Campasini Bay, where we lived isolated from everyone else on
the island, and while I have some fond memories of our life
on Saipan, I have only tragic memories of our taking of that
island.

We fought the Battle of Saipan during June and July 1944.
Saipan played a prominent part in the war because it was the
first time that the Allies captured an island within bombing
distance of Japan. The U.S. military was planning for the
soon-to-be-completed B-29 heavy, long-range bomber. With
the refueling requirements of the B-29 in mind, the U.S. gave
priority to taking Guam, Saipan, and Tinian, which were
located at distances that would allow the B-29s to reach and
return from the Japanese home islands. Also, taking Saipan
would allow us to cut the lines of communication between

the Japanese homeland and Japanese military on islands to
the south and west.

In our capture of Saipan, U.S. forces drove the Japanese
around the edges of the island to Marpi Point. I participated
in that operation. Saipan is a pretty good-sized island with a
volcano at the interior. Terrain drops steeply from the mountain center to the ocean and was the reason we drove the
Japanese around the edges of the island.

Earlier, Emperor Hirohito had learned that the Allies were
encouraging Japanese soldiers and civilians to surrender on
islands we took, and he had commanded the Japanese not
to surrender under any circumstances. He sent a message
to his people on the islands that suicide was a more honorable death—as honorable as dying a soldier's death. Japanese
soldiers posted on Saipan were living there with their families. Rather than allow surrender, Japanese fighters on Saipan
made their wives and children commit suicide with them.
When they reached Marpi Point, they all jumped off the cliffs
there.

What was even worse, the Japanese forced native islanders, the Chamorros, to jump off the cliffs with them. The
indigenous people didn't even have a hand in the game; they
had not taken sides in the war, although it's hard to think they
didn't resent their treatment at the hands of the Japanese who
conquered their islands. However, the Japanese disseminated
propaganda warning Pacific Islanders that Americans routinely raped and cannibalized the people they conquered. On
Saipan the Chamorros were as terrified of American forces as
they were of the Japanese. At Marpi Point, the Marines saw
both the Japanese and indigenous people throwing themselves off the cliffs and tried to stop them. Our boats circled
around in the water with loudspeakers telling the Japanese
and Chamorros in their own languages that we wouldn't harm
them, imploring them not to commit suicide, but it was no

use. I didn't witness this part of the taking of Saipan because I was elsewhere on the island, but I heard about it from other Marines. We took very few prisoners. Saipan is such a beautiful place, it's hard to imagine the horror there.

JASCO's small tent city on Saipan seemed far away from Japanese bombs that might strike elsewhere on the island. Once it was out from under Japanese control, Saipan became headquarters for the Second Marine Division in its entirety, the B-29 bomber groups, an Army division with maybe 20,000 men, and one of the biggest ammunition depots in the Pacific. Tanks, guns, shells, bombs, and anything else you might use in combat were stored there. Navy barracks were also constructed on the island. JASCO was lucky to be located far away from all that on our own quiet bay. I think we were placed off on our own partly by chance, because Campasini Bay happened to be a small, available location, and partly because we were encouraged to think of ourselves as a small band of brothers.

Today on Saipan you can't find any sign of JASCO's encampment; it's wall-to-wall houses. Also, the name Campasini is probably long forgotten; I think only the guys in the military called it that. Back then, our home base was an idyllic spot enclosed by coral cliffs. A reef kept the water warm and calm inside the bay. A truck brought us food. To solve the laundry question, we set up a windmill over a big barrel, filled it with sea water, and rigged a paddle to go up and down hitting the water. Into the barrel we threw special soap that had been issued to us for the purpose of bathing in saltwater. We were pleased with ourselves for making a washing machine. Our tents were mounted on floors, so they felt more like houses than tents. Life felt tranquil and easy until we had to go into combat.

I hate to report an example of our mindlessness when it came to the environment. In Campasini Bay a coral reef enclosed a basin of beautiful blue water. The coral formed arches and a scenic blowhole. We wanted to go swimming in the inviting blue water without cutting ourselves on the coral, which was so sharp it could slice right through our boots, so we blew off all of the coral's jagged edges. We simply pulled the plugs on hand grenades and tossed them into the water to solve the problem. And to think that nowadays the coral reefs are endangered.

In spite of our isolation and feeling of safety on Campasini Bay, the Corps dug slit trenches there, a form of bomb shelter for us. Whenever the alarms sounded, we were expected to retreat to the shelters. However, U.S. airfields were situated on the other side of the island from us, and life was so peaceful on our bay that we stopped running to the shelters. One night a Japanese pilot aiming at the airfield on the other side of the island lost his bearings and dropped his bombs on our side, and there we were, out in the open. No one was hurt, but afterward we went dutifully to the trenches. We may have had guts, but not that much.

As we worked together under difficult conditions, all of the men in our unit became a close, solid team. You had to be able to trust the man next to you, which we did unequivocally. Robert Waggle did either shore/beach or air/ground liaison. He and I never became close buddies, but we weren't unfriendly.

I never saw Waggle again after our unit left Saipan. By the end of the war, he and I were the only two survivors of the original nineteen in our JASCO unit. A third man, Robert Benkin, survived our work in JASCO, but afterward he was killed on Okinawa. Back in the States I was able to trace Waggle and learn his address so that I could send him an invitation to my wedding. The answer came back: "Anyone dumb enough to get married I don't want any part of." It seemed a shame to spend that much time together in combat, to operate as a cohesive unit under extreme conditions, not to consider ourselves friends of a sort.

Correspondence with Lucretia continued while I was based on Saipan, but my end of it was pretty uninteresting. The military had strict rules as to what we could say while fighting in the Pacific—strict, that is, depending on the officer who screened our letters. Lucretia said that mine arrived back in the U.S. with lots of blackouts. I limited my news to descriptions of landscape, terrain, and culture where I was stationed but didn't give too much detail about those things either. The censors felt I was too revealing even then. We had to be careful in our correspondence with folks at home because somehow the Japanese seemed to intercept our mail. I don't think anyone today has figured out entirely how they obtained all of the information they had about our troops. It was unsettling when we soldiers stationed in the Pacific heard details about ourselves in English-language radio broadcasts by a woman named Tokyo Rose. Actually, there were about a dozen women broadcasting Japanese propaganda in English, but Allied forces in the Pacific coined the term "Tokyo Rose" to refer to any female broadcasting to us in English on behalf of the enemy. During her airtime, she might say something like, "I see a William Walters has arrived in Saipan with the Second Division. Welcome! It's too bad you'll never get to see your relatives again because the Imperial Japanese Navy will eventually have to kill you." We'd tune in and laugh—except maybe during those moments when we heard our own names mentioned. Fortunately, we also received Armed Forces Radio, which broadcast entertainers like Bob Hope, Red Skelton, and the big bands.

One way that the Japanese were known to have gathered details about U.S. soldiers was by collecting mailbags
floating on the water from ships of ours that they had sunk.
Also, believe it nor not, the war had progressed a year or so
when the Japanese discovered the U.S. military was dumping
soldiers' garbage in the sea, and the enemy began to retrieve
discarded package wrappers and mailing boxes floating on
the surface that had been sent from home and indicated our
names, ranks, and serial numbers. (Clearly we didn't have the
environmental sensitivity that we do today.) If the Japanese
retrieved soldiers' names from floating debris, it was easy
enough for them to assume that these men could be found
on nearby islands. Quickly, the U.S. stopped dumping garbage that way and also began to place all mail traveling to the
Pacific in canvas bags weighted with canon balls or something
heavy like that so that they went to the bottom if the carrier
or submarine was sunk. Still, somehow, the Japanese continued mentioning servicemen's names in their radio broadcasts
as if they had intercepted personal mail.

We soldiers weren't smart about the environment, but we
were clever about other things. We received beer rations,
maybe six cans a week for each of us. The problem was how
to chill the beer, because on the islands we had no refrigeration. To get around this difficulty, a Marine on Saipan with a
science background guided us to dig a hole four or five feet
deep in the sand. We placed our beer into the hole and, at
his instruction, refilled the hole with sand. Then we poured
gasoline over the sand and lit it. The gasoline fumes drawn up
through the sand to feed the flames exerted a cooling effect
on the beer below. That's exactly how a refrigerator works.
Still, the process was risky; the fire could have traveled via the

fumes to singe us. The process didn't make our beer frosty, but at least it wasn't real warm anymore.

If we were planning a big beer bust, we chose another method. Everyone saved up their beer and hauled it by Jeep to the nearest airfield, where we bribed a pilot to fly it up to 10,000 feet while doing surveillance or making a transport run. They'd sack up our illegal cargo in the transport, and at that altitude, the beer did become ice cold. (The pilot stayed warm because he wore a flight suit and other protection.) However, we didn't do that very often, because there wasn't often the opportunity. At the time I didn't drink beer, so I traded my ration for goodies like cookies or candy or cakes.

I carried out other trades as well, with rations and the spoils of war. The Red Cross handed out cartons of cigarettes in addition to beer, so I turned around and traded both, many times working my way to actual dollars. At the fighter base on Saipan the pilots had no opportunities to obtain enemy souvenirs available to me and my buddies, such as Japanese swords, pistols, and flags. My friends and I went to the fighter base with those items to trade for whiskey, which the pilots did have. In turn, we traded the whiskey at regimental head-quarters for money. It was a roundabout way of getting more money, which I didn't spend but instead saved up along with my pay. On one occasion, though, I traded a samurai saber for a ride in a P-51 Mustang. There was only one seat in the P-51, so I had to crouch down behind the pilot and grab hold of his seat. There were no belts or straps, no nothing. The pilot did loop-de-loops and turned upside down. I didn't throw up, but it would have been easy. It was terrifying, but it *was* the thrill of a lifetime.

During my time on Saipan the beautiful brunette I'd met from a train car in the South came to the Pacific with a USO show. In her letters she'd told me she'd landed a part in a

Broadway musical, the 1945 revival of *You Can't Take It with You*. When she arrived on Saipan with the USO, this young woman asked for me by name to escort her around.

This was a big deal. Usually commissioned officers had the privilege of escorting USO performers. CO's accompanied them to chow, showed them to their quarters, and gave them a tour of the main camp. If a camp wasn't located close to the front, there'd be dances, and the CO's got to take the visiting ladies. This actress created quite a stir when she asked for me instead of a CO. As an NCO, I was a far cry from men who'd been to West Point and Annapolis. My pen pal insisted, and the Corps had to go along with it. It was fun serving as her escort around camp, and I was proud as a peacock as I ignored the stares of the colonels and the rest of 'em. The fact that the actress requested me was a little feather in my cap. I think personality counts a lot more than looks, and that must be what she was responding to.

As I wrote to Lucretia during my days off, I followed her rules. I didn't express feelings for her since she made it clear that ours was a platonic relationship. I soon felt that I'd gotten over her, but I did look forward to her letters with their news of our old neighborhood and what was happening at Newsboys'. Lucretia was pleased to tell me that she had earned her high school diploma and had found work at North American Insurance Company in Manhattan. She continued to live at home and was able to report the latest on fellows who still lived at Newsboys' or who had once been residents. After a while, though, she said that Newsboys' closed and was taken over by the Coast Guard. It looked like every older boy in the place entered the service, and other institutions provided homes for the younger boys.

During our correspondence, Lucretia impressed me
with her thoughtfulness in asking which books I'd like to
receive. Also, I was touched by the beauty of her cursive
penmanship. And then there was the way her mother sent
me care packages. There was much to enjoy in our platonic
relationship. The fact that Lucretia continued to write made
it seem my letters pleased her as well, maybe undoing some
of the poor impression she had from my days in New York.
I also wrote to other girls. Eventually I lost contact with the
actress, but I exchanged letters with Susan and even Mr.
Spadavecchia's daughter, although the latter finally gave up
on me.

As I read Lucretia's letters, I came to know her family better. I ate up information about all of them, vicariously enjoying the feeling of family life. Lucretia's father, Francesco Paeto
Anzilotti, had immigrated to this country from Italy. His job
for Pat and Jean Gallo's father was to gather used paper from
office buildings, after which he sorted and bundled it to send
to a recycling facility to be made into cardboard, I think. As
he sorted through office papers, Pop liked to tear stamps
off envelopes and stash them in a bag. Many offices where
he gathered paper were financial institutions, so he found
stamps from all over the world. Once a month a man came
to Lucretia's home, and Pop and this guy would sit and drink
wine while the guy looked through Francesco's stamps. The
fellow was a collector or stamp trader. He paid for certain
stamps, which gave Lucretia's father a nice little side income.
Her pop didn't do too badly in this country. He arrived here
on his own without any resources but eventually was able to
pay for first-class ship passage to bring over his wife, Rose
Marie, and their daughter Filomena. The three boys and
Lucretia were born in this country. In the old country, the
family home had been a town called Craco, a tiny hillside

fortress halfway across the boot of Italy between Naples and Bari on either coast.

Lucretia said her mother was the disciplinarian in the family and the more practical of her two parents. Pop was more the romantic. He liked to grab Mama on his knee and sing to her. I tried to imagine this. My only sighting of Lucretia's mother had been a night when our group of friends was walking home after an evening on the steps of Fraunces Tavern. Rose Marie stepped out of her building on the other side of the street about a half a block away from us. She was on her way to clean offices on Wall Street. Although Lucretia and I most definitely were not on a date, nor were any of us together as couples, her mother absolutely did not want Lucretia to spend time with kids from Newsboys'. Lucretia said, "Oh my God, there's Mama!" We quickly parted ways so that her mother wouldn't see. In that quick glance she looked like my idea of a typical Italian-looking mama with her slightly rounded, matronly body and her headscarf.

Lucretia's oldest brother was Joseph, and he'd had a difficult childhood. He'd fallen ill with pneumonia before the era of antibiotics. The doctors operated on Joey and removed two ribs, their surgery leaving what looked like a huge crater in the skin on his back. Pop and Mama didn't have enough money to pay for the operation, so they borrowed from the Gallos. That's when Mama went to work cleaning offices, in order to help pay off the debt. After the surgery Joey had to go away to a sanatorium for a long time, and that was expensive as well. Many years passed before Pop and Mama were able to pay off his medical bills. Joey had recovered and was serving in the Army, which took him to Alaska for the building of the Alcan (Alaska-Canada) Highway. His job was to guard the work site.

Lucretia's brother Angelo was the guy I tried to pick a fight with outside Newsboys'. A gentler person you'd never find. He was a peacemaker, despised quarrels, and became the arbiter any time there was a dispute. Angelo had lost much of his vision as a teenager. He was standing near a bonfire that kids built out on the street in Little Italy when someone threw something into the fire that made it flare into Angelo's face. From then on, Angelo, also known as Gus, wore glasses with lenses about a quarter-inch thick and, in spite of that, needed to hold things extremely close to see. He didn't use a cane but was quite handicapped. Two or three times he tried to enlist in the service, but of course it was hopeless. Gus was a nice person, salt of the earth, would do anything to help you, and at the same time was nitpicky and meticulous. For example, when he cooked beans, he first examined each bean, one at a time, holding them close to see.

Lucretia's other brother, Mikey, was a Seabee, so I watched out for him to come ashore. The Marines and Seabees were real tight, like brothers. If ships with Seabees arrived on Saipan, they did things like steal ice cream off their ships and share it with us. From what Lucretia told me, Mikey was a nice guy, and it was a disappointment when he didn't show up on our island. She said he was the live wire of the three. The smallest in size, he could be feisty at times, and had upset their parents by marrying secretly while home on leave. He and Mary began to date before he went off to fight but kept their relationship secret. The two of them married without telling any of the family except for Lucretia. Mikey confided the news and said, "You break it to Mama." Theirs was a very close family, and all of the brothers knew that Mama found it hard to let go of her kids and expected to know what was going on with them. The scene that followed was the maddest Lucretia ever saw her mother get. In fact, her mother slapped Lucretia, who cried, "What are you smacking me for?" "You knew about it and didn't tell me!" said her mother. Lucretia explained that she hadn't known either until after Mikey and Mary tied the knot. Mama was furious but didn't seem to hold it against Mary and was sweet to her.

The one family relationship that Lucretia didn't say much about in her letters was the marriage of her sister, Filomena, to a guy named Paulie. I learned later that this was the one marriage Mama and Pop didn't get over. They were polite to Paulie but didn't like him. Paulie was minor Mafia and known in the neighborhood as Big Paulie. He was ill-mannered and rude. A bully. To give you an idea, he liked to pick on Lucretia's brother Angelo. Nobody could figure out why Filomena married him. She was a genteel lady with good manners and was well educated.

During a break on Saipan I came down with dengue fever, a tropical disease spread by mosquitoes. I may have picked it up on Kwajalein or Tinian; it was hard to know. Dengue is a viral infection that can recur again and again over the course of many years.

A good nickname for dengue is breakbone fever. You feel terrific pain in your joints, pain so agonizing that you can't bend your knees or elbows. Along with a high fever and chills come a headache and skin rash, with the whole thing leaving you pretty weak. The first time I had dengue fever, it leveled me. Each time it reappeared I learned to expect a hospital stay of a week or two. There was no treatment apart from bed rest and drinking plenty of fluids. I'd recover and go along for a while before experiencing a recurrence.

The first time dengue fever hit, I decided to use my recovery time in the Saipan hospital to make a thank-you gift for Lucretia's mother. As soon as I felt well enough, I spent my days carving a set of rosary beads. I'd learned that Lucretia's mother was devout and went to mass every morning. With the help of a friend who visited me in the hospital, I traded a samurai saber and pistol with pilots at the nearby fighter base for silver wire and windshield glass from a Japanese bomber our forces had shot down. The wire was for the rosary chain and the glass for the crucifix and beads. The cross was fancy, with rounded octagonal edges rather than more typical sharp-edged, squared-off ones. Lucretia let me know that when her mother opened the gift she said, "Anyone who can do something like that has got to be a nice person." Rose Marie wrote back with a warm thank-you, so I felt comfortable asking if I could send money to her and her husband for safekeeping. They agreed. I think they came to see that I was frugal because I sent my pay regularly to be saved, and I guess they liked that about me as well.

In the Pacific I was wounded a few times. During a stay in the Army general hospital in Saipan with a Japanese bullet lodged in my knee, a nurse spotted me and said, "I know you!" She thought we'd met in a hospital back in the States. I said I was sorry, but we couldn't have. She was an Air Force nurse, and I was in the Marines, not the Air Force. The Saipan hospital provided care for Army, Marines, Navy, Seabees, and Air Force, but back home, we were treated in separate hospitals.

Later this same nurse returned to my room to tell me she remembered more about it. "I had a patient in the hospital at Quantico, Virginia, and he was a dead ringer for you." That was strange. "Do you have any brothers?" she asked. I told her about traveling west on an Orphan Train with my brother. "I swear," she said, "this guy has got to be your brother." On her own initiative she contacted the hospital in Quantico, somehow got the man's name out of the records, and supplied me with his contact information, which was an address in Rhinelander, Wisconsin. I was dumbfounded. I never expected to see my big brother again. I wanted to believe the nurse was on to something. This guy's name was Gerald, but I don't recall the last name he used. No telling what he was doing in Wisconsin, far from military bases, but he may have been on medical leave at the time because it turned out he tended to be sickly.

I wrote to tell Gerald I was in the hospital in Saipan and gave him my address. My letter brought a totally different reaction from what the nurse and I expected. Yes, he was my brother, he wrote back, ". . . but the only thing we have in common is blood and I can see no reason for us to maintain contact." He reported that he'd been abandoned by the people who took him off the Orphan Train and eventually was given refuge by a Catholic orphanage. The nuns treated him well and even sent him to college. Gerald's coldness seemed especially surprising because in the short history he provided he mentioned studying for the priesthood. You'd think he'd be a more congenial sort of guy. On the other hand, he said he'd quit his religious pursuits shortly before being ordained.

Gerald mentioned that while in the Air Force he studied physics and earned a degree in that field. He also said he didn't want further contact with me. That wasn't quite satisfactory to me, so I continued to write.

In late 1944 or early 1945, the doctors sent me back to the States with a shrapnel wound in my right leg plus a recurrence of dengue fever. They decided that the fever plus my wound were too much for them to handle on Saipan. The shrapnel damn near killed me but at the same time hit in such a way so as to be strangely beneficial, whirring like a saw blade as it struck my calf, searing the wound clean. I lost a slice of calf about six inches long, and pieces of shrapnel were left in my knee.

The military sent me to St. Albans Naval Hospital in
Queens, New York. I was lucky to be sent there because
sometimes you didn't get the location you requested. New
York was my choice because of Lucretia and her folks. They
were the closest thing to family I had. Filomena came to visit
while I was hospitalized, serving as a kind of a courier for the
family, and it was the beginning of a nice friendship between
the two of us. I appreciated the time it took her to make these
visits, since it took several hours by bus out and back from
Little Italy to the borough of Queens on Long Island—and
longer when she and her husband moved to New Jersey. I
spent two or three weeks at St. Albans and then was given
three months' leave of absence to recuperate. The Corps
provided a stipend to live on, so I went to stay at the Hotel
Astor again in Manhattan. I tried to see Lucretia during those
three months, but she wasn't willing. She must have been
nervous about giving me the wrong idea about the friendli-
ness she'd shown in her letters. Filomena didn't arrange to see
me during my time at the Astor, but she may have figured I
was no longer the lonely guy stranded in a hospital bed. After
I was well enough, the Corps sent me back to Saipan.

Until U.S. forces reached Okinawa on D-Day morning, April
1, 1945, we Marines had landed on islands no larger than
maybe twenty miles by twenty miles maximum. For Okinawa
it was decided that my JASCO unit was no longer needed.
Multiple other JASCO units were assigned there to do reconnaissance because Okinawa was a much bigger island than
any of our units had mapped so far. Okinawa was so large that
the war on that island would become more like that fought in
Europe, with large fronts and U.S. Army divisions numbering
about 180,000. The intention was to have a staging area for
the invasion of Japan.

The U.S. amassed more than a thousand ships to attack Okinawa as part of the Joint Expeditionary Force. We were joined by ships from other Allied forces, and all in all there were more than 1200 ships in the water. Today it's hard for me to conceive of, that the U.S. had that many ships in one area of the ocean. I'll never see a sight like that again in my life. I don't think anyone will. There were seventeen battleships, twenty aircraft carriers, and hundreds of destroyers, cruisers, destroyer escorts, baby flattops (small aircraft carriers), submarines, auxiliary ships, hospital ships, tenders, and transport ships. Our Fifth Fleet was unimaginable. I can't imagine what the enemy thought when they saw them coming.

Before those ships could reach Okinawa, though, kamikaze planes swarmed over us. By approaching Okinawa, Allied forces threatened the Japanese home islands like never before. Japan's D-Day air attack on us was carried out in sheer desperation. Kamikaze pilots flew over in waves and waves.

On D-Day morning I traveled offshore on the USS *Hinsdale*, an APA (attack transport ship) carrying about 1500 Marines and sailors. As we lay offshore, a kamikaze plane dive-bombed us. My next assignment was to be a telephone lineman after we arrived onshore, but the *Hinsdale* didn't make it to shore, and I believed it had sunk to the bottom with many, many other ships that day. Later I found out that the *Hinsdale* had been saved. All I knew at the time was the *Hinsdale* listed over so far that we had to abandon ship. An AKA was one of the ships that stopped to help; it sent a smaller boat, an LCVP, to retrieve about thirty of us in the water.

We made it on board the AKA, but soon it was torpedoed by another kamikaze. The torpedo took off the rudder and turned the AKA into a drifting hulk. Eventually I was picked up by the battleship *Iowa*, which had been part of the Third Fleet.

The *Iowa* dropped me back in Saipan, but first I had
the satisfaction of seeing the battleship fire its big guns at
Okinawa, a spectacular sight. From the deck we couldn't tell
what targets were in the rangefinder, but we could see explo-
sions where shells landed. The Fifth Fleet led the bombard-
ment of Okinawa, and as soon as it delivered troops there,
it took off for the Japanese home islands. I can still see the
Fifth Fleet as it traveled past, enormous, spread out across the
ocean, on its way to batter Japan.

Liked the prisoners too much

As part of a conquering force, William made an ideal soldier for postwar administration of territory. He was sympathetic to the underdog because he had been one himself. He could see the humanity in people who had been labeled "enemy" or "alien." In 1945, in the course of his work for the Corps, he made friends in Japan. People there seemed to like him. If health problems overseas hadn't pulled him home, William might have chosen to continue living in Japan.

By 1949 William's young family had lost their first home and the good life they'd created for themselves in New Jersey. They boarded a train to travel west for the health of their first-born, who had narrowly escaped death from polio. On the way to Albuquerque, as they watched one town after another fly past out the train windows, William from time to time told his wife, "I was in jail there." He was thinking of his days as a vagrant and the likelihood of being picked up for not having two dollars in his pocket. Finally his wife told him to hush: "The other passengers will think you're a criminal."

About a decade later, after they'd moved to California, after the debacle at the Ford plant, more successful stints at Lockheed and Pacific Airmotive, and the waxing and waning of an upholstery partnership, William decided to seek out better pay and greater security. With a certain poetic justice, he landed a job that put him on the other side of jail bars.

At first in Upland, California, he secured full-time work with the city as a fire engineer. The position called for him to drive a fire engine and operate pump equipment but not actually fight fires. He learned to run the complicated American LaFrance engines and was relatively happy in his work. After a while, the fire department consolidated with the Upland police to become the Public Safety Department, and William was assigned to the police desk. He continued to be called out on major fires, so when he drove to a fire, a patrolman subbed for him at the desk.

And so in Upland, William and his wife landed on their feet once more. Their three kids, who by now were preteen to midteens, appeared to enjoy life in Upland. His wife, always one to make friends easily, became acquainted with a local bakery owner and was offered a job at his shop. She rose at four in the morning to help bake bread and other items, and William saw the kids off to school.

However, there were problems for William at his workplace. William was constantly at odds with the fire chief and the police chief. Neither seemed to like him. The police chief complained that William was too liberal and liked the prisoners too much.

The man had a point. William was a sucker for a prisoner's tale of woe. A jail trustee told William that he wasn't really guilty of car theft; his car had broken down, he'd taken it to be repaired, and the repair shop overcharged him. He couldn't afford to pay, so one night he stole his car back. Maybe that was true, maybe it wasn't. Whatever the case, while working the police desk William let the trustee take time off from jail to go to the movies.

Then there was William's practice of hanging up his gun in his locker when the chief wasn't around. To William it seemed ridiculous to wear a gun for a desk job. The gun was heavy and a bother to wear. Of course the police chief eventually noticed the latter and heard about the former.

Eventually William's sympathy toward the prisoners spelled doom for him in terms of job advancement—or maybe even job retention. He seemed unable to resist requests for help. The wife of an inmate regularly came to see her husband while the latter awaited trial. During William's swing shift, the woman told William that she needed to go see her mother in the hospital but didn't have a way of getting there. The woman was in tears, so William said she could take his car and bring it back afterward. However, she must return his car by midnight.

Come twelve o'clock and she wasn't back. William told some of the patrolmen to be on the lookout for his car, because now he considered it stolen.

No one spotted it. William knew where the prisoner and his wife lived, outside city limits in Pomona, a town near Upland. He asked one of the patrolmen to drive him there. Sure enough, his car was parked in front of the house. The woman came to the door half naked. She admitted that she'd been to a bar, gotten drunk, returned home, and forgot about returning his vehicle. She'd never been to the hospital. William told her to hand over his keys. She asked why he was so upset.

"Because I'm now in serious trouble," he said. "That patrol car over there is outside city limits on my personal business, and I'm standing here talking with a scantily clad woman who borrowed my car and didn't return it."

At this point, another Upland patrol car pulled up to the scene. William's fellow employees took him back to the station and into the interrogation room for questioning, as if he were a criminal.

The next morning the police chief said, "I don't know how many times I have to tell you, crooks are crooks and you've got to treat them as such. How are you going to explain this to your wife?"

"Hopefully I won't have to," said William.

"Well, you're going to have to explain something because I'm giving you a four-day rip."

That meant suspension without pay. So William did have to tell his wife. She knew him and trusted him and didn't worry about the scantily clad woman. But she did ask the same question as his fellow officers: "Why did you let the whole thing happen?"

It was a good question, he knew.

It was in his nature, he supposed.

Deeply.

CHAPTER TEN

Nagasaki and Beyond

The Japanese surrendered a couple of months after the taking of Okinawa. I was sent to Japan with other Marines, but as usual I didn't learn my assignment until after we arrived. Our first stop was Nagasaki. We landed toward the end of August 1945, a couple of weeks after the atom bomb dropped on that city.

As we sailed into Nagasaki's winding harbor, the power of the bomb was evident. A 10,000-ton ship had been blasted right out of the water and onto the shore. It lay on its side on the docks about a quarter of a mile from where the bomb hit. All we could see were the underside and sides of the vessel, which didn't look damaged. We guessed that the superstructure was gone, but we couldn't tell for sure because that part of the ship faced away from us.

On Nagasaki's docks I was amazed to see piles of steel girders lying neatly in piles and rows. We learned they'd come from a New York elevated rail system and were sold to the Japanese before the war. All I could figure was that the girders had been shielded from the blast by the dock itself.

Entering Nagasaki proper, we saw that parts of the city remained intact while others were totally wiped out. The city lay over terrain that was a combination of mountain, hills, river, and large harbor. Residential and commercial buildings sprawled down in the valleys and climbed up hillsides. Portions of the population had been shielded from the bomb blast by the hillsides. On slopes that faced the epicenter, or more precisely, the hypocenter, nothing was left of residential or commercial life. Nothing. On slopes facing away from the blast, houses and businesses remained intact. Forty thousand people were killed immediately and an estimated 60,000 to 80,000 total died in the weeks after the bomb dropped. Approximately 200,000 were still alive. Cars and bicycles traveled the streets, and people walked about. By the time we arrived, evidence of the dead had been removed.

We were shown to our temporary living quarters up on a hillside and then given some leisure time. I walked through the city with a few other guys to see what we could see. A Japanese soldier spotted us. He looked kind of shabby. Cloth wrappings held his uniform to his legs. He walked over to stand before us and stated in English that *he* hadn't been whipped, he was still unbowed. A big old Marine in our group punched him in the chest, knocking him to the ground, and said, "Okay, now you can say you've been whipped." The Japanese man gasped for breath, but he stared up at us in defiance. Then he got up and hurried away.

That soldier was in the minority; most people in Nagasaki were subdued. Many residents looked like they were in shock, wandering aimlessly about without any clear direction. Enormous numbers had lost their houses and jobs and families. With conquerors arriving, they were bewildered by their circumstances. Their government had not let them know how the war with the Allies was going. Japanese citizens were used to thinking of themselves as dominant. Their armies had invaded China and Korea. As soon as the B-29s were able to reach them, their home islands had been bombed every day, but propaganda had encouraged the populace to expect victory.

The atom bomb had missed the planned hypocenter in Nagasaki proper and instead fallen a short distance inland from the harbor. The hypocenter of the blast appeared to have been directly over a radio tower. While the other guys and I walked about, we came upon the remains of the tower, which had been vaporized down to four charred stumps. No one had warned us about touching anything; we had no knowledge about the terrible effects radiation can have. We crumbled the ash from the charred remains of the tower in our fingers.

For the short time our group stayed in Nagasaki, we bunked in former Japanese barracks on a ridge of one city slope. From there we had a view of a sheltered cove that wasn't part of the main harbor. Down in the cove I was surprised to spot rows of submarines parked side by side in the water. This was curious, because I knew that Japanese subs had done very little damage to the U.S. Navy; they were supposed to be in scarce supply. I walked down to the cove to have a closer look. The submarines were fakes constructed from concrete. They were built to lure American bombers to drop their payloads and in this way waste bombs. Clearly this had happened. Many of the concrete forms were blown all apart, bomb craters pitted the land nearby, and bombs had destroyed the slips around the fake subs.

Soon the Corps gathered a battalion of us on an LST (landing ship, tank) to travel around the island of Kyushu heading for the town of Miyazaki. There were no tanks on board, only us infantrymen. We didn't go directly to Miyazaki. About three miles outside that city, we stopped and disembarked. We were instructed to walk the railroad tracks into town, going into what you'd call combat dispersal mode, spreading out with a point man and a rear guard. The U.S. still

William and his older brother, Jared (Gerald), in Pennsylvania.

William and Waggs in Gallup, New Mexico.

Sixteen-year-old William, dressed in the first fine clothes he ever purchased.

William (center) with Marine buddies in Miyazaki, Japan, 1945.

William and his intended, Manhattan, 1946.

William and his intended, Manhattan, 1946.

Wedding portrait of William and his bride, August 4, 1946.

On her wedding day, William's love at St. Joachim's, Manhattan.

William and his wife departing on their honeymoon, August 1946.

William with Jerry, Willie, and Dorothea.

Steve and Molly on a tricycle.

Pat dressed as Shirley Temple for Halloween.

Steve dancing with Sally.

Willie, Jerry, and Dorothea, 1950s.

Willie, Jerry, and Dorothea with their parents in Upland, California, 1959.

Poster advertising the services of Macy's interior design manager.

William Walters, Santa Rosa, California, 2013.

wasn't sure that the Japanese in the hinterlands were going to give up without a fight. Total defeat of the Japanese was very much up in the air. Emperor Hirohito had announced Japan's surrender, but the news didn't circulate everywhere, and there were Japanese who still considered themselves combat troops.

In our walk to Miyazaki we did encounter Japanese citizens. Each time they spotted us, they turned their backs on us. We became angry about being insulted this way. Some men grumbled that they were going to force the citizens to turn around and show respect, but our provost marshal told us their behavior was a sign of respect. He'd been briefed on Japanese culture and understood that Japanese citizens felt they didn't have the right to look on the face of the conqueror.

Our primary purpose in Miyazaki, we learned, was to accept the surrender of weapons by Japanese troops, particularly from the Kwantung Army returning from Manchuria. At that time, the Kwantung numbered maybe 700,000, and we didn't want a large group of enemy troops arriving back in Japan all at the same time with their arms and their officers, which would have made it easy for them to continue Japan's fight. The U.S. intended to dismantle their army and do it carefully, so they shipped the Kwantung home in small groups to various bases around the islands. Allied forces brought many of the Kwantung by rail and by truck to the Hagarashima Racetrack near Miyazaki, where they were required to surrender their arms. Then they were allowed to go home.

In Miyazaki, a city of maybe 50,000 people, we found a single large building left standing in the commercial center. The structure was ten or twelve stories high and about a block square. It was pockmarked by shrapnel and bullets but still usable as Marine headquarters. During the war, U.S. military brass had instructed bombers to leave this particular building standing so we could employ it eventually as a base of operations. This kind of thing was done during the bombing of many Japanese cities, apart from Tokyo, where Allies dropped incendiaries and created a firestorm. The fact that we found this large building in Miyazaki intact proves that there was accuracy in U.S. bombing raids.

Walking through Miyazaki, we saw that civilian homes were pretty much left unharmed. It was the town's commercial core and infrastructure that were destroyed. I don't believe our troops restored roads, bridges, water, or electricity. All of those eventually were repaired or replaced, but I believe that happened after we left. However, in the aftermath of the war, all rubble was cleared quickly by the Japanese; otherwise, outward signs of physical destruction seemed to remain pretty much the same in Miyazaki during my nine months there.

American bombers flying over Miyazaki Prefecture had focused in particular on destruction of a naval base located several miles outside town. Now approximately three hundred Marines went to live in barracks still standing at that base. Each day soldiers from the base reported to the nearby racetrack in order to take weapons from returning Japanese soldiers.

After confiscation, Marines ran over enemy weapons with tanks so that they couldn't be used again. Although, if our guys found ancient samurai sabers, these were not crushed. I'm not sure what was done with those antique sabers. The really good swords take forever to make. First the steel is hammered into a flat sheet. Then the sheet is folded over and pounded so that the two pieces weld together by the sheer force of hammering. Ancient sabers were sometimes folded and hammered thirty-two or sixty-four times in a process that actually changed the molecular structure of the steel. Not only do these sabers hold a razor edge, they are so strong you can't bend them. A really good one is worth many thousands of dollars.

At the headquarters in Miyazaki I became part of a group of five officers who comprised a city management team. We were headed by a provost marshal. I served as an interpreter and had some of the PM's authority in regard to closing houses of prostitution and directing other activities within the city. Our team also included an Army RTO (railroad transportation officer) and an Army highway officer who controlled roads and bridges in the area. We were situated on the ocean, and I think the fifth person was a naval officer who oversaw the movement of Japanese boats.

Managing city sanitation was part of my responsibility. For example, when we first arrived there were no bathrooms. The Japanese are very meticulous people, but their toilet facilities left a lot to be desired, and as a result, their cities were not that clean. On the one hand, the Japanese swept their streets every day, removed their sandals before stepping into buildings and walked about indoors in socks, and kept their homes immaculate. On the other hand, people relieved themselves in gutters, which were like trenches at either side of roadways.

Eventually we created public restrooms that were much like porta-potties, but until then, it was customary for honey carts to go around town picking up poop from the roadside gutters. We were warned not to eat vegetables from Japanese gardens because human excrement was dumped there as fertilizer.

I directed the honey cart people as well as local street sweepers, who walked the city using crude brooms devised from tree branches. This type of broom was simply a pole with small branches secured around it; it puzzled me how it could sweep anything up, but it did remove leaves and other detritus from the streets. The honey carts picked up those sweepings as well. The excrement and sweepings were removed to compost piles in agricultural areas outside town or to ponds used for irrigation/fertilization.

A frustrating part of my duties in Miyazaki was the assignment to close down houses of prostitution. The Japanese naval base had encouraged the appearance of these houses. This led, I think, to a very high incidence of venereal disease among the women in that city, with local men carrying VD like a plague to their wives. Soon our Marines contracted VD as well. The U.S. brought in a medical team to examine the girls in these houses and to give treatment, and when they discovered carriers, they forbade them to engage in prostitution. My office tried to steer Miyazaki women with VD to Red Cross and medical facilities, and while many women were treated there, we had no success whatsoever in closing the houses. We'd find a brothel, go in and throw everyone out, and post signs outside saying that no one could enter. The only thing this achieved was to scatter the women to hit the street and eventually wind up in other houses.

Finally, the base commander came up with the solution to VD among our servicemen. A prophylactic kit was issued to each Marine who went out on liberty. Upon returning to base, each soldier returned a used kit and signed a statement to that effect. If you returned a kit unused, you signed a statement that you hadn't needed it. Later, if you were diagnosed with VD, there was a severe punishment for having lied. Punishments included loss of rank down to private, six months of extra duty like guard or KP, no liberty, and the loss of points toward going home. This system proved to be the best solution.

A word about earning points toward going home: During World War II you were required to enlist in the Marine Corps for the duration of the war plus six months, with duration determined by the government. Since the definition of "duration" could be hazy, depending on the need for military involvement after enemy surrender, the Corps also set a number of points you could accumulate toward going home. Points were earned based on number of months in service, combat duty, wounds suffered, and medals received. Still, even if you had the necessary points, you weren't allowed to go home if they decided to declare you "essential."

At first we saw citizens going about their business on the streets of Miyazaki but no kids. Families hid their sons and daughters for fear that American soldiers raped little children. In wartime propaganda, the Japanese government had convinced the population we were monsters. With the passage of time, the adults relaxed. Their children found out we had gum and candy and became our friends. One little girl was a tot as cute as a button. Whenever she and the other kids came to say hello to us, I toted her around on my shoulders. It was relatively easy for me to make friends because I spoke the language. It also helped that I'd learned a bit about Japanese culture while studying the language back in the States.

I noticed that an old guy often walked by our headquarters, and we became friends. He carried a wooden game board and two wooden bowls, and when I asked about the board, he told me it was a game called Go. He offered to teach me, so we played during my lunchtime, sitting in the sun at a table outside headquarters. The old man kept small, round, stone pieces in the wooden bowls, one for black and the other for white. He explained that one player took black, the other white, and showed me how the stones could be placed on the board's grid during game play. Go looked deceptively simple. I don't think I ever won a game. It's strictly a mind game, and some say it's harder than chess. You definitely have to think ahead before you put the next little round stone down on that board. We concentrated on the game and never talked about life in Miyazaki or the war. The old people in particular seemed afraid to broach the subject for fear of offending.

As the days went by in Miyazaki, local attitudes toward us seemed to shift rapidly. The Japanese appeared to be good at adapting to changing situations. Also, it wasn't clear what the Japanese thought about their government at the time war was declared. They may have been dead set against the conflict, which could have helped them adjust to our presence more easily. Our oversight was not brutal or harsh, at least in my experience, and this may have helped many local people accept us.

My work group of five lived at a house in town. The dwelling was a traditional structure with sliding bamboo doors, rice paper windows, a modestly pitched roof, and a lovely garden out back. There was no shower or bath, so we all frequented public bathhouses. There were several in town. In our backyard the Seabees threw up an American-style outhouse with a few holes, locating it as far away as possible from the house.

The military hired a few servants for us. These people were not at our house full time, but instead came and went after cleaning, making beds, doing laundry, and serving our meals. There was a food shortage on the island, so prepared food was delivered to us from the base.

An important aspect of my assignment in Miyazaki was translation of U.S.-generated documents intended for residents. I was fluent in the spoken language but not the written language. A local translator was hired to join our team and work with me at the Miyazaki headquarters. The town elders selected a woman of about thirty years of age, Sadako Yamagata, to serve as an interpreter alongside me. If the provost marshal wanted to issue a statement of any kind, I translated it aloud from English into Japanese, and Sadako put it into written form. Then she'd read back the statement to me. Occasionally she altered my wording, but usually we agreed on vocabulary and phrasing. Certain Japanese words can be interpreted in a variety of ways; if we issued an official document, we wanted to be certain that we chose the correct wording.

I had found Japanese pretty easy to learn because there's relatively little inflection required, unlike Chinese, for example, where there are complexities in pitch or tone related to meaning. There's a big difference, however, between speaking Japanese and writing or reading it. Japanese calligraphy is fairly complex. I may have picked up the spoken language in six months, but learning the written form would have taken a lifetime. Sadako showed me how certain words in Japanese calligraphy could change with a small brush stroke. A subtle change in direction of a single stroke could alter the word's entire meaning. In the old days, the Japanese used a brush on a bamboo shaft to write the classic form of their language. By World War II they used typewriters and a more modern, simplified written form of the language that Sadako tried to teach me. Nevertheless, this simplified form was also demanding. I developed a modest ability with written vocabulary but needed to spell words out slowly.

Trust between Sadako and me developed quickly. I found that Sadako's and my translations agreed almost all of the time, which led me to feel confident about her interpretations. From the outset she spoke English quite well, which surprised me. So few Japanese seemed to speak English at all. It turned out she'd studied languages in Germany before the war and was assigned to do propaganda for the Japanese government upon her return.

I did discover a nasty side to Sadako; she was an anti-Semite and a Nazi sympathizer. I got a glimpse of her thinking, but that aspect of her character was usually kept hidden. Mostly she was friendly and generous, which was also surprising considering what I learned after a while about her brother.

Sadako told me that she'd been engaged to a Japanese naval captain but had broken off the engagement at the war's end. She was a pretty young woman, with a round face and well-endowed body compared to many Japanese girls then, even a little on the chubby side, probably because she was able to eat well as an employee of the U.S. government. To the office she wore typical peasant pants that gathered tight around the ankles and then ballooned out. Over those she wore a loose, one-size-fits-all blouse in a kind of olive drab. Underneath the blouse a white garment was visible where its collar stuck up. Around her waist she wore a traditional sash so that a couple of pieces of fabric hung down at her side. On her feet she wore the traditional split-toe sandals and socks.

Sadako and I became friends and eventually went to a public bathhouse together. Social attitudes in Japan were much different than back home in the States. Men and women bathed naked together at community bathhouses, and the public bathrooms were unisex. At the bathhouses the Japanese held to a very strict cleanliness routine. These buildings had an indoor pool. You had to shower first with soap and water before dipping into the pool, which looked like a lap pool and was waist high. No one actually swam in the pool. Sitting and soaking in the pool, men and women did not stare at one another. There was no shame; it was simply a natural way of life. I often wondered how men and women came to have passion for each other when they were so used to nakedness and there was no suspense. They knew everything about each other.

Going to bathhouses made me uneasy, but soon I became acclimated and it felt natural. I suppose it helped that the

Reidhead-Harrises had been relaxed about bathing in front of one another. The locals did stare at first, observing the physical differences between me and them, but my body was about as hairless as theirs, and they got used to me while I got used to them. One thing I found kind of funny, though: When you first entered the pool, everyone bowed.

When Sadako and I began going to a bathhouse after work, I had already visited various bathhouses in town, so I wasn't unprepared for being undressed in front of her, but I can't say I was entirely comfortable with the prospect either. At first when she suggested it, I said I didn't think it was a good idea. We worked together; it didn't seem right to see each other naked. She reminded me that there was nothing improper about men and women in her culture bathing together, that there was nothing sexual about it, and finally we agreed it would be okay. Still, leaving the men's dressing room nude in front of her was difficult the first couple of times.

Sadako and I began to socialize as well, but our relationship was purely platonic and stayed that way. At age twenty I still had not had sexual relations with anyone, not even close. Besides, Sadako was ten years older and had to consider me a mere kid and not a love interest. She mentioned that she had horses, and I more or less invited myself to her home by saying I'd enjoy riding them. In response, she invited me to ride as well as for dinner.

Sadako's family home was in Osaka, but her parents had died during the war, and she and her brother, who was a cavalry officer, had been transferred to Miyazaki in wartime. They lived on a property at the edge of town that resembled a small ranch. Sadako's brother, who had been a colonel in the war, made it clear he didn't like me. He was extremely discourteous and unpleasant and seemed to wear a sour look on his face all the time. If I asked a question, his answer was as near to one word as possible. For my benefit he made it very plain that he was not defeated, that the emperor may have surrendered, but he would not have done so.

By then most Japanese soldiers had returned to civilian dress, but he never took off his uniform. I didn't say anything about the latter because there was no law forbidding the wearing of uniforms. Few Japanese people at the time had a source of income or the ability to buy civilian clothing if they didn't already own it. As time passed and their uniforms fell apart, soldiers managed to change to civilian dress. The colonel came from an affluent family, though, and he could have afforded civilian clothing at the war's end.

Sadako invited me for dinner several times. Eating with the two of them was my first experience of a formal Japanese dinner. It was excruciating learning to eat seated with my legs crossed under me. The traditional approach for a man is to get on your knees with your legs behind you and then let your knees go to either side, swinging them outward so that you land sitting on your heels and sides of your feet. Talk about painful, if you're not used to it. I never did become accustomed. Women lowered to their knees and then sat back on their calves with their feet kept straight back.

During my first dinner at Sadako's, her brother pulled a fast one on me. I had no experience with sake; I still wasn't a drinker at all. Her brother kept pouring sake into my small porcelain cup, and to be hospitable I drank. A pot of hot water sat on the table for use in diluting the sake so that you drank half sake and half water. This I did not know. Sadako's brother continued to pour sake, and I continued to swallow it down. I became so damn drunk that when I drove home afterward I parked the Jeep on the steps of our house. It was a wonder I found my way home at all.

The day after that dinner, Sadako didn't show up for work. I went looking for her and learned from her brother that he'd sent her back to their house in Osaka. Japanese women were required to be subservient, so there was nothing Sadako could do about it, but I could. I let her brother know in no uncertain terms that I was in command, that she must come back and report at her job, and that he dare not do anything like that again. Within a week Sadako returned to the office. She confided that she didn't like the way her brother treated her but that she had no choice.

Upon her return, Sadako also confided that her brother had forbidden her to have contact with me apart from work. Again I went to the former colonel and told him, "I'm the boss now, not you. I determine who does what, where, when, and why." Which of course didn't endear us to each other. We clashed often. He saw Sadako and me ride what had been his cavalry horses and complained about it. I said the U.S. military could take the damn horses away from him if he didn't like it. He spoke a little English, so we were able to communicate either in his limited English or in my Japanese, but we never had much conversation. I wasn't too sure he wouldn't do something physically aggressive toward me or toward Sadako, he was that hostile.

As soon as Sadako saw that she was under our protection, she felt free to be friendly again. One time when her brother was out, she invited me to her house to show me traditional dress. While she put on the clothing, she explained the various layers and pieces. I think she wanted me to see that she could dress up in a beautiful garment, not just the peasant clothes she wore to work.

We became good pals and often went riding her brother's horses out in the countryside or along the nearby beach that faced the Pacific. Japan is fairly mountainous, but Miyazaki lies on a flat coastal plain bounded by mountains, so there were lots of good areas to ride. I considered myself a good rider because I had lots of experience riding at the farms and ranches where I worked as a kid. Most of the people I

worked for in the 1930s couldn't afford saddles, so I learned
to ride bareback, holding on largely with my legs. If you ride
that way, you make yourself part of the horse. I also could
ride with a Western saddle, which was relatively big and had
a horn to grab if needed. At Sadako's I rode on a military
saddle, which was smaller, did not have a horn in front, and
was more like an English saddle or dressage. There wasn't that
feeling of connection to the horse that bareback riding gives.

I'll never forget the first time Sadako and I rode out
together. We were galloping along the beach when my horse
abruptly turned back toward the house and stables, leaving
me stunned in midair. The horse flew off, and I landed in the
sand. My body wasn't hurt, only my dignity. Sadako turned
back, saw the look on my face, and laughed out loud. Japanese
women didn't usually belly-laugh. If they were amused, they
giggled and snickered behind a hand held to the mouth. After
Sadako stopped guffawing, she said she could have warned me
about that horse but hadn't thought of it. From then on I rode
keeping a close eye on the animal and never took a fall again.

Sadako and I kept in touch by mail after I returned to the
States. Upon learning about my coming marriage, she even
sent a wedding gift, and she and my wife became pen pals.
Sadako also sent my wife a complete Japanese geisha outfit.
The two women were quite alike in terms of height, so Sadako
was able to judge the correct size. Her gift included the *obi*
(sash around the waist), the *obiage* (additional sash peeking
out from under the *obi*), the inner and outer *kimonos* (red
outer with beautiful flowers, maybe hibiscus, and creamy
white interior), and traditional flat sandals that split your
big toe from your other toes with a wooden knob. We sent
Sadako presents in return, but that beautiful outfit had to be
quite a sacrifice for Sadako in those postwar years.

Time and distance caused our correspondence to peter
out. Often I've wondered about Sadako and what became of

her. Years later we visited Osaka but were unable to locate Sadako's family home using her old mailing address. The city had grown to such a point that the street may not have existed anymore.

For me, it was a good life in Miyazaki. City management duties and other work didn't keep me busy all day long, making it possible to come and go as I pleased. We ran a kind of loose organization. The provost marshal didn't mind as long as we accomplished what we were supposed to. If illness hadn't been a recurring problem and I'd been able to return to the States occasionally for recreation rather than recuperation, life in Miyazaki would have seemed like an ideal kind of existence. In my experience, Japanese people were mostly welcoming and the culture fascinating. Many of us were aware of young women in postwar Japan looking for soldiers to marry them and take them back to the States, away from the dire conditions following the war. On the other hand, it would have been a trick to find a woman bold enough to marry a foreigner and remain on Japanese soil.

Naiveté

In spite of his hard-knock experiences—or maybe because of them—
William retained a certain kind of innocence in one-to-one relationships
until the end of his life. Lacking good parenting, he hadn't absorbed certain crucial clues about human behavior that, if you're lucky, are delivered
along the way while growing up: for example, parental guidance that
might take the form of warnings about people who seem friendly but
might do you harm or, on the other hand, role modeling of affectionate
behavior and gentle advice about intimacy.

William's innocence led to passivity in business dealings, in friendships, and in romance. He was both shy and hungry for reassurance. If
another person expressed admiration, that alone could mean connection.

Sometimes in his reticence, William was lucky. It's doubtful that he
initiated friendship with Sadako. She invited him to the bathhouse and
home to dinner. Since her actions would bring down her brother's wrath
as well as disapproval from others in town who hated the occupation
force, Sadako made her invitations at great risk. She may have wanted
their relationship to go further. William described how Sadako invited
him home when her brother was away in order to show him a traditional
kimono. His take was that she simply wanted him to see her in something
beautiful rather than the peasant tunic and pants she wore to work. The
fact that she completely disrobed in front of him and then slowly dressed
herself again didn't make much of an impression. He figured they'd been
naked together at the bathhouse, so it couldn't be a big deal. Maybe,

maybe not. She was about thirty, he was about twenty; she couldn't be interested in him, he thought. He was just a kid; they were just pals. Maybe, maybe not. Given that she was a Nazi sympathizer and anti-Semite, and he knew by then that he most definitely was not, he was fortunate to escape entanglement.

Sometimes in his shyness and passivity, William was not so lucky. In the early 1950s, in the months following his family's move to Albuquerque from New Jersey, William located work in a furniture store where he was given a chance to learn the upholstery trade. A fellow employee tutored him in reupholstery and wood refinishing. William's attention to detail and the fineness of his craftsmanship drew attention from one of the customers. The man came into the shop one day, admired William's work, and the two of them got to talking. They'd known each other about a month when the man suggested that they go into business together. The stranger seemed like a nice guy, and he was very positive about William, which was the important thing. They didn't draw up partnership papers, and William didn't try to check him out. Their plan: The man would look at incoming jobs and estimate prices for the customers and William would do the shop work. William had never been in business for himself, knew nothing about business agreements, but being self-employed was something he'd daydreamed about, and the stranger's idea fell right in line with his own inclination.

They leased a shop in a convenient location near William's home, and William took out a loan to purchase tools and supplies. William's wife waitressed at a local restaurant, and her pay was modest, but they figured they'd manage to support their three kids, make monthly loan payments, and keep up with the lease as well as their home rent with the help of income from the upholstery shop.

And no need to worry: From the very first, things looked promising. Soon after their shop opened, William landed his first job. A lady came in to ask about a sofa with elaborate wooden arms that she wanted refinished. The arms should appear black, but when you looked closely, you should be able to see red deep down inside the highly polished finish. He stripped down the arms, stained them a brilliant red, fogged black lacquer over that, and then applied twenty-four coats of hand-rubbed varnish. It turned out that their customer was the governor's wife. She loved William's work. The governor and his wife retained William to refinish numerous pieces of furniture from the governor's mansion.

Word spread. Next came a call from the University of Colorado with a huge order to refinish classroom desks and chairs. It looked like they were off to the races! They really had a thing going! But how much did the partner contribute? Not that much. Still, William was grateful. His partner had pushed him to make it happen, and the man's glib way with customers made him an ideal front man. The shop had top-notch equipment, and together they created displays with examples of William's craftsmanship.

Then it all turned around.

One night William returned to the shop after dinner to continue work on an order and was planing a piece of wood on a jointer when someone walked in the door. As he looked up to see who it was, he sliced off the tips of four fingers on the jointer's whirling blade. At the hospital William was stitched up, but the doctor said he couldn't resume work until his hand healed some, at least a few weeks.

While William was home recovering, his partner cleaned him out lock, stock, and barrel. William returned to their shop antsy to check in on things even though he couldn't yet get back to work, and found both their money and equipment gone. His partner was also nowhere to be found. The guy had skipped town and there was no way to find him. William and his wife were back to broke again. Or worse than broke: They owed money on the vanished shop equipment and the lease. William took whatever jobs he could muster as soon as his hand was somewhat usable.

Even in his senior years, after many decades in a nurturing marriage, William was naive when it came to relationships. A desperately lonely widower, he made a cross-country train trip hoping that his old love of travel would help him feel better. In a train station lounge in the South, a much younger woman picked up on him and glued herself to his side on the train. Some of the other passengers in the dining car assumed she was his wife, but when they learned she wasn't, warned him. Still, she initiated long-distance contact, speaking of future home stays and trips together, including a trip she had already planned out for the two of them without input from him. Fortunately, once home, William heeded warnings from family and backed away.

Within the year, well into his ninth decade, in spite of many hours each week with his daughter, William continued to badly need steady companionship and reassurance. This led to an online meeting with another much younger woman, quick entanglement, and troubled romance that he pursued in spite of ominous signs. At his urging, the woman moved in, and after he realized his mistake, William was able to extricate himself only with legal aid and help from the police.

All of that puts William's sixty-five-year marriage in clearer perspective. His greatest stroke of good fortune came when someone else made the proposal that led him to marry the woman who would become his much-adored wife.

CHAPTER ELEVEN

Homecoming Surprise: Wedding and Honeymoon

Dengue fever struck again in the spring of 1946 while I was in Miyazaki, and once more the doctors sent me back to the States. The fever hit particularly hard this time because I was recovering from various war injuries. For my second time returning to the States sick, I was lucky to be sent again to St. Albans. As soon as I was well enough for weekend leaves, I took the bus to Manhattan. My continued correspondence with Lucretia's family made me feel I could pay them a visit.

I arrived at Lucretia's home in Little Italy on the day of her mother's funeral. The family had just returned from the cemetery. Her brother Joey opened the door to me and explained what was going on. I was shocked. No one had told me Mama was sick. Rose Marie died of cancer; I'm not certain what type. In those days it didn't much matter what part of the body was affected, because as soon as you were told you had cancer of any kind, you knew you were doomed.

In the living room of their apartment, Lucretia's father sat crying over the loss of his wife, with the rest of his large family gathered around him. Apart from Lucretia and Filomena and that unfortunate incident with their brother Angelo, I'd never met any of them in person. To the others I was a stranger, so I gave my apologies and my condolences and figured I should get out of there. Lucretia stood by while her father rose to put his arms around me and give me a kiss on the cheek. Then he stood back to look at Lucretia and me and said, "Mama always wanted you two to get married."

His words caught me entirely off guard. I was struck dumb. I could have given *him* a big kiss. But he had placed me in an extremely awkward position. I couldn't fathom where his statement came from. How did Mama decide that? I'd never met her or her husband in person. He smiled through tears and said, "After a reasonable time has passed, you two will get married."

Lucretia appeared to be as shocked as I was. The last time I'd seen her she was a teenager, a high school student, and now she was a young woman of twenty-one. If anything, the passage of time had made her more graceful and lovely. Lucretia gestured for me to follow. We withdrew to a bedroom. She closed the door. She stated that she had nothing to do with her father's announcement and that she had no idea he was going to say this. I was still speechless. She waited. Then she asked, "What do you think about it?"

The fact that she was not rejecting me outright came as the second big surprise.

I knew that Lucretia had dated other guys and that at least one or two had proposed. One guy she dated was named Bernard Schwartz. Later he would become Tony Curtis, the movie star. Lucky for me she wasn't interested.

I still loved Lucretia but had learned to ignore the feeling. In spite of her earlier rejection of me, she always treated me beautifully and had done nothing to destroy my love. Even if she didn't approve of my past behavior, her tone was kind and gentle in the letters we exchanged.

I suppose our correspondence had deepened some kind of feeling in her. Knowing about the special love and respect she felt for her father gave me the bravery to say, "I'm willing if you are." It didn't occur to me to declare my love. That felt beyond the realm of possibility. I didn't know how to say words like that. She had to get the picture; she had to know how I felt.

To my continued amazement, she didn't hesitate, as if she'd given the matter some thought. "Okay," she said, "but you're going to have to change." She said I had to get the chip off my shoulder.

I told her I'd do anything to please her. Then I leaned forward and kissed her on the cheek. Her sister Filomena's little boy, Paulie, ran past us into the living room shouting, "That man kissed my auntie." He'd sneaked into the bedroom without our noticing or been there all along hiding behind a piece of furniture.

We were embarrassed as hell. We left the bedroom to rejoin the others. Everyone fell silent. A kiss was a big deal in those days, especially for me. But conversation resumed and no one said a thing about little Paulie's announcement. I excused myself a short while later and said I'd return at a better time.

Lucretia told me later she knew her mother liked me, but she didn't think anyone knew about Mama's wishes apart from Pop. The fact that I looked to the future and saved my money during the war must have made a big impression on her parents, and also the rosary I carved for Mama.

It's still hard to believe how quickly Lucretia accepted her father's announcement. Maybe she secretly liked me during those Newsboys' days but didn't want to say so because I seemed dangerous. In all the years of our marriage, I never asked about her change of heart and she never offered to explain. I suppose I was afraid to question my good fortune. I wanted to believe that all along she secretly found me attractive and that our correspondence led her to believe I could be a better person.

Lucretia and I spent relatively little time together in the few months before our wedding. She was working full time at North American Insurance, where she read and rated policies, and now that my health was better, I was told to report to Camp Lejeune in North Carolina. On some weekends I was able to take the train back to New York, where I checked into the Hotel Astor and either asked Lucretia out on a date or spent time with her and her family at their place. A few weeks before our wedding date, I was transferred to the Brooklyn Navy Yard, although I was given time off because I was getting married. I moved into the Hotel Astor full time.

Paulie, my future brother-in-law, asked where I was staying and informed me that I had to move out of the hotel and into his house. This wasn't a request, it was an order. I was in love with Lucretia, so I did it without question. Lucretia hadn't told me what a completely despicable person Filomena's husband was, maybe because she didn't want to turn me against a member of the family.

One night I was home alone at Paulie and Filomena's when two guys came to the door. Like classic hoods, they wore their hats pulled down low over their eyes and kept their hands in their jacket pockets. I was still in my Marine shirt and pants because I had no civilian clothes. The two men eyed my uniform and asked my relationship to Paulie. I said I was staying at his house and was going to marry his sister-in-law. They asked if I had a black tie. I said no. They said, "You better get one, because if we find Paulie, you'll be wearing it." I guess nothing came of the death threat, at least nothing bad for Paulie. At the time, he owned a plumbing business, but that had to be a front because he didn't seem to know a thing about plumbing. When his pipes needed to be repaired, Paulie called a plumber.

Later on Lucretia confided a few things about her brother-in-law. One day Paulie flattened his own brother right in the street, knocking him out cold. Also, Paulie often made overtures to Lucretia, no matter how many times she told him off, and he even informed Lucretia he would marry her when Filomena died. Lucretia said that Paulie never hit her sister, but I saw him do it. At their house before our wedding, I walked into the living room just as Paulie threw a book at Filomena from short range, smacking her right in the side of her face. Fortunately nothing more happened once I entered the room. Since I was a guest in their house and not a member of the family yet, it seemed a good idea not to get in the middle of whatever was going on, so I didn't do anything or say a word, although I did imagine punching the bastard.

Filomena stayed with Paulie until he died, for thirty or thirty-five years of marriage. It was revealing that Filomena suffered from a rash all up her arms and on her neck, bright red and itchy, during those decades. We saw her rub at it and apply Calamine lotion. After Paulie died, the rash disappeared. You could see what a nervous wreck Filomena was while Paulie was alive. Around him, she was a ghost of herself; when she was away from Paulie, I could get her giggling like a schoolgirl. Why Filomena ever married that guy, I don't know.

Lucretia's way of relating to me changed as soon as we agreed to wed. I felt total acceptance from her. She became more affectionate, although I soon learned that she was a hugger and kisser with other people as well, especially when it came to Pop and her brother Mikey. Still, in spite of the new feeling of warmth, it took a while for us to feel we really knew each other. I still didn't find a way to say "I love you" out loud, and I never did say it much until far too late, when I was losing her. But as our wedding day approached, she had to see how happy I was—how much she meant to me. I bet I walked around grinning like a fool.

Anytime Lucretia saw me revert to the behavior she hated, she talked to me about it, always in private. Her approach was gentle but strong. She made it clear that she would not abide by violent behavior. I did screw up a number of times, more so early on. The worst instance happened shortly after we became engaged, on a weekend when I came to New York from Camp Lejeune. I picked up Lucretia early at her father's apartment so that I could take her to Nedick's on Park Row for breakfast, to order their famous ten-cent meal of orange juice plus donuts and coffee. At the cash register I gave the guy a dollar. He handed me change, but I pushed it back and told him he'd shorted me a nickel. He then made the huge mistake of sliding it back across the counter saying, "*That's* your change." Without further ado, I reached over, grabbed him by the front of his shirt, and yanked him toward me over the counter. Lucretia was horrified. The guy scrambled to get me my nickel. This was one of the few times Lucretia physically intervened in a situation. She wrapped her arms around me to pull me away from the counter and said, "Let's get out of here, let's go." Outside Nedick's she quietly but firmly told me what she thought.

Even if I screwed up in front of her family, Lucretia didn't talk to me about it within earshot of them. Her approach was always subtle. She never dictated to me but instead stated what she could and could not accept. I loved her so much that it mattered.

Very quickly I came to love Lucretia even more dearly. Feeling her warmth, seeing the kind way she treated me, I wanted to do anything to keep from upsetting her. I lost my temper at times but learned to curb it. At first this felt impossible. It was hard to believe there were people like Lucretia and her family who could accept other people's bad behavior without comment. For example, where Lucretia worked at North American, there was a woman who liked to call her an *Eye*-talian. Lucretia never let that throw her. Hearing about this, I said I would deck the woman. Lucretia said that was never how she wanted to deal with it.

When an incident set me off, Lucretia and I discussed it. My first reaction tended to be, "You never stand up for me for anything. You always think the other person is right." Lucretia said my statement hurt her feelings more than anything else, my claiming that she didn't take my side. It wasn't a question of sides, she said, it was simply that she didn't want me to kill anybody.

Often I became angry over things that weren't going to make any difference in our lives. To me, other people's criticism was always an attempt to put me down, to deride me. Lucretia's reaction to other people's negativity or bad behavior was, "That's just people. You don't have to retaliate. What will it accomplish?" It was true, I was easily angered. I didn't want other people to walk all over me. I was proud of the way I could stand up for myself.

Lucretia saw all of me, the warts and everything. She realized my flaws fully before we were married, which of course was the reason she rejected me at first. I understood why she hadn't wanted to date me. By the time I was a young man, I honestly couldn't control my anger. It took her love to get me to control it.

Lucretia's family treated me like one of them almost instantly. Which astounded me. They were the most openhearted people I'd ever met. If Pop said Lucretia and I should marry, that was good enough for all of them. Their welcoming attitude took me aback. Even the boys in the family were expressive. They could be protective of their sister, but they were very friendly with me.

At first I may have seemed cold because I didn't know how to respond, but that didn't keep Lucretia's family from treating me warmly, even Angelo, the brother I'd taken a swing at during my Newsboys' years. Everything about these people was different from what I was used to. The Reidhead-Harrises were nice to one another, but I hadn't seen overt displays of affection in their home. Each time we met, the men in Lucretia's family hugged me and the women both hugged and kissed me. It took a while to hug and kiss back. Soon I felt very comfortable, very welcome. I loved that family.

I wish I could have known Lucretia's mother. Lucretia told me that if Pop had a little wine and got tipsy, he'd try to dance with Mama. Lucretia said it was obvious her mother loved that. When Pop grabbed Mama and hugged her, singing "Rose Marie, I love you so," her mother laughed and struggled, sometimes giving him a playful slap. He'd keep it up, though. Everyone could see that Mama liked his affection even if she protested. Eventually I used Pop's behavior as inspiration and occasionally did the same with Lucretia, grabbing her and singing one song or another to her. Lucretia also told me that if she and her brothers hugged and kissed Mama, their mother gently shooed them away and didn't show her feelings openly, but again it was clear she loved them. She expressed her feelings in the way she made a home for her family, the way she enjoyed baking and cooking for them. Her kids liked to tease her a lot, and you don't tease someone if they're harsh. Even as a grown man, Mikey would hang out the window of their third-floor apartment and say, "Look, Ma, no hands," which made her go ballistic. Mikey was that way as a kid and was still a daredevil as a grown man, but all he had to do was put his arms around his mother afterward, and they'd laugh.

As we got to know each other, Lucretia's brother Joey and I began to spend time together. Mikey was already married, so I didn't see as much of him. Angelo, with limited vision, mostly stayed home with Pop. Joey had particularly dark, swarthy skin and was the only family member with a pronounced Brooklyn accent. Like Mafia guys, Joey wore a soft-brimmed hat with the brim turned down in front. His hand was always in his side pocket as if he had a gun. He seemed to cultivate the Mafia image, but it was only a pose. The better I got to know him, the more I saw that Joey wouldn't hurt a soul. He loved films and often suggested we go down to Times Square to see a movie.

Filomena offered to go shopping with me to help select rings, and she and Paulie helped me make the wedding arrangements. Filomena clearly wanted to be helpful, but my impression was also that she enjoyed opportunities to get away from Paulie. I came to see what a nice person Filomena was and how intelligent. She was a college graduate and had been employed as a schoolteacher, but right after the war ended she didn't work outside her home, so we were able to spend more time together than Lucretia and I could. A devout Catholic, Filomena seemed to take great comfort from attending church every Sunday. But she was fair-minded about spiritual belief. She said it was fine with her if Lucretia and I didn't go; we upheld the Ten Commandments, and in her eyes that made us upstanding.

I came to see for myself what a cheerful man Lucretia's father was. Pop and Lucretia were close. If Lucretia and I were returning to the family's apartment, she'd go sit in Pop's lap, put her arm around his neck, and chat with him or sing to him, and he'd sing back. He was affectionate with his other kids, but Lucretia was the baby of the family, the youngest of the children and special in his eyes. The two of them were a lot alike. They were both tiny people and both very loving toward others, like two peas in a pod. Lucretia said that when she was little, Pop liked to take her to the Bronx Zoo and the Museum of Natural History. Seeing that her father couldn't read English, she brought home her kindergarten books to study with him, and eventually he did learn. Lucretia could get anything she wanted from her father. She'd simply go sit in his lap and ask.

Then there was Lucretia's godfather, Goombah Pete. He was Greek and didn't speak much English. Pop was fluent in Italian and not nearly in English, but the two of them regularly sat together speaking like two old chaps, drinking their wine. Goombah Pete was blind—or maybe I should say nearly blind. He had a pushcart and sold peanuts and flowers in summertime, hot chestnuts and snack foods in the winter. He didn't have a license, so about every six months the cops busted him, took him in, and fined him twenty-five or fifty dollars. He told his friends, "That fine was my license," and he'd go another six months before the cops brought him in again.

I'd known Goombah Pete before my engagement to Lucretia. His territory was just across from City Hall Park. While I was working at ITT, I used to buy peanuts and chestnuts off him. I wore a suit for the ITT job, and whenever I came near, he'd say, "Ahh, Il Professore." How he could see what I was wearing, I didn't understand, because he didn't seem able to see much. Almost from the start, Pete refused to take my money. Maybe he sensed that I was poor or someone told him I'd lived at Newsboys! He said he didn't want my money, but I silently paid him anyway. Sometimes he recognized me and other times he didn't and took my money with no complaint. After I returned from overseas, he seemed to recognize my uniform and absolutely refused to take my money, now calling me "Il Generale." Like Pop, he was a lovable old man.

In talking with Lucretia about her godfather, I said, "Poor old guy, he has to push that cart." She said, "*You* should have what that poor old guy has." Goombah Pete had saved money from the proceeds of his pushcart sales to buy a huge apartment house in Brooklyn. The rents allowed him to purchase more real estate. He built a bloody fortune for himself, his wife, and children with that pushcart. But you'd see him there on the sidewalk year-round. Apart from the flowers, everything he sold was bought in bulk and kept in the basement where he lived in Little Italy.

Lucretia and I were married on August 4, 1946. Lucretia was so tiny in comparison with me that, for our wedding portrait, the photographer had her stand on a box. She weighed all of 103 pounds and stood five feet, one inch tall.

Our wedding was elegant. The ceremony was held in Manhattan at St. Joachim's, a very large church. Lucretia's father gave her away. I wore my uniform, and she walked down the aisle in a beautiful gown with a long train. Her brother Joey was my best man. Her matron of honor was Filomena. Filomena and Paulie's daughter, Rosalie, was our flower girl. The ring bearer might have been Mikey, Jr.

Filomena's husband participated in our wedding ceremony even though we didn't want him to. He went up to the altar and stood there like he was part of the wedding party. Paulie's main contribution to the wedding was to take my money and hand it out. During planning, he'd said to give him my wallet and he'd arrange everything. On the day of the event he acted like a big shot, handing out tips and various payments to the florist and caterer and priests and altar boys. He'd requested a nuptial mass, the whole shebang. Lucretia's family was pretty well known in Little Italy, and there may have been four hundred people present at our wedding. Unfortunately I had no one to attend from my side of the family.

The wedding reception afterward was held at a hall on Vandewater Street. The Italians usually had a wedding cake or a tray of cookies stacked to look like a cake, and Lucretia wanted both. Her father gave her both. Italian-Americans also had a custom in which wedding guests handed envelopes containing money to the bride and groom as they offered congratulations. I thought those envelopes contained only greeting cards, and, being a brash young man ignorant about cultural customs, afterward threw them unopened into the trash basket at the hall. Back at the Hotel Astor after the reception, Lucretia asked where the envelopes were. I told her about tossing them, and she was astonished. I ran out of the hotel and rushed back to the hall to retrieve the money-filled envelopes.

The next day we left on our honeymoon to Quebec City.

Since there wasn't much time for Lucretia and me to go out on dates prior to our wedding, there was still a certain awkwardness between us leading up to our wedding day. Even though she'd become more affectionate, Lucretia and I weren't intimate before the wedding, and, in fact, that didn't change right after. It may sound strange, but it turned out that this was fortunate for both of us. I, of course, was extremely nervous about sex, which she didn't know. There was a physical reason on her part: She was plagued by fibroid cysts that bled from time to time. She worried about telling me and felt humiliated by the problem, but once she confided that we couldn't have relations just then, the problem kept both of us from feeling too much pressure on our wedding night and during our honeymoon. We could relax and smooch and become acquainted gradually.

As I look back now, I see that our love life was awfully slow to develop after the honeymoon, no matter the physical reasons, and that it was very cut-and-dried. There was no experimentation with anything outside Victorian thought, nothing playful. I was limited in my approach to sex because of what had happened with Eleanor Walters. I had a feeling of disgust with my body and anything sexual. Lucretia never complained and seemed to have a similar lack of interest in sex but for a different reason. She wasn't a regular churchgoer, but she was devoutly religious in her own way. She worried about having immoral thoughts and grew up thinking that anything sexual was sinful. That's not to say that we weren't passionate about each other. Our passion showed itself in other ways. She was beautiful. She was my little Lucretia. My feelings for her deepened with the passage of time.

For our honeymoon trip we traveled by train to Canada, talking much of the way. By the time we arrived in Quebec City, we knew each other a bit better. Still, we slept in separate berths on the train, upper and lower, and never the twain did meet. Our honeymoon felt more like two friends going on vacation.

In advance of our honeymoon I'd booked a room for us in a famous Quebec hotel, the Château Frontenac. Unfortunately, a member of the British royal family chose to arrive in the city at the same time as us, and our reservation had been canceled because the royal party booked into our hotel. No one notified us about the cancelation until we showed up at the front desk. We also learned that none of the other hotels had rooms available. A Travelers Aid office in Quebec City found us a rental in a beautiful, beautiful home in Montreal. The rental was located near Mount Royal Park, a nice part of town, and was an older home with antique furnishings. It seemed like a mansion to us. As far as we were concerned, it was better than the hotel. The only trouble was the landlord, who was an alcoholic and liked to drop by when we weren't there, which was not part of the rental agreement. We had a bottle of Scotch that Pop had handed to me at the wedding reception saying he wanted us to enjoy it on our honeymoon. Each day after Lucretia and I returned from touring the city's museums and parks, we discovered the bottle depleted a bit more.

About a week into our two-week Montreal stay, Lucretia and I were sitting in a restaurant eating breakfast when I was alarmed to spot a Marine captain walking along the sidewalk outside our window. Even though the war was over, I was in the Marines with four years to go and was still subject to wartime regulations. In Miyazaki I had reenlisted and, like all other Marines serving after the war, was supposed to be in full uniform while out in public. That morning I wore only my Marine pants and khaki shirt—no tie and no jacket. The captain glanced at us through the window, stopped, and took two steps back to have another look. I told Lucretia I was in big trouble.

The captain entered the restaurant, waltzed up to our table, and greeted us with, "Thank God I found someone who speaks English. Can I sit down?" We laughed with relief. I think the guy was with the U.S. Consulate. He was a delightful fellow and asked what we were doing in Montreal. He heard how we'd lost our reservation at the hotel in Quebec City and said, "I've got a gift for you. I have a room at the Château Frontenac for another five nights. All I want is to get the hell out of here." He was tired of being in a place where mostly French was spoken. The two of us were in love, and not being able to speak with the locals didn't bother us. The man gave us his suite.

With the fairy-tale hotel as our lodging, we escaped the snooping, alcoholic landlord and very much enjoyed the remainder of our time in Canada. We saw the sights and dined in restaurants, and it felt to me as though we were boyfriend and girlfriend getting to know each other and enjoying every minute. My loneliness was gone forever thanks to this beautiful girl.

As good as that?

To hear William speak, you'd have thought Lucretia was a saint. I had to wonder if anyone could be that good. If saints are subject to occasional fits of anger, maybe she was.

Two years into work on this book, William let drop that there were a couple of times when Lucretia became enraged at him. He was quick to say these incidents were not at all characteristic of his wife. Interestingly, he could not recall what he'd done to inspire her fury. Both happened in the early days of their marriage at the home they purchased in New Jersey.

The first glimpse of an infuriated Lucretia popped up in William's introduction of Pat, a teenage girl who babysat for them. Wanting to give an illustration of Pat's unusual poise, he described how the girl happened to walk up to the Walters' house just as an alarm clock came crashing through a pane of glass in the front door. Lucretia had thrown the clock at William but missed. The clock lay on the grass with its alarm going off. "All the neighbors had to be wondering what was going on," said William, "but Pat strolled up the front path, picked up the clock, and entered the house, never saying a word about it. Lucretia and I were so embarrassed, we dropped our argument."

Another time, reacting to William, Lucretia kicked over a jug of her father's wine that sat on the cellar steps in their home. The bottle crashed and splattered on the basement floor. William insisted that this sort of thing never happened again. Either Lucretia developed a tighter rein on her anger toward him or there was an improvement in his behavior, or both.

Marriages require compromise, and in her marriage, Lucretia had to accept many related to her husband's wounding as a child. How often did she ask herself whether she was his wife or his mother? How often did she wish she didn't need to soften William's harsh words toward their children and others? How frequently did she yearn for words of love from him and maybe even sexual excitement, in spite of the fact that William didn't seem to need it? Lucretia's patience and fortitude seem admirable.

Always, William emphasized to me Lucretia's fine qualities. Separately, his daughter, Dorothea, expressed the same things. Generosity, concern for strangers, selflessness, a loving and demonstrative nature. Not unusual memories for a grieving widower and his daughter. Maybe to be taken with a grain of salt.

And yet. As he unfolded his tale, William said that Lucretia had worked for a while at Hardisty's Homewares in Santa Rosa, California. It had been twenty years since a certain experience of mine in that store, and I hadn't thought about it since, but I could still summon up the sensation I carried away afterward.

Hardisty's was an old-time kitchen and home-supply store located in downtown Santa Rosa. I patronized Hardisty's only a few times because I was a weary young mother and one-stop shopping at local department stores was more convenient. On this particular occasion a petite, middle-aged woman helped me find an expensive item I needed to get precisely right but that I've now forgotten. Her, I have not forgotten. She was one of maybe two employees staffing the cavernous store. There was nothing physically remarkable about the lady apart from her short, slight stature; her face, hair, and dress made no big impression. Her smile was something else again. She radiated goodwill in a combination of kindness and interest that seemed genuine. I left the store with my purchase having been helped in more ways than one. Thirty minutes with the stranger felt like an embrace.

Lucretia, I think now.

Which makes it easier to trust William's recollections of her, including his earliest reactions.

When she came by Newsboys' with her girlfriends, Lucretia hung back but was watchful. She was both wary and interested. She seemed to care about the young men who lived at Newsboys'.

People took it for granted that the guys at Newsboys' were poor, but Lucretia asked questions of them—for example, whether they were getting enough to eat and where they'd lived earlier. She asked William about his childhood. He gave what had become his new stock response. At age sixteen he still worried about being returned to the Walters. He said he'd grown up in an orphanage. Forget Lucretia's physical loveliness; her concern for William and other residents of Newsboys' alone would have grabbed his attention. Others might have simply called her "nice." To him, her kindness was a beacon.

Lucretia watched William and the other boys, and he watched her. She gave pennies to people begging on the street. A disabled man lived downstairs from her family; Lucretia went out of her way to run errands for him or assist him in other ways. She spoke out against prejudice of any kind. She'd been sensitized at an early age because people often thought you were Mafia if you were Italian, and she had an absolute abhorrence of prejudice against any race or religion.

The more he knew about her, the more William loved Lucretia. That held true all the years of their marriage.

Had he idealized her? Possibly. But I can tell you that it made you feel good to be in her presence.

CHAPTER TWELVE

Easing into Marriage and Civilian Employment

After our honeymoon, Lucretia continued to live with her father and brother Angelo while I reported for service at the Brooklyn Navy Yard, just across the bridge from Little Italy. I saw Lucretia every weekend and returned to the navy yard at night. There was no room at her father's house for me to stay; she had her room, but it held only a single bed, which was too narrow and small to hold both her and tall, gangly me. So it continued to feel as if we were dating. We had no privacy and no opportunity to be intimate. Believe it or not, it never crossed my mind to get a hotel room. This might have been avoidance on my part. However, there was an occasion when Lucretia and I went to her sister Filomena's house in Teaneck, New Jersey, and we were making out on the couch when Fil came downstairs. Boy, did we fly in opposite directions. That may have been the first time Lucretia and I were at all intimate.

Still, deep down, I felt an unbelievable love for Lucretia right from the start of our time together. No one had ever

loved me the way she did. I was on top of the world. It's hard
to put into words what Lucretia was to me. A companion,
a friend, a mentor. She knew all the proper things to do in
life, having come from a family like hers. She taught me a lot
about manners. She taught me a lot about affection. She was
exceptional.

We were married only a short while when I came to see
that Lucretia was physically awkward and clumsy. In the
Pacific during the war, we saw birds called gooney birds that
didn't walk straight. So I began to call Lucretia my Gooney
Bird and had this name engraved on a gold bird charm that
I gave her. My gesture pleased her, especially since I made
the gift for no special occasion except that I loved her.
Unfortunately I didn't find it within me to write that on the
charm or on a note attached. Still, that was the beginning
of surprising each other with gifts large and small over the
more than sixty-five years we were married. A lot of times I
couldn't afford much, so I'd save up. She'd do the same. Or,
she'd let me know she was thinking about me by putting notes
in the lunches she packed for me to take to work. We both did
things like that.

Lucretia continued to work at North American Insurance
in the months following our wedding. In our free hours, we
found fun things to do in the city. Sometimes we took the el
to the Polo Grounds to see the Giants play. At the time there
was a big rivalry between the Brooklyn Dodgers and the New
York Giants. We called the Dodgers "Dem Bums." Rivalries
then were not like the rivalries now. There was not a strong
underlying dislike. Our loyalties were more in good fun.

Upon reporting back to the Brooklyn Navy Yard after our
honeymoon, I had something of a scare. I came close to being
court-martialed. During the war, you weren't allowed to get

married without your commanding officer's permission. There was a good reason for this: In the U.S. during wartime, a lot of girls quickly married servicemen so they could receive the government allotment for wives, but they had no intention of honoring their vows. Guys married quickly, shipped overseas, and had no idea what was going on back home. Their wives collected government checks based on their husbands' service but went catting around with other guys, and the next thing the soldiers knew, they received Dear John letters. So you were required to tell your commanding officer if you planned to wed so that he could look into the situation.

I hadn't informed my regular commanding officer before the wedding because I didn't know who he'd be. In the weeks leading up to the wedding, I reported to the commander at the navy yard's Sands Street Gate, an officer who was not going to be my regular commander and didn't really care what I did; he was the one who gave me time off to marry and go on a honeymoon. After I reported back for service and told my new commanding officer, he got real upset. He pointed out the rule about seeking permission. I explained to him that our marriage wasn't sudden and that I'd known Lucretia for four or five years prior to wedding. He took some time to think it over and decided not to create a problem for me. It must have helped that the wartime mobilization was winding down, things were relaxed, and there wasn't much opportunity for women to grab up guys in that way anymore.

At the Brooklyn Navy Yard, I had another close call with military brass. It linked back to my time in Saipan and a day when I'd been driving a Jeep along a coastal road. A sergeant sat in the back seat and another Marine was up front with me. These guys were always kidding around. The sergeant said, "You'd better pull over, there's a civilian behind you." Our Jeep had a snorkel to feed air to the engine if it was necessary to drive through water, but it lacked a simple rearview mirror. I figured the sergeant was joking about being followed and said, "Yeah, right," and kept driving. All of a sudden, out of the corner of my eye, I saw this big black Buick trying to pass us. It didn't belong to a civilian; it belonged to big brass. There were little flags on the front bumper, and one of those flags had four stars. I damn near ran into a ditch getting off the road, out of the way of a four-star admiral. He stopped, got out of the Buick, and ordered me out of the Jeep. I did what he said and stood at attention. Boy, did he read me the riot act. "Do you know who I am?" he yelled. I said, "No, sir, but I know *what* you are." He informed me that he was Admiral Kinkaid. Kinkaid was one of the most important admirals of World War II. He was commander of Allied Naval Forces and the Seventh Fleet under MacArthur in the southwestern Pacific. You might say we won the war in the Pacific thanks in large part to leadership from him, Admiral Halsey, and Admiral Nimitz.

Admiral Kinkaid instructed his driver, who was a lieutenant, to get my name, rank, and serial number. I thought to myself that I wasn't likely to run into Kinkaid or his lieutenant again, so I gave a fictitious name, rank, and serial number. No way were they going to trace me.

Now, back to the Brooklyn Navy Yard: I was put in command of the Sands Street Gate. There were only two entrances to the yard, that gate and the Washington Street Gate. The Sands Street Gate closed at six o'clock at night. One evening I was on duty in the guardhouse at the gate when a private stationed at the gate came over and said, "There's a lady at the gate who wants in." I told him that it was after six o'clock and the gate was closed. "She can go around to the Washington Street Gate if she wants in." The private came back a few minutes later and said, "This lady is awfully angry and still wants in." I said, "Go back out and tell her I don't care how angry she is, she doesn't get in after six o'clock."

The next morning when I reported for duty, there was a notice to report to the colonel's office. He asked me, "Do you know who you kept out of the Sands Street Gate last night?" "No, sir, I don't." "That was Admiral Kinkaid's wife. And he ain't exactly happy. So you write a report to me and say why you did that." In my report I pointed out that orders were orders, and that the orders didn't say that the gate should be opened for the admiral's wife; they said that all visitors after six at night had to report to the Washington Street Gate. The colonel read my report and said, "You know, you're right. You obeyed the orders you were given and you cannot be court-martialed for following orders." He took care of it, and that was that. But believe me, I was shaking. I thought that if Admiral Kinkaid saw me and remembered me, I'd be a dead duck.

Military attitudes can be funny. There are rules and there are rules, depending on who interprets them. In Japan one time I was leaning in a doorway smoking a cigarette. Someone cleared his throat behind me. For some reason I didn't move. He cleared his throat again, and when I looked, it was a two-star general. I had failed to jump to attention, but he smiled as he passed by and said, "You're lucky it wasn't a second lieutenant who saw you."

In combat on Saipan I witnessed another example of insubordination. General Holland M. Smith was known to us as Howlin' Mad because he liked to yell at the troops. A group of us infantrymen were taking fire from the Japanese when he walked up and stood among us. All of us stood up to protect him. We knew that he'd draw fire from the enemy because of his high rank. The Japanese knew it was smart to shoot officers because this would cause chaos among the ranks. In combat, officers wore their stars under their collars and revealed their rank to the men only if it was crucial. No one was supposed to even say "Yes, sir" if the Japanese were near.

Generals were more obvious targets for the Japanese because they had stars right on their helmets. We stood up to protect the general, but Howlin' Mad yelled at us to lie down and resume fire. One guy yelled back, "We will if you get the hell out of here." The general didn't say a word of reprimand and backed away. Smith knew the guy was right.

A few months after Lucretia and I married, I was medically separated from the service. The dengue fever recurred, so I was sent again to St. Albans in Queens. The long bus trip from Little Italy was demanding for Lucretia, but she came to see me often, and it warmed my heart to have her there. I couldn't imagine her making the journey on a regular basis, riding several hours round trip. It looked like dengue fever was going to be an ongoing affair. The doctors said the illness could return repeatedly for as long as fifteen years. They reviewed my case with me and said that if I wanted to continue military service, they first wanted me to stay in the hospital for a year or so of treatment. I asked if there was an alternative. Yes, an honorable discharge from the service. That was my choice. I didn't want Lucretia to continue traveling to the hospital over that many weeks and months. Also, we were still in dating mode. We were married but didn't feel like it entirely. There had been no real intimacy. We couldn't continue on that way, not for another year.

The doctors said I'd have to find a sedentary job. There was no recommendation of follow-up medical care or monitoring, but there wasn't much they could have done, because there's still no treatment for dengue fever except for strong painkillers and bed rest. I tried to return to ITT, where I'd been told that my employment would be secure. Not true. This kind of deception still happens to vets today. At ITT's personnel office I was informed that my job no longer existed and they had nothing else for me. The promise had been pure hogwash.

Lucretia and I needed to set up housekeeping on our own. We rented an attic apartment in Woodhaven, Long Island. The new privacy and time by ourselves made it easier to finally become intimate. I found a job with Chubb & Son insurance, right across the street from the office where Lucretia worked. At Chubb & Son I rated policies. If you ever saw the movie *The Apartment*, with Jack Lemmon's desk in a sea of desks, that's how mine was situated. All day long I sat there rating commercial fire insurance policies using Dunn & Bradstreet. A policy came my way, I looked up the business, and I rated the policy according to the owner's financials. They paid me something like twenty-eight dollars a week, which went up to thirty dollars a week after I complained. I lasted only a few months, quitting in frustration. It was absolutely tedious work. Higher pay would have helped, but my supervisor, who said I was doing fine, said he couldn't arrange it.

Next I hired on at a watch crystal factory in Manhattan. The workplace was a dingy sweatshop, but I was paid thirty-five dollars a week. Workers sat in a line of chairs facing a bench that ran the length of one wall. Before us were wheels that looked like grinding wheels but were covered in felt. Underneath each wheel sat a pail of water and pumice. My job was to grind tiny watch crystals using the felt and wet pumice. At the end of the day, I held up my hand with fingers pointed downward and watched blood drip off. The wheel and pumice had ground the tips of my fingers along with the crystals. I decided that I wasn't going to bleed to death for thirty-five dollars a week. I lasted one day.

There were other jobs, none of them decent. It was now winter, and Lucretia's brother Joey said, "Hey, I'll tell you how we can earn some money. The City of New York pays you two dollars an hour to shovel snow." That was big money, although snow shovelers could only be employed for a maximum of four hours a day. "But I've got a plan," said Joey. "We'll shovel snow uptown for four hours, and then we'll get hired downtown to work another four hours." If New York City had a serious snowstorm, it spelled trouble for everyone, so they hired a big raft of people to scoop away the drifts from streets and sidewalks as quickly as possible. Joey and I had a great time. He was a good guy with a positive spirit, and the work he'd found us was helpful, but spring would come, and I needed to find better. I was determined to be a good husband and a good father to the kids I imagined for us, and that included being a good provider.

Talents

She was a countess and a fashion icon. Photos of Countess Consuelo Crespi wearing Valentino and Fendi graced international fashion pages. She modeled, she edited the Italian edition of *Vogue*, and her name repeatedly landed at the top of American "best dressed" lists.

The countess may have been a fashion icon but she was also an iconoclast. In the early 1960s, when hems were short, the American-born Pauline O'Brien O'Connor, now married to Count Rodolfo Crespi, arrived in New York from Rome wearing skirts four to five inches longer and initiated her own fashion trend. In the globe-trotting world where social elites still held sway, the countess also was unafraid to recognize emerging talent and showcase it. Valentino credited her for giving him his big break. Fendi and Missoni said much the same.

Fashionistas would not have recognized the same woman on the streets of Cloverdale, California, in the early sixties. Sporting beat-up boots, a flannel shirt, worn-out dungarees, and a cowboy hat, and driving through town in a Jeep, the statuesque woman with streaks of grey in her hair looked for all the world like a local ranch hand.

One day the countess in a cowboy hat walked through the door of Interior Accents by Lucretia, the shop established by William and his wife in their new hometown. He was in charge of carpets, flooring, upholstery, and drapes. Mama handled the china, crystal, and gifts end of things. Beginning in Upland, where he had been briefly encouraged by artist Millard Sheets, a representative of the California School of Painting,

William had been trying his hand at oils and other media. Now he sold his art in two of the region's galleries and hung his work in their Cloverdale shop as well. Cloverdale may have boasted fewer than 3000 residents, but the population had more than doubled between 1950 and 1960 and was continuing to grow, and their store served a wider swath of the region than the immediate vicinity. Though it was the time of a back-to-the-land movement, not all newcomers were hippies aiming to live modestly.

Especially not Countess Crespi. The commanding stranger wanted William and Lucretia to help decorate her home. At least half the year the countess lived at residences owned with her husband in Italy and on Long Island, but when she came to northern California she didn't want to socialize. Here she was looking for privacy and a slower pace. If William and Lucretia wanted her patronage, the couple must promise to tell no one about her or where she lived, an estate located off River Road in the hills east of town. A crude barbed-wire gate was the first thing you saw before starting up the simple dirt drive. The next thing to capture your attention was a racetrack for horses and then, on the hilltop, a Tuscan-style villa, its wraparound balcony providing views of lawns and woods and the racetrack below. Indoors there was a swimming pool. The only other person in town who was in on the countess's story was Bob at the hardware store. Consuelo Crespi asked him to transport to her property three freight-car loads of chain link fencing for the perimeter.

William and Lucretia installed carpeting and drapes at the countess's home. At their shop she picked out crystal and various knickknacks as well. Then she spotted one of William's drawings, a pastel of an old Native American man he'd done on newspaper and glued to plywood. The countess purchased the piece but William worried that she should have something more durable. He painted the same subject in oils on canvas, but she turned it down. She was right, he decided. She had a good eye.

In William's home before he died were multiple examples of his painting, woodworking, and upholstery talents. In the living room, an intricate wooden screen carved from four two-by-four-foot panels brought to mind Asian art, reflecting hours of minute attention with scroll saw, files, and coping saw. Among the screen's dense vines and leaves were

woven a Victorian home with a couple sitting atop the porch railing, a boy
and his dog on the way to the fishing hole, and children on swings.

Arts, crafts, superior memory, intellectual curiosity—who knows
what William might have become if he'd had a formal education and
opportunity.

Looking back on his hobbies and his various jobs, William said these
didn't amount to much. He maintained that he never accomplished anything significant. He would have liked to make contributions in one of a
number of fields: inorganic chemistry, pathology, or archeology.

It's easy to imagine the envy William felt when he learned his brother
had a degree in physics. William sounded like an educated man when you
spoke with him, thanks to extensive reading and frequent travel, but he
knew better. He knew what he might have been.

William's belief in what he might have achieved was one of the few
instances in which he thought of himself not in demeaning terms but
with a positive understanding of his own potential. A potential he didn't
fulfill. Which he blamed on himself.

In some ways, William wished he'd stayed in the Marine Corps after
the war, which would have offered the possibility of advancement. Or he
could have applied himself to getting an education. Following the war, the
GI Bill made it easy for vets to attend high school and college, but he didn't
take advantage of that opportunity, allowing his feelings for Lucretia to
carry him away. He might have asked her to wait to get married. At the
time he told himself that he'd hardly been to grade school, and it would
be a long haul to reach college. In retrospect, that seemed to him like an
excuse: "Now look how many years have passed. It's been a long life, and
there was plenty of time for schooling. I made the wrong choices, and
after that, I didn't have much control. I had family obligations. No, that's
something of an excuse as well. I read about people who had families to
support but didn't let that become an obstacle to achievement."

William insisted that he wasn't bitter about not getting an education.
He didn't want to say that his life had been unhappy. "As long as I had
Lucretia, I was happy. We had our ups and downs, we had disasters, but we
had a good life."

Countess Crespi recognized something special in William. Lucretia did, too. As did others, including inventor and entrepreneur Isidor Goldberg.

CHAPTER THIRTEEN

The Pleasures of
Meadowbrook Farm

It was late 1946 or early 1947 in New York, and a series of jobs
had led nowhere. Then, to my great good fortune, I spotted an
ad in the newspaper calling for someone to manage the farm
operation on an estate in Westchester County, New York. To
apply, I had to meet the estate's owner at his corporate offices
in Manhattan. This is when I came to know a man named
Isidor Goldberg, head of the Pilot Radio Corporation.

My first impression was of a short, stocky guy seated
behind a large desk and smoking a big cigar. Before I could
say anything, he called an engineer into his office and read
him the riot act for doing something or other. I thought, oh
no. The engineer didn't react much to the dressing down. He
didn't seem nervous and didn't apologize; he simply walked
out again, apparently able to shrug off the episode. Goldberg
turned to me, laughed, and said, "I have to keep them on their
toes."

Mr. Goldberg asked what I knew about farming. I told
him I'd grown up on farms and ranches in the West and had

pretty extensive experience. My guess is he took this statement with a large grain of salt because of my age and my
appearance. I was twenty-one, which may have seemed young
for a manager. I also looked pretty citified. For the job interview I wore a suit and tie. Mr. Goldberg asked what I knew
about farm machinery. I told him that I'd operated almost
every type of farm machine there was. "Okay," he said, "I'm
going to tell you . . . there's an aircraft hangar on my property,
and in that hangar is a side-delivery hay rake. It's all in pieces.
If you can put that thing together so that it operates, you've
got the job." I'd never used one, but I knew what a side-
delivery hay rake was. It might be a challenge to assemble,
but I said I'd do it.

Within a few days I took the train north from the city
to Yorktown Heights. A dignified black man met me at the
station in a limousine, identified himself as the Goldbergs'
butler, and drove me the half a mile or so to the estate. On
that day Homer wasn't wearing a butler's uniform; the only
time he did that was when the Goldbergs had rich guests up
from the city. Usually he dressed in a white shirt and black
pants, and that's what he wore when I first met him. As we
spoke, it seemed that he was well educated, although he did
have something of that broad New York accent.

Homer drove us to a property he told me was
Meadowbrook Farm. It was located on 325 acres in Yorktown
Heights, not far from Peekskill. Giant maple trees stood on
either side of the winding drive as we entered the estate and
came to a stop in front of a two-story colonial-style house.
The buildings and land were beautiful. The large house sat on
a knoll with rolling lawn all around it.

In addition to the mansion, Meadowbrook Farm included
the airplane hangar, a silo, chicken coops, a milk house
with refrigeration, and two barns—one of which never saw
a cow and was used for dances. Various smaller houses for

employees were scattered out of sight of the main house. Homer told me there were four horses, a couple of bulls, and many cows whose milk provided the farm's only income. Across the driveway from the main house he pointed out a two-story frame structure painted white with green trim to match the mansion. Downstairs was a three- or four-car garage. If I got the job, my wife and I would live in the quarters above.

Homer told me to take my few things up to the apartment and then come back to see him. The apartment didn't look like it had been used in a long while. It was pretty antiquated, dusty, and dirty. The furnishings were sparse. Outside, a privet hedge had been allowed to grow about eighteen feet high.

I followed Homer to the airplane hangar, which was empty apart from the side-delivery hay rake. Within a couple of days I assembled the piece of equipment. At mealtimes, Homer's wife, Daisy, came looking for me to invite me over to the main house to eat with them. Her husband was a bit shorter than me and of average build; Daisy, who matched Homer in height, was quite rotund. Their company and my work made the days go quickly. Daisy and Homer liked to laugh and were the salt of the earth.

After I was done assembling the hay rake, Homer came down to the hangar to take a look and had me run it around to prove it worked. He phoned Mr. Goldberg to make his report, and Mr. Goldberg told Homer to let me know I had the job and could move in whenever I liked.

I loved that job. It was one of the best I ever had. My assignment was to run the farm operation and dictate what the other workers should do, as well as to work alongside them. Lucretia and I would live there happily for almost a year.

First, though, I had to convince Lucretia that it was a good idea to move to the country. She wasn't thrilled with the prospect, having been raised on the sidewalks of New York. I talked it up, though, and she agreed. One thing Lucretia didn't mind was giving up her own job, because she'd come to hate it. She didn't like the people at North American and the way that one woman in particular treated her, the one who liked to call her an *Eye*-talian.

After we moved to Meadowbrook, Lucretia came to love the place. Daisy liked to grab up Lucretia in big hugs and took her under her ample wing like a daughter. Our attic space on Long Island had been hardly big enough to turn around in. Meadowbrook was Lucretia's first real home away from home. She never had to worry about a thing as she learned to set up housekeeping because Daisy was always there to help out and advise her.

At last we felt like a happily married couple. Lucretia and I were closer than ever, I had a regular job that I liked, and with some fixing-up, we had a nice place to live. Finding ourselves in such a good situation at Meadowbrook Farm made us feel lucky.

Homer and Daisy lived in the main house and generally looked after the mansion as caretakers. Homer took the employees on regular shopping trips into town for their groceries and other supplies and also kept the acre or so of lawn around the house neatly trimmed by using a riding mower. He and Daisy kept a storehouse stocked with food and other items for the times when the Goldbergs were on hand. Daisy was strictly a cook; the Goldbergs employed maids who came in to do cleaning and laundry but didn't live on the premises.

Homer and Daisy soon became our good friends. We learned that Mr. Goldberg and his wife visited the estate infrequently, him more often than her, although his work in the city didn't give him much opportunity. At times when the

Goldbergs were in residence and other people descended on the estate, Homer served as chauffeur and would take all the ladies to Peekskill to shop. During the many days and weeks when the Goldbergs weren't there, you wouldn't believe how many times Daisy had us over to dinner at the estate house, always insisting that we come spend time with her and Homer.

Meadowbrook had approximately seventy cows. They were Ayrshires, a handsome red-brown breed of dairy cattle known for being healthy, long-lived, and good grass-converters. Their milk has high butter content—not as high as Jerseys or Guernseys, but still pretty high. Apart from the chickens and a small garden that provided fresh produce for the Goldbergs and for Daisy and Homer, the farming operation was dedicated almost entirely toward raising, supplying feed for, and milking the cows. We men concentrated most of our efforts on plowing, planting, and harvesting grass and grains to feed the cows.

Three other farm employees lived and worked at Meadowbrook: Mr. Peniotta, who lived there with his wife; an old man who was a bachelor living alone; and a third man who shared a house with his wife and son. That boy, who was about twelve years old, was one of the meanest kids I've ever known. The boy used to throw rocks at me when I was plowing and was cruel to the farm's animals. I'd see his father chasing him with a stick after he caught his son doing nasty deeds like that. One day the kid told the old bachelor, "I don't like you and I'm gonna hit you." Knowing what I did about the boy, I warned the old guy to watch out, but the man didn't believe me. Just days after the boy threatened the old man, I walked into the milk house to find the guy laid out on the floor. The boy had hit him over the head with a metal pipe. I found some ice and held it to the man's head. We were located pretty far away from medical care, and maybe because of that, the old guy insisted he was okay and didn't require further treatment. He quit the farm shortly after, and if he hadn't left, I believe sooner or later that kid would have killed him.

Two bulls resided at the estate: Thistle and Quaker. Thistle was a big, big, big bull with a heart of gold. Thistle was gentle, but Quaker was a short, stocky, mean son of a bitch. They were as opposite as two bulls could be. Quaker was so bad that Mr. Goldberg decided to build a special breeding pen for him alongside his regular pen. He and I worked on it one weekend when Mr. Goldberg was up from the city. Quaker stood watching from his adjacent pen, and as soon as we finished and let him in, he immediately tore the new pen to shreds. Mind you, the fencing consisted of concrete posts connected by two-and-a-half-inch metal pipes. When Quaker laid into them, he bent the pipes like bowstrings. Mr. Goldberg and I built the breeding pen again but stronger. Still, the pen was destined to be a failure because Quaker was not a breeding bull. Two reasons: Quaker was damn mean, and he was so small that he needed a ramp to reach the females.

In general, you couldn't trust Quaker in any way. All you had to do was put your arm atop one of his pen's posts, and he'd put his head down to take aim. He was so vicious that we decided to sell him.

A potential buyer showed up. He was interested. I asked him how he was going to take Quaker away.

"I'll just put a nose ring on him and lead him away," he said.

I said to let me know when that was going to happen, because I'd climb to the top of the silo before he did. The sale didn't go through.

Mr. Goldberg didn't understand the situation. Our mouths fell open watching him deal with that bull. One day, a couple of us were trying to clean Quaker's pen, at the same time using cattle prods to keep him away. Mr. Goldberg spotted us and said, "What's the matter with you guys?" He opened the pen, walked in, and when the bull came at us, he kicked Quaker in the ribs. The next thing we expected to see was Mr. Goldberg being killed, but Quaker only walked away in shame, head down. Maybe he was so surprised he didn't know what to do.

There was much I didn't know about Mr. Goldberg. He never mentioned his many accomplishments developing and introducing a range of groundbreaking products in communications for both civilian and wartime use. It would have been interesting to ask about those and other products his company pioneered, but I didn't know enough to ask and he wasn't the kind of guy who boasted.

As weeks and months went by at Meadowbrook, the dengue fever recurred only once. Civilian doctors knew very little about the disease. During that last bad episode, Lucretia called a doctor. As soon as he walked in, I told him I had dengue fever, and he said, "Why do you think that?" He was an old country physician and thought I might have something else, maybe polio. He grabbed my foot and bent my leg. The pain sent me through the roof. I said, "If you do that again, I'll kick you out the window." Tropical diseases were a whole other ball game than what American doctors usually saw. Elephantiasis, malaria, and dengue—the illnesses we brought back from the Pacific and elsewhere—were not commonly known. I told him what to prescribe.

After that, dengue fever went out the window. Occasionally I experienced mild fevers, but not much more. Soon I became the healthiest I'd been in my life. I plowed and planted and harvested and milked morning 'til night. We ate well, we slept well, we breathed in the country air.

Lucretia seemed very happy, especially since her family came up to visit every weekend. We had our own vegetable plot, as did each Meadowbrook employee, and on the weekends Filomena taught Lucretia how to cook using bounty from our garden. Lucretia's father loved spending time at Meadowbrook. There was a big old tree about fifty yards from our house, and Pop used to sit under it on a stump and smoke his pipe as he watched the rest of us working or relaxing nearby. Those weekends were the only times I ever saw Paulie act like a real human being. Not only did he drive Pop up for visits, he helped out with projects like removal of the towering privet hedge at the back of our house and installation of a lawn in its place.

In time I became aware of a fire siren perched on the roof of the main house. The idea was that if Mr. Goldberg was in residence for the weekend, Daisy could blow the siren to call him in for dinner from wherever he was on the estate or sound an alert if a phone call came for him. The siren went off one evening as Mr. Goldberg and I were working on something out by the barn. Whatever it was we were doing, Mr. Goldberg was so interested that he ignored the signal from Daisy. The siren went off again. Again he ignored it. Before we knew it, Daisy came waddling down to the barn and grabbed Mr. Goldberg by the ear. She was taller than him and, as I said, a big woman.

Daisy said, "Mr. Goldberg, did you hear that goddamn siren?'

"Yes, Daisy," he said.

"Do you know what that means?"

"Yes, Daisy."

"Well, the next time you hear that siren, you get your ass up to the house."

"Yes, Daisy."

Daisy was a wonderful cook, and I don't think Mr. Goldberg wanted to lose her. Or her husband. It seemed they were well paid, because in addition to their quarters in the mansion at Meadowbrook, the couple owned what sounded like a nice apartment back in New York City. It's hard to say when they used their city apartment since they were always at Meadowbrook.

Daisy had a dog, a black mongrel that was allowed to wander the estate. One time I saw Mr. Goldberg walking to the main house along a pathway when he tripped over Daisy's dog. His response was to kick the dog, and it let out a yowl. I wasn't the only witness. Here came Daisy again. She took Mr. Goldberg by the ear and said, "You ever kick that dog again and I'll bash your head against that rock over there." "Yes, Daisy," was all he said.

Mostly Mr. Goldberg treated us employees pretty nicely. However, I began to notice he had a horrible attitude toward many of the people who came to visit him and his wife. On Sunday mornings when the couple was up at the estate, he'd throw pebbles at our bedroom window. I'd go to the window and peer down, and he'd ask, "You want to go horseback riding?" I'd saddle up the horses and we'd ride for an hour or more all over Meadowbrook. Mr. Goldberg was an easy companion, very friendly. One Sunday, Mr. Goldberg and I were setting off on a ride when he realized he forgot something. I dismounted and walked back to the house to get whatever it was and ran into Homer at the side door. Homer asked me to tell Mr. Goldberg that Dr. and Mrs. So-and-so were leaving on the afternoon train and would like to say goodbye.

I gave him the message about his guests. Mr. Goldberg said, "Tell Homer to tell Dr. and Mrs. to kiss my ass."

I said I couldn't do that.

Mr. Goldberg said I could do that or get fired.

I knew Mr. Goldberg well enough to know that wasn't the case. "You don't mean that," I said.

He was silent.

I asked why he disliked rich people so much.

"In 1929 I had a million dollars," he said. "You wouldn't believe the friends I had. We had parties, we had friends all over the place. Then I lost my million and I couldn't find a friend anywhere. Now I've got ten times that much money and I don't need no damn friends."

At times he also seemed hard on his wife. One time she arrived at Meadowbrook on her own to spend a week supervising renovation work on the main house. Part of this work involved an enclosed sunporch with a big brick BBQ on the side of the mansion facing our place. Toward the end of the project, flooring people sanded and varnished the sunporch floor.

Then Mr. Goldberg arrived for the weekend. He liked to have his breakfast on the sunporch. Daisy would bring it to him there. It was summer, and the windows of our house and of the porch were wide open, so we could hear what was said when Mr. Goldberg showed up to have breakfast there.

Daisy must have come up behind him as he stood in the doorway from the house to the sunporch. "You can't have your breakfast out here," she said.

"Why?"

"Because Mrs. Goldberg just had the floor refinished. It needs to dry."

Daisy told us later exactly what happened. Mr. Goldberg disappeared, put on his work boots, and returned to run across the freshly finished floor, skidding to a halt and leaving huge scuff marks.

He said, "Now, Daisy, I can have my breakfast out here."

• • •

Actually, I can't claim that Mr. Goldberg was always sweetness and light to us employees either. One time I left the pasture gate unfastened with the result that the cows found their way onto his lawn. Their hooves dug into the beautifully kept spread of grass, and they relieved themselves wherever they liked. Mr. Goldberg got a look at this and stormed out to find me. He jumped all over me about leaving the gate open. However, about half an hour later, he came looking for me again and apologized for yelling. That he cared enough to say he was sorry made a big impression. I was surprised to have a wealthy man—my employer and my superior—apologize for anger. The Walters stayed fresh in my mind.

I also appreciated the way Mr. Goldberg liked to joke around. Handing out paychecks to the men who worked at Meadowbrook, he liked to include Cuban cigars. Except for me. For me, he'd begin to hand over the cigar but pull back. "Oh no," he'd say, "you're too young to smoke." Then he'd laugh at his own joke.

He also liked to give the cows funny names, like Lady Plushbottom. Cows that he called Esther and Lillian were named after friends.

Even though the milk produced at Meadowbrook was sold, I don't think the farm was intended to be profitable. The profit-and-loss picture didn't seem to be a concern for Mr. Goldberg. We never talked about it, but given the way he spent money on his farm, that was my impression. For example, he had built a barn that was the epitome of barns in terms of size, features, and quality of construction, but it was intended for dances and parties only.

Mr. Goldberg was generous with us employees. There was a wagon and manure spreader at Meadowbrook that we could use on our own personal garden plots. Our gardens turned out to be prolific providers because of the farm's abundant fertilizer.

He was generous in other ways. An orphanage was located not far from Meadowbrook in Pleasantville, and Mr. Goldberg liked to throw big parties for the kids and have them over. He treated working people and the poor like princes of the earth. What I didn't realize was that Mr. Goldberg had lived at that orphanage—or, at least, one in New York City run by the same organization. Recently I learned that he arrived there at the age of four. It's too bad we didn't know we were given up by our families at the same age. We might have had a lot to talk about.

After a few months at Meadowbrook, Lucretia told me she was pregnant. The news made Mr. Goldberg protective of her. He decided he didn't like the banister on the exterior stairs leading to our living quarters and hired a carpenter to replace it. The guy must have been Michelangelo, because the new banister was a work of art.

Also, one day Mr. Goldberg grabbed Lucretia and said, "Since you're going to have a baby, I'm going to show you what the birth of a baby looks like." He dragged her down to the barn to show her a calf being born. If it worried Lucretia to see the process, she didn't make much of an issue of it one way or the other. She seemed to take most things pretty much in stride.

Life at Meadowbrook was wonderful for both of us. However, as Lucretia's pregnancy progressed, we decided that the estate wasn't a place we should stay. There was no future for me there, no possibility for advancement. We'd never be anything except a farm family. Raising our kids in an environment like that seemed like a bad idea—I'm not sure why, because it was generally a great place. In retrospect, I was wrong in my hurry to leave. It would have been

good for our children. And, if we'd stayed in the country, our
first-born might not have gotten so sick. Still, Lucretia and I
wanted our future kids to see what city living was all about,
and we wanted to own our own home. We had the money
I'd saved while in the service, and we could take advantage of VA loans for housing. I suppose I wanted to leave
Meadowbrook because I felt subservient and felt destined for
better things.

We arranged our departure as the baby's due date drew
close. Daisy and Homer seemed to understand. Mr. Goldberg
didn't seem surprised. If anything, he said he was surprised at
the way city girl Lucretia had adapted to living on a farm and
at how long she'd been willing to stay.

I went looking for a home and found property for sale in a
new development in Saddle River, New Jersey. We purchased
a lot, and while we were having a house built on it, Lucretia
moved back in with her father. I took an apartment in Saddle
River near the construction site so I could oversee the work.

At the same time, I took a job with a plumber named
James Butler. Paulie had hired Butler to do some work on
his house during the months I first returned from the war,
and while Butler was working for Paulie, I'd briefly served as
Butler's go-fer. Butler had told me then that if I ever needed
a job, I should come see him. Now he taught me the heating
and plumbing trade. Many, many homes were being built for
returning vets, so we had plenty of work installing coal-fired
boilers and plumbing in new houses. Butler's nephew and
I became a team as we worked our way from one house to
another in the new developments.

On some weekends, I came into the city to spend time
with Lucretia, and now we felt fine about my joining her in
her narrow bed. Most often, though, Lucretia came out to
Saddle River to view the construction, and on those weekends

we stayed with Filomena and Paulie, who lived close by in Teaneck. As construction progressed and Lucretia's belly grew, it felt like we were moving along just fine toward our goal of a family and a home of our own.

A visit to the Walters

Lucretia learned about William's early life in bits and pieces. She never seemed to become infuriated by his descriptions of the Walters, perhaps because she heard the story gradually and incompletely. She may have felt betrayed by William's initial lie that he'd grown up in an orphanage. If he hadn't been truthful about that, maybe he hadn't been entirely truthful about other things. Her lack of outrage on William's behalf made him feel that Lucretia as well as the kids thought the stories he told about the couple were exaggerations. And of course he would never tell any of them about the especially terrible things that Mrs. Walters had done to him.

It had to be hard, telling others only part of the story. And, if he didn't make clear the frequency of the horsewhippings or the nudity and hand-binding involved, the exile outdoors overnight, and many other examples of the harshly restrictive atmosphere of the Walters' home, listeners may have figured that William experienced the common "spare the rod, spoil the child" attitude of early-1900s America. It wasn't until William sat down for the writing of this book that he laid out the full story of the abuse he suffered.

Still, Lucretia knew quite a bit. It was enough, he thought, and yet she didn't seem very upset. It was important to him that she believe his version of events. Around 1960 or a bit later, while they were living in southern California, William decided to take his family to meet the Walters if he could find them. During one of his family's summer vacations, when they often piled into the car for road trips, they could stop to see the Walters in New Mexico or Arizona. Lucretia could experience those two people herself and form her own opinion.

Didn't it occur to William that the Walters were expert at hiding their true natures? Didn't he assume that Eleanor Walters' treatment of him as a child might cause her to shun him because he was now an adult capable of confronting her about the abuse?

Desperation and even his own long-term avoidance of speaking about the sexual aspects of the abuse narrowed William's focus on the concept and made it simplistic. Visit the Walters; seek validation.

So they got in the car and drove, eventually arriving in New Mexico, stopping to check out their old haunts in Albuquerque, where they'd moved after leaving Saddle River, New Jersey. Here and there in Albuquerque, William mentioned, as he'd done in other towns, that he was looking for his foster parents, who'd long ago lived in Gallup and Winslow. (It wasn't until doing some sleuthing later that William learned he'd been formally adopted.) From a real estate man in Albuquerque he learned that Mr. Walters now owned a peach orchard and 6000 square feet of real estate on the main drag in Farmington, way up in the north-west corner of New Mexico adjacent to Monument Valley and north of the Shiprock Butte landmark.

William drove his family to Farmington. He asked around town, and a pharmacist was able to give him the Walters' home phone number and address. William called, and Mrs. Walters answered.

When he identified himself, she said, "William? William Walters?"

"Yes."

"That's all I wanted to know," she said and hung up.

William returned to the car and drove the family to the Walters' house anyway. He and Lucretia walked to the front door and knocked, but no one answered.

"Witnessing this rudeness, Lucretia immediately concluded that any-thing I said about the Walters was correct," William reported years later.

And of course Lucretia had no idea what the woman might be afraid of in the way of conversation.

"It's possible that Mrs. Walters feared I would confront her face to face, now that I was an adult who was able to stand up to her," said William. "Showing up after all those years was in-your-face kind of behavior on my part, but I didn't intend to make accusations. In addition to letting Lucretia get a look at the Walters, I wanted to prove something to those two: that I was not the scum they claimed I was, that I had grown up, married a lovely woman, had children, and was an upstanding human being. By then I was working for Upland's Public Safety Department. I wanted the Walters to see that I had survived and was well employed in spite of everything they'd said about me. As far as my showing filial love, at that point there was none of that in my thinking. However, I didn't have a chance to prove myself, because they didn't come to the door. They had the last word."

News of the attempted visit to the Walters intrigued Lucretia's sister, Filomena. She asked William about his childhood and was so appalled at his description of life with the Walters that she wrote them a blistering letter. Maybe this was the effect of having heard his censored account all at once. The answer Filomena received back from the Walters enraged her even more. Filomena wouldn't let William see what the Walters had written, and, unwilling to let things stand, she wrote them a second letter. If she received another response, Filomena didn't say.

CHAPTER FOURTEEN

Family Matters

Lucretia was living at her dad's during the building of our house when our son William Francis Walters was born at St. Vincent's Hospital in New York on September 18, 1947. A phone call came that Lucretia was having contractions, so I traveled from New Jersey to meet her at the hospital in Midtown Manhattan. It was nighttime, and by the time I arrived, Lucretia had already been taken into the delivery room. If I'd been able to make it there earlier, the doctors wouldn't have let me into delivery room with her. In those days, men were kept apart from their wives in hospital waiting rooms as childbirth progressed.

I was sitting in the waiting room when a nurse appeared, told me my wife was fine, smiled, and asked me, "What do you want?"

"Anything, as long as the baby is healthy," I told her.

"Well," she said, "what you got was a baby elephant." At ten pounds, two ounces, Willie was very big for a newborn.

I went immediately to look at our son in the nursery. He was beautiful. The sight of him was thrilling. We were connected, he and I and Lucretia. He would never have the childhood that I'd had. I'd make sure of that. Looking down at that vulnerable little human being, I felt more than ever that I needed to earn a good living and provide well for my family.

It had been a long and difficult labor, but Lucretia was very cheery, very happy, right after the birth. Willie was definitely big and healthy, and all three of our kids would turn out to be this way, not all wrinkled like a lot of new babies are. On the day each was born, he or she looked about a month old. William, like his brother and sister, was born bald and took a while to grow hair.

As far as Grandpa was concerned, Willie was the apple of his eye. Certainly he was the apple of mine. Our baby was adorable. By the time he was a toddler, maybe little more than a year old, Lucretia would dress him in a brown snowsuit and mittens and hat, and we'd put him on a sled going down a gentle slope. He'd fall off and lie there like a beetle thrashing around in the snow because he was so bundled up. He'd be laughing, and we'd laugh, too. He was such a happy child.

In our new community we became part of a group of ex-servicemen and their wives starting families. It was a new experience for all of us, becoming property owners and learning how to take care of our children. As we settled into our neighborhood in New Jersey, life seemed to have come full circle for me as Lucretia and I created our own family in our own home. I couldn't have asked for more.

Except, maybe, for my brother. I continued to write to Gerald in the hopes I could see him in person. Every once in a while he wrote back, so gradually I learned more about him.

Before the war, while Gerald studied to be a priest, he'd come to Albuquerque during summer vacations aiming to get outdoors and enjoy a change of scene. He was hired by a lumberman there who also owned the motel where Gerald lived. Gerald proved himself, working his way up to become a scaler, a key job in the lumber industry. He explained that the work takes memory and skill; scalers are highly regarded, and he was paid accordingly. That summer he met a woman he decided to marry and gave up his plans for the priesthood.

At the outset of the war, Gerald enlisted in the Air Force, and they provided his education in physics. Now he worked for the military in Albuquerque at Kirtland Air Force Base. His job was extremely specialized: He was employed in connection with atomic weaponry.

In Gerald's third or fourth letter to me, he asked if I had any money. He knew of a ranch for sale in Grants, New Mexico, and thought if we shared the cost, we could buy it and stock it with a few head of cattle and go into the ranching business. I turned him down because the venture seemed risky. I was extremely frugal and didn't want to blow my hard-won savings on the unknown, especially not with my new family responsibilities. Years later I read in the papers that gas, oil, and uranium were found at that ranch. Uranium was required in the making of the atom bomb, and it was scarce. If Gerald and I had bought that ranch, we would have been so rich we would have made Midas look like a pauper.

Finally, Gerald wrote to say I could come see him. In 1948, on a vacation from my plumbing job in New Jersey, I traveled alone by train to visit my brother and took a room for a week at a hotel in Albuquerque. I was overcome with emotion at the idea of meeting him in person. It was an awfully long time since I'd seen anyone from my original family. I barely remembered my brother, only the time we spent together on the Orphan Train. But we were linked. We had a bond. Maybe if we saw each other, he would feel it, too. My son would have an uncle, and I would know my brother.

Gerald's home was located up on the West Mesa, an area within city limits but still kind of isolated. Only three other houses stood on his street. The four of them looked alike, with fake adobe exteriors and parapet roofs in Taos-style architecture.

I rang the bell, and Gerald opened the door. The person standing before me was tall and slender and had a full head of blond, wavy hair. It could be said that he was a good-looking man. I didn't see any resemblance between us; when I look in the mirror, all I've ever seen is ugliness. Still, within a few days, I came to understand more clearly that my brother and I could be taken for twins.

There was no question of embracing Gerald. His attitude from the moment he opened the door was grim. He invited me in, but my spirits sank lower and lower as we talked. His wife worked at the base and wasn't present during that first visit. From our letters, I knew that Gerald was a lot brighter than I was, so I took his attitude at least partly to be the result of his superior education and his knowing that I didn't measure up in that way.

Meeting in person changed nothing between us. We saw each other just a few times during the week I was in Albuquerque. A general unease pervaded our visits. I did meet his wife, and she was friendly—you could say overly friendly. On the other hand, the two of them were rude to each other. Gerald's demeanor changed for the worse when his wife came on the scene, maybe because her welcoming attitude toward me disturbed him. I know it disturbed me. Anyway, it was hard to read Gerald. Their son was maybe six or seven, but I didn't see my nephew enough to form an impression of him because I visited Gerald's home mostly during school hours.

My brother and I didn't talk about our birth family. I wish we had shared what we remembered. We spoke mostly about Gerald's job and about my experiences in the service. In my brother's presence I felt kind of paralyzed. I suppose that's what kept me from asking about his memories of us as kids. In my discomfort, that didn't occur to me.

It took me by surprise when Gerald handed me a photo of myself as a boy. The snapshot showed Waggs and me. In my first letters to my brother during the war I'd told him about the Walters. He had contacted them, and they had written back. Their letters caused him to form a good impression of the couple. They'd sent him photos of me as a child and did their best to convince him that they'd given me a lovely life and I was an ingrate. I couldn't believe that the couple had managed to follow me here, into the home of my brother.

In the picture Gerald handed me, I'm maybe seven or eight years old, standing in the Walters' yard, dressed in one of the white sailor suits the Walters liked to parade me around in. Waggs stands upright beside me, with me holding his front paws. We look like a typical American kid and his dog, the two of us well fed and healthy. Of course, Gerald didn't understand how two-faced the Walters could be. I told him about being horsewhipped, but nothing I said changed his view of the couple. He thought I had nothing to complain about compared with his own experience at the hands of people who took him off the Orphan Train and then abandoned him. I didn't feel comfortable enough with Gerald to tell him about Eleanor Walters' twisted treatment of me. But then, I didn't plan to talk about that ever, with anyone.

In between visits with Gerald, I walked around Albuquerque. During one of my strolls a woman greeted me. She called me "Gerry." I told her I wasn't Gerald, but she insisted, "I've known you for fifteen years, Gerry, and I certainly know you when I see you." That's how close in appearance he and I were.

Gerald told me he was often sickly as a young person, and his poor health had kept him from qualifying for combat during wartime. Nevertheless, he made it clear he was extremely valuable to the military because of his intelligence and his training. He emphasized that he was one of only a small number of men who knew how to arm the atom bomb. The Air Force assigned him to accompany nuclear weapons on B-36 bombers capable of delivering their payload to the Soviet Union. B-36s were assigned this job at the onset of the Cold War in 1948, but in 1955 the job of nuclear deterrence was taken over by B-52 jets that our Strategic Air Command kept aloft day and night, directing them toward Russia but never crossing over a certain line.

Gerald had to be the first one to leave a B-36 if any kind of incident occurred. Arming the bomb required a series of procedures with various safeguards so that not just anybody could set it off, and as a result the Air Force designated him as "superior cargo" or "special cargo" or something like that. Given his special expertise, they couldn't afford to lose him if a plane went down. A protocol stated that if the plane carrying him malfunctioned, the crew had a matter of minutes to correct the problem, and if they couldn't, they had to ensure Gerald's survival. He described a mission when one of the plane engines caught fire. Immediately the crew put a parachute on Gerald, stood him in the doorway of the bomber, counted down the time as they dealt with the fire, and when the time expired, kicked him out the door. Just as his parachute opened, Gerald looked up to see that the fire had been extinguished. The B-36 flew home with no problem. I bet that Gerald peed his pants during his fall from the air, because, from what I learned of him during our short time together, he was not used to physical challenge.

Observing Gerald, I realized how different we were. I tried to tell him about riding the rails and finding farm work, but he didn't have the foggiest notion what I was talking about and didn't seem to care. I suggested we throw a few hoops in his backyard, so he found a basketball that belonged to his son and we fooled around on an old hoop installed by the house's previous occupants. Gerald was so clumsy with the ball that I got the impression he'd never shot hoops before. I tried to make casual talk about other sports, but he didn't know anything about football or baseball. He seemed to fit the picture of an egghead.

Gerald's wife appeared during my second visit to their home. She returned from getting gas for their car to tell us that the guys in the gas station had been all over her. She was a plain woman but very busty, which may have caused men to call out to her. The next time I saw her, I arrived at the couple's house before Gerald returned. His wife took out a tape measure and asked me to measure her boobs. "No, thank you," I said. "Not interested." "Well," she said, "the guys at the gas station were making such an issue of it, I thought I'd see how large they are."

Gerald's specialized job in the service meant he probably had a higher military rank than I did. He did act superior, talking down to me as if he were a national hero and exceeded me in every way. I began to feel angry. He'd never experienced combat or faced the wartime obstacles I had. While he expected me to show him respect, he didn't show any toward me. His education and intellectual achievement were intimidating, but I soon felt something other than respect.

We had an argument about something or other before I left town, so we didn't part on particularly good terms. Gerald made it clear he was not receptive to further contact.

And that was that. Lucretia wrote to Gerald to see if she could learn more about my early childhood, and he responded by sending a couple more photographs: another the Walters had taken of me and one showing Gerald and me as tykes in Pennsylvania sitting side by side in front of a house, him looking maybe five and me two years old. He'd carried that little picture with him on the Orphan Train as a memento of home. I continued to write to him but Gerald didn't write again.

A year or two later we moved to Albuquerque, and I looked for Gerald but couldn't find him. One of his former neighbors told me that Gerald had been kicked off the base in Albuquerque. This happened because of Gerald's wife, the man said. She couldn't get along with anyone and called Gerald constantly while he was at work. I located the lumberman who owned the motel where Gerald had lived before the war. He told me that Gerald's wife came to Albuquerque from up north after becoming pregnant by another guy. She traveled south to have the baby, and when she met Gerald, it seemed to the man that she conned Gerald into marrying her. The lumberman said he had a bad feeling about her and warned Gerald she was not the kind of woman you marry.

It pains me to think of my lost brother, especially when I see the snapshot of us sitting close together as little boys on the curb in front of what might have been our Pennsylvania home. Online searches for Gerald turned up nothing. It seems that he and I were lost to each other from the moment he was removed from the Orphan Train. Events carried us far apart, and when I found my brother again, it was too late for us to understand each other.

Adopting others

Family was nourishment. Family was solace. The young boy who walked alone by the railroad tracks in Depression-era America believed the passage of time would bring him both. Marriage did, not just because William and Lucretia had each other and their children but because they opened their home to young adults in Albuquerque, where they would relocate in 1949 after leaving their New Jersey home. William tended to be passive in social interactions, but Lucretia wasn't. She was both bold and motherly, and it drew people to her.

In Albuquerque the couple's intent was to help others, but an expanding household also meant assistance during their own hardships. Going West had forced William and Lucretia out of reach of her family circle with their ethic of mutual support.

Instant family was not an idea alien to William. At Boys Town, acceptance into a large, created extended family felt like rescue. His more intimate experience with the Reidhead-Harrises seemed both startling and entirely natural because of the way these generous people quickly slipped him in among themselves as if one of their own.

In choosing Albuquerque, William had in mind both the dry climate and the presence of his brother, but when they arrived, Gerald was gone. William's repeated attempts to connect with Gerald over a number of years—unusual for him because in this particular case William was not passive—in the end amounted to nothing.

It was in Albuquerque that William worked at a furniture store and subsequently opened an upholstery shop with the partner who left him high and dry while Lucretia first waitressed and then managed other dining room staff at a Chinese restaurant. Her ready smile, seriousness about the work, and easy handling of customers made her a natural for the job.

It was Lucretia's nature to take strangers under her wing, so William wasn't surprised when Mama said she wanted to provide a home for one of the other waitresses. Molly had confided to Lucretia that she lived with her aunt and uncle but that her uncle liked to peek at her in the bathroom and that she feared worse. The young woman's move to their home worked out well: Lucretia could schedule restaurant shifts so that she or Molly was almost always home with the kids.

In Albuquerque their third child was born: a boy named Gerald after the uncle he would never know. Will, Dorothea—who was born a year after Will in New Jersey—and Gerald all were named for their father's mostly disappeared side of the family. If another daughter had been born to them, she would have been called Marian.

On occasions when Lucretia and Molly couldn't juggle their work hours to be home with the kids, a next-door neighbor, Irene, babysat them. An older woman of independent means, she had the time and she liked kids, and they were crazy about her.

So now they were a family of six—or seven if you included Irene as grandma.

Soon their family grew again. Mr. Toth, a former neighbor in New Jersey, phoned to say that his daughter Pat was suffering from asthma and needed a drier climate. The girl had been Will and Dorothea's babysitter in Saddle River. Mr. Toth wanted to know if Pat could come live with them; he could pay his daughter's share of the rent. William and Lucretia said that wasn't necessary, that Pat could help with the three children.

Molly and Pat shared a room with little Dorothea. Molly helped pay for food, and Mr. Toth sent money to augment Pat's income from a part-time job, making it possible for her to contribute to the food budget as well.

And then they were nine. Molly announced that she had a boyfriend. Steve was homeless, so he was invited to sleep on the couch. He didn't appear to be ambitious and didn't make much money, but Steve was a good kid, and his contributions were to help out around the house and drive family members here and there in his car.

Next came Sally. She also worked at the Chinese restaurant and had no family, so Lucretia took to mothering her as well. Sally didn't move in with the Walters, but she spent many hours at their house.

The kids had affectionate names for two of the young women: Sally-O and Molly-O. In snapshots from that period, Sally-O and Steve are seen dancing in the Walters' small living room; Steve is seen joking around in the yard, pedaling a tricycle with Molly-O riding on the trike behind him; and Pat is shown dressed as Shirley Temple as she dances and sings in the living room while little Will, clad in his own Halloween costume, watches. William and Lucretia were barely making ends meet, and eventually they'd go broke, but around them they had created a feeling of warmth and protection.

It followed that when William and Lucretia decided to leave Albuquerque and move to California, along came Molly, Steve, and Pat. Which was especially crucial, as it turned out. After the loss of his job at the Ford plant in Long Beach, William found employment at another large furniture store. The owner, Aaron Schultz, learned that William knew how to refurbish furniture and offered him a side job for extra pay. All was proceeding smoothly when back pain crippled William. He was admitted to the veterans hospital in Long Beach and told he was not going to leave there quickly. By his late eighties, William had long forgotten his diagnosis and treatment, but not the pain that bent him over, stabbing in the area of his kidneys.

Schultz calmed William's fears somewhat by promising to hold his job for him. To keep the family together during her husband's two-month hospital stay, Lucretia took a waitress job an hour away from home. By this time, Pat had moved on, but Molly watched the kids, and Steve drove Mama the long commute back and forth to work each day.

Schultz was true to his word, and William was able to resume employment. Lucretia kept waitressing, and soon they were able to put aside savings. In short order they dreamed again about buying property as well as opening their own business.

This time they set their sights on a motel in the southern California mountain community of Lake Elsinore. A resort town on a lake—how could they go wrong? The motel pulled in far more money than they were presently earning, there was even a small building on the property where William could take in upholstery work, and the lake was a great place to raise the kids. Lucretia, Molly, and Steve would take care of the motel by registering guests, making beds, and doing the cleaning. They settled into the Olive Grove Motel and put their plan into action, only to watch the lake go dry soon after. As the water level fell, the fish died, and the stink of rotting carcasses could be smelled miles away. Their motel venture failed, and they had to move again.

Up and down, up and down in abrupt swings, that's how their lives went.

By the time of a move to Upland, California, where William eventually found work as a fire engineer and then on the police desk, Steve and Molly had split up and moved away.

And yet, as William and Lucretia's fortunes rose and fell, there would always be extended family. Friends became like aunts and uncles to the kids and stepped in if help was needed. It's easy to imagine Lucretia striking up friendships and encouraging close ties. In addition, the children's blood relatives were now able to visit periodically or host them when the Walters clan traveled back East to see Lucretia's large family.

Family provided nourishment. Family provided solace. Thanks very much to Mama.

CHAPTER FIFTEEN

Polio and Moving West

We settled into our New Jersey home in the late 1940s, but problems cropped up at my plumbing job. James Butler complained that my brother-in-law Paulie had never paid him for the steam heating Butler had installed at his home. I told him I had nothing to do with it, but Butler continued to ask when Paulie was going to pay up, and that made the job somewhat uncomfortable. I'd worked for Butler about eight months when he assigned me a job at a rendering plant. We were supposed to run steam pipes to the presses where workers pressed fat out of the meat. It was a large job, and I got stuck doing it by myself. The customer had a nasty way about him, always on my case about every detail. I was there a week or so when he jumped all over me for placing a six-inch pipe too far from a wall. I told him he was going to run two hundred pounds of steam through the pipe, enough pressure to stretch the pipe and knock down the wall if I did what he wanted. A day or two later the man accused me of stealing a couple of brass valves, which cost a fortune in that day. That was it for me. I threw down my tools, said no more, and got in my truck. Back at the office Butler said, "You either work there or not at all." I was finished with him and the job.

A competitor of Butler's hired me immediately. A few days later Lucretia was wheeling the baby carriage along the sidewalk near our home when Butler pulled up alongside her in his truck and said, "If your husband ever wants to come back, tell him I'll hire him." I wasn't interested.

It turned out, though, that my new employer didn't have enough jobs to give me steady employment. Instead I found a job with the Erie Railroad doing the same kind of steamfitting. We ran steam lines to the tracks so the switches wouldn't freeze up in winter. It was a good job but cold and miserable part of the year. One day the boss said, "I've got something better for you. The railroad owns Pier 67 in New York. We're going to resheet that dock. I want you to meet Captain Hook." It's funny, I know, but my co-worker-to-be was named Hook and had been a captain in the U.S. Navy. "He's a nice young fellow, and the two of you can work together on that dock."

Pier 67 was the largest pier on the wharf in New York City. You talk about a job, that one was a plum. The dock was almost entirely covered by a warehouse whose sides were made of corrugated zinc sheets. A footpath went all the way around. Our job was to remove the zinc sheets and replace them with aluminum ones. The zinc was riveted on, so we were to drill off the old rivets, replace the zinc sheets, and drill on new rivets. This was union work, and the union called for fifteen sheets a day to be replaced. The warehouse had huge rolling doors made of zinc sheets, and we were also to replace those sheets as well as their bearings. The huge old doors rolled upward on bronze bearings, quite a few bronze bearings. Some doors were to be eliminated entirely, along with their bearings. The boss explained that we had to haul the zinc sheets and bearings back to New Jersey, which would cost the railroad for both fuel and truck driver pay, so if we could get away with deep-sixing any of them, go ahead and do it. We could let the old sheets and bearings "accidentally" slip out of our hands into the Hudson River.

As we undertook the work, Captain Hook and I arrived at a few conclusions. One, fifteen sheets could be replaced in half a day rather than a full day. Two, several blocks away was a guy who bought metal. Selling the discarded metal was the smart way to go. Bronze bearings would bring good money. It turned out that the guy with the metal business didn't want zinc sheets, but every lunch hour we loaded up a couple of bronze bearings and brought them to him. Of course, we kept the proceeds for ourselves, figuring the bearings would have been dumped in the river otherwise. In the afternoons, our work done, we went to the movies or sometimes sat on the dock watching ships come and go.

Each morning we reported to our shop in Secaucus, New Jersey, where someone then drove us to the pier in New York. We were paid from portal to portal for our time plus fifteen sheets' worth of labor. I'm not sure how long we went along like this before we reported for work one morning and the boss told us to come into his office. He gestured for us to follow him to his window.

He handed me a pair of binoculars and said, "Look directly across the river and tell me what you see."

Well, I'll be damned. It was Pier 67. Our pier.

"The union contract calls for fifteen sheets a day," he said, "not fifteen sheets in a half-day. And I won't mention hauling the bearings up the street to the metal place. But from now on, fifteen sheets a *day*."

But he didn't make a big deal out of it. We stopped visiting the guy with the metal business. From then on, as much as we could, we dumped both the sheets and the bearings into the river. It wasn't possible to do this all the time because there were too many people around.

Can you imagine that happening today? Being told to let slip all those zinc sheets and bronze bearings into the river? There must be thousands of them lying down there from all the jobs like ours.

The winters were harsh in New York and New Jersey. The day we moved into our new home with baby Willie, there was twenty-eight inches of snow on the ground, and I had a hard time keeping the house warm. A snowstorm had prevented coal deliveries. We depended on truck deliveries to feed a coal-fired boiler in the cellar. The boiler was mounted on the concrete floor with pipes running to the various radiators. Until deliveries resumed, I burned everything else I could find to keep the house warm enough for our newborn and also went to neighbors begging for coal from their supplies. By the time the coal trucks drove down our street again, I owed all the coal I could buy. In those days you could purchase different sizes of coal—nut coal and pea coal—and we needed both. Nut coal went into the big boiler, and pea coal went into a smaller boiler that provided hot water. Eventually most people switched to oil heat, which was much more convenient.

But for the time being, we depended on coal. Since I was gone all day and Lucretia was taking care of the baby, it was a demanding task for her to shovel coal into the boiler every hour or so. Not only that, but whenever you opened the draft on the furnace, the house heated up really hot. Too hot. If you shut the draft, the house cooled down too much. Lucretia constantly ran up and down the stairs to readjust the baffles and send the proper amount of heat up. So I figured out a way to make life easier for her. I rigged a chain through a hole in the floor that allowed her to use pulleys to make adjustments to the draft without going to the basement. In addition, I rigged a half-horsepower motor and belt system to carry coal over to the boiler. All Lucretia had to do was throw a switch upstairs to move the belt with a load of coal. Alongside the chain I ran a cable to open the furnace door so coal could be deposited there. Word spread about my invention, and our neighbors copied it. They came over to look at our setup, and if they had any kind of technical skill, they were able to recreate it at home.

Until Willie got sick, those were pretty good days. I'd given up boxing in the Pacific, but I decided to set up a speed bag in the cellar to help me stay in shape. On the weekends and after work, I went down to the cellar to practice with the heavy bag. Lucretia and I were clowning around in the kitchen one day, and I invited her to box. "Come on," I said, "take a poke at me." She hauled off and hit me in the chin and knocked me down. She was horrified. Little Lucretia with her 103 pounds of power! I was stunned but fine, and she had a good chuckle after she saw I was really all right.

Our second baby, Dorothea, came along on September 29, 1948, after Willie had just turned a year old. To give you an idea of how poor we were at the time, we didn't have a crib for her. Willie had a crib, but Dorothea slept in a baby carriage that her grandfather bought for her. We didn't have much furniture at all. Our home had no refrigerator, and there were no furnishings in the living room and dining room, although in the months just after Dorothea was born we were able to buy a used dining-room set. It was pretty nice, with a china cabinet that had a curved glass front. We also had a kitchen table and chairs that I built.

Summers were hot and humid in New Jersey, which inspired me to find a way to create a pool in the backyard. The Erie Railroad used what were called Bradleys. These were shallow pools in the rail yard shop where engineers or others working on the railroad could wash up after work. Bradley washfountains were terrazzo, and the sides were a couple of feet high all around. A pipe brought water to the center of the pool. I saw workers removing one of the Bradleys from the railroad shop and asked the manager if I could have it to make into a small pool in our backyard. He said first I had to have a space dug out in our yard, which I took care of. The railroad placed the Bradley on a flatcar, and when one of the freights was due to come through our town, they carried it there. Next they used a crane to haul it from the tracks the ten or twelve blocks to our home. I installed a fountain in the center and built a walkway around the pool plus a patio where the neighborhood ladies could sit and watch their kids splash around. All of the neighborhood children came to our house to enjoy that Bradley.

Well, it wound up that seven kids in our neighborhood contracted polio, including Willie, and the doctors blamed it on the Bradley. Willie had bulbar polio, which affects the brain stem, and the others had paralytic polio of the spine. In the 1940s there was a huge scare about polio, and swimming pools took a lot of the blame. Many public pools were closed. Chlorine is effective in deactivating the virus, and it began to be widely used in public pools around that time. I'd been using bottles of chlorine purchased at the hardware store, but I can't say I knew the precise science for determining how much to use.

Willie became terribly ill when he was not yet two years old. The first symptoms were flulike. In those days, family doctors routinely came to the house to see patients. Our doctor paid a visit during which he told us that Willie had bronchitis. Our baby didn't get any better, so we kept calling the doctor back, and he kept saying it was bronchitis. For nearly a week the doctor called it bronchitis. The next time Lucretia called him, the man said that she was being a hysterical mother. When I arrived home from work, Lucretia said, "I don't care what the doctor says, this kid is dying. He's turning blue."

We took Willie to a hospital nearby in Rochelle Park. A young emergency room doc gave him a cursory look and said, "We're going to keep him here. You go home, and we'll call you as soon as we diagnose his problem." I think he recognized instantly that it was polio and was trying to get rid of us because we were distraught young parents who might create a scene and get in the way of our baby's care. We weren't home long when he called us.

Lucretia answered the phone and fainted. I grabbed the receiver.

The doctor said, "Your boy has polio. We've transferred him to Bergen Pines."

That was a hospital in New Jersey I knew we couldn't afford. We took off for Bergen Pines. It was after midnight when we got there.

The doctor was German, a Dr. Lenz. He lit into us.

"WHAT IS THE MATTER WITH YOU PEOPLE? This boy is going to die, and it's all your fault. He should have been here days ago."

We told him that we'd been trying to get help from our doctor.

He asked for the name of our doctor and said he wouldn't be a doctor much longer.

Dr. Lenz also told us that so far doctors had not been able to cure bulbar polio, and this is what Willie had. Most of the deaths associated with polio were caused by this form of the disease. Willie couldn't swallow and had to be on an IV. He was paralyzed from the chest upward. They put our little guy in an iron lung. Willie was in there for two months. Every day the staff told us, "If he can make it a bit longer, he may make it."

That Dr. Lenz was a great doctor. He knew what he was doing. He may have had a cold demeanor, but he was capable, and I credit him for saving Willie.

Meanwhile our family was placed in quarantine by the public health department, who put a "Quarantine" sign on our lawn. People walked across the street to stay away. Added to the blame placed on our backyard pool, the isolation was humiliating.

Dorothea was almost one year old when Willie was diagnosed with polio. Soon after we went into quarantine, she also became ill. Immediately the doctors assumed Dorothea had polio as well. They tested her and determined she had a bad cold and bronchitis, so she wasn't hospitalized, but before that was confirmed, public health told us we had to burn all of her clothes and anything else in her room. It was a wonder they didn't tell us to burn her.

Lucretia and I explained to Bergen Pines that we couldn't afford the daily rate they charged for Willie's care, but they said to pay what we could, and they'd take the rest of the cost out of the hide of people who could afford it. We checked with the March of Dimes, the only organization set up to help in cases like ours, but learned that they couldn't assist us; so many people were suffering from polio by that time that their funds were depleted. To make matters worse, I couldn't report to work because of the quarantine.

Every single day, Lucretia's brother Angelo, who still lived in downtown Manhattan, traveled by bus across the bridge from New York to Teaneck, caught another bus to Saddle River, walked to a grocery store, caught another bus, and delivered food to our door. We didn't have a refrigerator, so our perishables didn't keep very long, especially in warm weather, but I think he made the trip that often also to make sure we were all okay. It took him hours. Every single day. He was an angel.

During our quarantine we were allowed to visit Willie at Bergen Pines. I'm not sure how this worked, because we were supposed to be isolated. Still, I think we went to see Willie at the hospital every day, traveling there by public transit.

After two months Dr. Lenz told Lucretia and me, "We're going to give William a teaspoon of liquid, and if he can swallow it, he'll survive. Otherwise we'll have to keep him in the iron lung, and eventually the disease will be fatal." We held our breath and watched. It was a huge relief. Willie was able to drink fluids. The hospital staff still had to give him oxygen in an iron lung, but at least our little boy could drink. We were grateful beyond words. If Willie was going to continue to improve, though, the doctor told us we would have to move him to a high, dry climate with clean air.

Albuquerque came to mind. I was familiar with the city from my travels as a kid and from visiting Gerald there. As soon as Willie was able to breathe on his own and leave the iron lung, we set off for the Southwest.

Thinking back to those times, I feel bad about the hard life Lucretia experienced once we left Meadowbrook Farm. My meager pay, our baby's crisis, our unknown future as we traveled west, and the many challenging years that lay ahead, all of it. But Lucretia supported me without fail and pointed out that she had a husband who made sure he was never out of work for long.

As soon as the doctor told us to relocate and Willie was able to leave the hospital, Lucretia and I put together the little money we had. We'd been unable to pay our mortgage because the quarantine had kept me from working, so we lost title to our home and there was no money from the sale of it. Lucretia's father helped us buy tickets on a train west. We left behind our modest furnishings, giving away everything that we couldn't easily carry on the train with us.

Willie continued to have a hard time breathing. As we found our places on a sleeper to Albuquerque, Lucretia and I worried over him. It would be a while before he seemed entirely better. I comforted myself that Albuquerque had the right kind of climate for Willie and was a relatively big town where I'd have a decent chance of finding a job. What I well knew was that you don't hold out for the job you want, you take the job you can get.

In Albuquerque we rented a house on the West Mesa near where I'd visited Gerald, and in the process I learned he no longer lived in town. On our street there were six identical houses all in a row, simple and plain. For a really good price I found a used Shopsmith, a multipurpose woodworking tool that I used to build us a kitchen set, bed frames, and cabinets for storage. In short order I made everything we needed for our new home, including chairs.

My career in upholstery began when I found a steady job in the warehouse of the Modern Furniture Company, one of three furniture stores under a single ownership. Each shop had a different quality of furniture. The high-end store sold an array of fine furnishings. The middle-range store sold nothing but Franciscan, furniture with woodwork inspired by traditional Spanish designs that had been simplified in California's Franciscan missions. Furniture at the Modern, where I was hired, was like what you'd find at Kmart. My job was to remove new arrivals from their boxes, assemble pieces where needed, take them out to the floor, and sometimes make deliveries to customers.

Modern also took in customers' old furniture and restored it for sale in a used-furniture shop on the premises. Modern's manager, a guy named Bales, said I could assist the upholsterer when I wasn't busy with warehouse work. The upholsterer showed me how to remove worn fabric and prepare pieces for reupholstery. However, there was a problem. My teacher was a drunk. One night he came back to the shop after closing time to complete a job with me and reported, "I just saw the ugliest man I ever saw in my life, and he scared the hell out of me. I threw a hammer at him, and the problem was, he was me. Broke a mirror." In the morning, Bales saw the shattered mirror on a brand-new dresser, fired the guy, and hired me. In the process I turned out a lot of bad work, but I learned as I went along, and Modern did a pretty good business selling used refurbished furniture out of that shop. From there I left to start my own furniture upholstery and refinishing business—with the partner who eventually made off with our money and equipment.

Meanwhile Lucretia found employment at the Chinese restaurant in the heart of town, across from the Hilton Hotel. We moved off the West Mesa, where the wind and sand blew something terrible, and found a rental closer to our jobs, down in the valley where the real Albuquerque was. Our new place on the eastern outskirts of the city was a Taos-style ranch house on two-and-a-half acres of more or less desert land. That's where we met Irene Gibson. She lived in the duplex next door and owned twenty-two sawmills in the Southwest. Irene was quite wealthy, but you wouldn't know it to meet her. Before we came to know her, Irene's husband had bought their fifteen-year-old son a gun for Christmas, which she was dead set against, and the boy killed himself by accident a week later. Irene took the sawmills in the divorce and cleaned out her ex. On the surface Irene seemed like a gruff, troubled woman, but for us she was a lovely neighbor and especially sweet to our kids. She took to Lucretia immediately.

Soon Gerald, our third child, came along. He was born on October 18, 1950, and his birth was uneventful apart from the fact that he weighed in at twelve pounds, eight ounces. And thankfully, by then, Willie was doing a whole lot better. Irene offered to watch the new baby and our other two kids at times when Lucretia and I and Molly, a waitress from the Chinese restaurant who was living with us at that point, weren't able to coordinate our work schedules to have one of us at home.

With the idea of selling food to the restaurant where Lucretia worked and bringing in a little extra money, I built pens on our property for turkeys, chickens, rabbits, and ducks. The turkeys grew from eggs we purchased and hatched. I don't think there's any other bird quite as stupid as the turkey. Someone had once told me that a turkey will stand out in the middle of a rainstorm, look up with its mouth open, and drown. Sure enough. There was a shelter for the birds in our yard, but during a downpour we caught sight of the little turkeys standing out in the rain drowning and had to bring them into the house. We dried them off, opened the oven, and set them in on "low" to warm them up. It was pretty funny. Eventually, as big birds, they'd end up in the oven at a much higher temperature, but for now we wanted them to be safe and grow up.

The Chinese restaurant did a terrific business thanks to the Hilton located across the street. A bar was attached to the restaurant, and the Albuquerque Dukes baseball team came in there all the time to eat and drink. So we were doing pretty good until my upholstery business collapsed.

I found a series of temporary jobs and did the best I could with the hand injury I'd suffered at my shop. Then the owners of the Chinese restaurant announced they were relocating to Houston. They invited us to go with them, but I ruled that out. I figured the opportunities were better in California. I didn't see much of a future for us in Albuquerque, although there might have been. Maybe the loss of my business made me bitter. Maybe I was an impatient young man. Maybe the need to move along after things didn't work out was ingrained in me as a kid. An Albuquerque friend who'd relocated to Long Beach wrote to say that Ford was hiring there. So we packed up and went to Long Beach.

The loss of her sons

The last ten years of Lucretia's life were miserable because of a series of devastating illnesses that struck in her mid-seventies and because of lack of contact with her sons. The first seemed to be fate, the second not. Lucretia was a loving, demonstrative mother and an easy confidante. Of her three kids, Will was her favorite, says daughter Dorothea. "We were thick, Mom and I. But Will held a special place in her affections, probably because he was her first and because of almost losing him to polio. Gerald was Dad's favorite."

How, then, did Lucretia lose both Will and Gerald?

William and Lucretia formed a strong parental unit, according to Dorothea. They were a package deal. Rejection of William by his sons may have seemed to necessitate rejection of Lucretia.

It's a common source of drama in human interaction: Anger and hurt erupt from the simple fact that people fail to say what they need to. Or too easily blurt out words that convey the opposite.

Of their three children, Will seemed to take it hardest that William could not speak his love and was prone to harsh outbursts. To make matters worse, in 1963 his parents chose to leave Upland, California, where quiet, high-school-age Will had established friendships. His dad had a good job, they all had a good life in Upland, and he couldn't understand why he was yanked away to Cloverdale in northern California. Apparently his parents didn't confide that William's job prospects in the police department had been ruined by his excessively sympathetic attitude toward the prisoners and his unwillingness to wear a gun. To me, William frequently remarked with sarcasm that the Walters never clued him in on the reasons for various decisions they made, including their choice to move across town in Gallup and then to leave Gallup altogether for Winslow. And yet William was guilty of the very same failure with his children. Two of his three were happy about the choice to leave Upland, but somehow William failed to see that his oldest was not—or maybe he noted Will's displeasure in passing but didn't worry about offering justification. Maybe William had adopted more of the Walters' attitudes toward children than he'd ever want to admit: Withhold praise, never voice affection, and maybe, at least in part, children should be seen and not heard. In fact, William responded to his children's expressions of pride in their own accomplishments by telling them that this was not seemly. Let others sing your praises, he said, not you. But then, of course, he didn't sing their praises either, at least not within earshot.

The rupture between father and son was fueled further by Will running off to Reno with a local girl and marrying at age eighteen. William said he and Lucretia were shocked: "The girl came from the worst possible family. Her father had robbed a post office and her mother had a drinking problem." They thought they saw signs the girl was following in her parents' footsteps. But Lucretia said they must hold their tongues. Knowing William, Lucretia may have said this in response to him initially *not* holding his tongue. Will and his young wife had two children and divorced when the oldest was five. The children went to live with their mother, and William and Lucretia never saw the two grandchildren again—not until William had a reunion with the mother and children in the last years of his life. "She's a nice person," William reported, surprised. "She turned her life around. Her kids are lovely."

By the time of her brother Will's divorce, Dorothea was married and working in banking in a distant state. Soon Gerald followed a friend to Mississippi, fell in love, married, and found a position in the procurement office of Northrop Grumman. Only Will stayed local, working for a brake business in Cloverdale.

Not long after his divorce, Will married again, this time to a girl from a successful Cloverdale family. William and Lucretia liked Susan, although they found her parents aloof. A daughter and son were born. Years went by. It was the late 1980s. William and Lucretia lived thirty minutes south of Cloverdale in Santa Rosa, and William was commuting more than an hour farther south to a job at Macy's San Francisco each day, but when they could, they attended their grandkids' basketball and baseball games. Then Will cut off all contact and forbade his kids to see their grandparents.

The precipitating event was a high school graduation party for Will's daughter. William and Lucretia attended the graduation ceremony and afterward met other family members at Will and Susan's home in Cloverdale. As William described it, he and Lucretia felt left out at the gathering. Sitting with the others in the living room, they had a strong sense Susan's parents did not care for them. William reported that everyone adjourned for dinner without inviting him and Lucretia to join them in the other room, so the couple decided to leave. They told Will they were heading home because William needed to rise early for his long commute to San Francisco. Will exploded. He expressed outrage that they intended to walk away from the dinner gathering in his daughter's honor.

Afterward Will wrote a letter to his parents, attacking their rudeness to their granddaughter and saying that he had never felt love from them. They seemed to care more for their pet dog, he said, than they did for him or their grandchildren. William did not see Will, Susan, or their kids again until well after Lucretia's death in 2012.

Could William have been right about being left out at their granddaughter's graduation party? Did he and Lucretia require an invitation to step into the other room for dinner? Was he correct about Lucretia sharing that view? A sense of rejection and inadequacy in other people's eyes was a lifelong curse for William, but there's no evidence of that for Lucretia. Was she swayed by her husband's thinking after decades living with him? Or was she compelled simply by her husband's demand that they leave the party, torn between soothing him and celebrating with her son's family? She must have been horrified at the outcome.

In ruling out contact with both of his parents, Will may have acknowl-
edged the inseparable link between his mother and father. He may also
have been angry at his mother for bending always to her husband's will.

In this way Lucretia experienced two of the greatest losses of her life:
separation from one son and soon the other, because it wasn't long before
a wider family schism opened as well. Dorothea read the letter from Will
and was puzzled by her brother's claims about not feeling loved. William
may not have been the father she would have wanted, but Dorothea
believed she and her brothers had had a wonderful childhood, and she'd
always known their parents loved them. "Mom was a hugger," she says,
"and she always felt fine expressing her affection strongly. Will was wrong
about never feeling love from our parents. I could see in many of my dad's
actions that he did love us. I think I may have been different from my
brothers because I realized how Dad was raised, understood how it could
have influenced his behavior, and tried to overlook it."

Dorothea stood up for their parents when she spoke with Will, which
led to a falling out between brother and sister as well. Dorothea and Will
did not communicate with each other again for twenty-five years, until
William sought reconciliation with his sons in 2014.

By the time Lucretia became chronically ill, Dorothea, now divorced,
had returned to northern California, purchased a home in the town where
her parents lived, found work there, and looked out for Lucretia and
William as her mother's health deteriorated.

A year or two after Will cut off contact, Gerald stopped talking to
William and Lucretia. Puzzled at first over his sudden silence, William
and Lucretia decided that Will had convinced Gerald their parents were
no good. Not true, but William wouldn't learn that until much later. After
a while, dismayed by her younger brother's behavior, Dorothea stopped
communicating with him as well. The family was effectively split.

It turns out that Gerald's removal from their family dynamic was the
result of a misunderstanding. Gerald continued to live in Mississippi after
he and his wife divorced and, during the time that his mother's health
had begun to decline, had called home for help when arrested for a DUI.
William and Lucretia were by then aware that Gerald had a drinking

problem. William flew out to find his son an attorney, visit Gerald in jail, and meet with his son's boss at Northrop Grumman to see if Gerald's job could be held for him. In a friendly meeting between the two men, William felt comfortable asking Gerald's boss to look out for his son and to keep William informed if more assistance was needed. Immediately after, William flew back home to be with Lucretia, who was disabled from a stroke and other illness. Gerald was released from jail in favor of rehab, but his drinking problem continued, and eventually he did lose his job. Gerald reported many years later that he believed his parents were disgusted with him and wanted no further contact, and that's why he made no further attempt to contact them.

Neither son visited Lucretia during her final years. Neither learned about their mother's impending death or her funeral. William's fury at his sons' lack of contact while Lucretia was alive kept him from reaching out in any way with news of her failing health and demise. Dorothea followed suit.

A stroke, polymyalgia rheumatica, Bell's palsy, diabetes, heart trouble, osteoporosis, breast cancer, a fractured spine, sepsis. Lucretia's final years were torture. She never complained. She did worry about the burden on William, who became an attentive caregiver. He insisted that he would do anything for her and she must not worry.

What did Lucretia privately feel as she slowly approached death? She had to be missing her boys terribly. She told William and reassured herself, "They'll come around when they're ready." She was weak, she was disabled, she depended on William for most of her needs, and whatever regrets she had, she couldn't have had much energy to deal with them.

Loss of family was a crisis that William and Lucretia never would have imagined for themselves. It was a tragedy for each, Lucretia because she'd savored family connection all of her life, and William because he'd been starved for it. But it happened, and no remedy was sought until well after William's beloved Lucretia was gone.

CHAPTER SIXTEEN

Macy's and After

By 1963 I understood that there was no possibility of advancement for me in the Upland Public Safety Department. A much different career was going to open up, but it was beyond the realm of anything I imagined.

I was still working the Upland police desk when our family took a vacation with British Columbia as our destination. On the way, we drove through northern California, through what is now wine country. Just past the town of Cloverdale, the Redwood Highway wound along the Russian River. We saw lovely open countryside. The air was fresh, the river ran clean, and the hills all around were studded with oaks and pines. The kids asked to have a picnic. Back in Cloverdale we found a small grocery store. The owner chatted with us and asked where we were from. He was familiar with sprawling, smoggy San Bernardino County. "Where you're at," he said, "is a whole lot nicer than where you're from."

The kids started to bug me after our vacation was over—at least, two of them did. I suppose now that Willie didn't. "Why don't we move up there?" they said. "Northern California's so nice." My job in Upland was going nowhere. Lucretia and I decided why not.

That began our life in Cloverdale. I traveled north to rent a house and was hired on as a sales clerk at the local hardware store. Lucretia and the kids followed. By February 1965, we opened our own business, Interior Accents by Lucretia, which offered china, crystal, art objects, carpeting, upholstery, and drapery. We felt we could do this for a few reasons. Lucretia grew up without much money, and we certainly didn't have a lot, but she had an awareness of fashion and a natural sense of style. She preferred to save whatever she could to buy one nice thing for our home or nice clothing for our kids rather than shop for armloads of stuff at thrift shops. Mama's talent showed when we had friends to dinner: She was a good cook, and she served up meals in a very attractive way, on special platters, with elegant table settings. Meanwhile, I'd spent a lot of time thinking about home furnishings because of the work I'd done refinishing and upholstering. I also wanted to think the paintings I'd been doing, which were beginning to hang in a couple of local galleries, meant I had an artistic bent.

It was a while before our business took off. Cloverdale was very provincial. At first the locals viewed us strictly as outsiders. We had to work our way into the fabric of the town. Lucretia joined the Business and Professional Women's Association. I joined the Lions Club and the Citrus Fair Association, and eventually I became president of the Lions Club. Our kids seemed to fit into the community pretty easily.

While the kids were in high school, we hosted parties for them about every two or three months. We may have had as many as 130 kids for a party following a major victory by the high-school football team over St. Helena in Napa, and still there was not one bit of trouble. Other parents saw that parties at our house went just fine, and they offered to chip in with cases of soda. That helped a lot. We told our kids, if there's any trouble, there won't be more parties. And if anyone does something wrong, I said, come get me and let me handle it. If you try to take care of it, that will only lead to trouble. Those parties were wonderful. Mama was a favorite with the kids. Little Lucretia. She'd put on a mock authoritarian pose. For example, at a Christmas party, she said, "If anyone breaks one of my ornaments, you'll never hear the end of it." A big football player lifted her up and set her down in another spot to tease her. "Don't worry," he said.

Jerry, our youngest, graduated from Cloverdale High School in 1968 and went off with a friend to Mississippi, where he married and found a job in the procurement office at the Northrop Grumman shipyard in Pascagoula. Willie was married and working at a brake shop in Cloverdale, and Dorothea was following a career in banking that took her from San Francisco to Texas and eventually to Georgia. Jerry's departure left Lucretia and me alone at home for the first time in more than two decades. This felt pretty damn good. We missed the kids, but at the same time we had a new freedom. We began to travel, where we never felt we could before, at least not by ourselves. We enjoyed each other's company, and it was a nice time of life. Sometimes we'd close up the store and go to Disneyland.

However, there came a point when our little shop faced such fierce competition that Lucretia and I decided to close it. In the early years, a supplier like Lees Carpet would agree not to have any other retailer carry its merchandise within a seventy-five-mile radius of us. Then they began to violate this agreement. The problem happened over and over with various suppliers. We'd been able to support our family and put aside savings, but now our shop was too much work for too little money. Around 1969 we sold the shop and moved down the road to the county seat in Santa Rosa, a much bigger town, where we used the proceeds of the sale to buy our own home, the first house we owned since losing the one in Saddle River, New Jersey.

I found upholstery work with an interior design shop in Marin, the next county south. The owner agreed to let me work at home. At the time I had a two-and-a-half-ton truck, so Lucretia and I would drive down, pick up maybe four to six couches and some chairs, quote a price on each, take fabric supplied by the design shop, and haul everything back to Santa Rosa. For nine or ten months, maybe a year, we did just that. Mama worked in the shop with me, and we had fun working side by side. I set up a bench for her. She tore the stuff down, removing the fabric, and I moved it to my bench, where I cut and sewed new fabric. We turned out several pieces a week and made good money.

A neighbor lady named Esther Hart liked to join us in our workshop and help Lucretia a bit. The two became almost like sisters, hanging out in our workshop, having their conversations. We didn't pay Esther; she came over mostly to kibitz and chat.

Over the months, the design shop cut its payments to me lower and lower, I think because they observed what nice money I was making. I heard through the grapevine that this shop previously had been burned down in order to collect insurance money, and now a second fire happened, maybe for the same reason. Only this time the place went bankrupt.

It was 1969 or 1970, I was about forty-four, and I was out of work again. An ad in the *San Francisco Chronicle* caught my eye. It said something like "interior designer" or "manager of interior design studio." Specific job qualifications weren't listed. If they had been, I wouldn't have bothered to apply. All I knew was that the job was a position with Macy's in San Francisco, which was about seventy miles from my home. I drove down to San Francisco for the executive hiring call and learned that there were 150 applicants, both men and women. Lucretia kept me well clothed in those days, so I was dressed to the nines in a suit and tie. As I sat with the waiting crowd,

I realized that extremely well qualified decorators were applying, some of them educated at the New York School of Interior Design. It was obvious I had no chance. We filled out written applications, and that same day I had a conversation with a group of Macy's executives who questioned me about my resume.

The whole exercise seemed like a waste of time. I didn't know anything about decorating apart from our small Cloverdale shop and my furniture work. I was told that the new hire would head up Macy's executive office in charge of home design. The manager of the design studio oversaw seven women and five men home decorators in the San Francisco store as well as decorators in the sixteen other northern California Macy's locations.

A few days later a letter arrived saying that the number of applicants had been whittled down to fifty and Macy's wanted me to appear for another interview. It had to be a mistake, but I made the trip south again. This time I met with a group comprised of the vice president in charge of interior furnishings, the VP for window dressing, and the VP for store design. They were noncommittal. Clearly there was no reason to feel hopeful. When it came to questions about design, I didn't know the first thing. I just made do and answered the best I could.

Another letter arrived. The applicants had been narrowed down to fifteen. I was astonished to find I was one of them. I returned to Macy's for more interviews with more people. Some of the store's interior designers were in on those sessions. Again, I spent a whole day in San Francisco. At the end, I was sent home with no expression of interest from anyone.

Then another letter arrived. The selection process was now down to three people, including me. I was flabbergasted. I went back for a final interview with two people: the store manager of Macy's main San Francisco store on Union

Square, and the man who ran Macy's in northern California and was the West Coast CEO. They told me I had the job.

Later I asked one of the executives why they'd picked me. He said they weren't looking for someone with design experience so much as they were looking for a manager. They felt I had the qualifications, and as far as they were concerned, I knew enough about interior design to get by. Also, he told me it was important that I wasn't "light on my feet." Which shows how backward the thinking was in those days. It certainly wasn't my thinking, and it was particularly odd because it seemed that every decorator they had, both male and female, was gay.

Macy's advertising and promotions department printed up posters with my photograph and disseminated them to all seventeen Macy's stores in the region. The posters announced: "Need assistance in planning your room settings or decorating an entire house? Mr. William Walters, Macy's Interior Designer, will be glad to assist you. Please call . . . ."

I was happy to land a solid, well-paying job, but the prospect of heading up a big-city design studio was kind of frightening. Each morning during the commute I had plenty of time to think about how unprepared I was. I rose early to beat rush hour traffic, but the drive still took more than an hour. Returning home took ninety minutes if rush hour went smoothly. My office and the design studio were located on the seventh floor of the west building on Union Square. Those first mornings, I stepped out of the elevator amazed to find myself reporting for work at the executive offices of a major department store chain.

The funny thing was, no one paid much attention to me. No one looked over my shoulder to check what I was doing. I was left to my own devices and was able to work out for myself how to operate. This took me by surprise. Of course, I'd had to figure out new jobs many times before, but

a managerial position with a large company was far different
from all of my earlier employment. My co-workers seemed to
assume I could do the work. Most of them were welcoming,
and I quickly came to feel I belonged.

What I needed to know I learned from observing the decorators who worked at Macy's, talking to the other executives,
and asking questions of the buying office. The latter were the
most helpful, especially Macy's buyer for hard goods, meaning furniture and bedding. Macy's buyers wanted the store's
decorators to sell their merchandise, so of course they catered
to the design studio.

The first thing I organized was a redesign of the design
studio itself. The studio looked shoddy and rundown at
the heels. We turned it into an elegant pavilion and gave it
an upscale look, like something you'd find in *Architectural
Digest*. Construction was done by an outside firm using a plan
created by Macy's designers.

Gradually my nervousness went away. I was proud to be
working at Macy's and did my best to dress the part. Lucretia
made sure of it. At one time I had fifteen suits. For two weeks
straight I never wore the same suit two days in a row.

I was making the best salary of my life, with benefits,
and I was having a great time. It was hard to believe my luck.
When I stopped to think about it, I shook my head. Macy's
and the Marine Corps were the two times in my life that I
think I performed well at a job. I guess this is because in both
cases teams of other people seemed to feel fine about my
work. In the Marine Corps, they rewarded me for being tough
and being a good shot, they respected my language skills, and
they thought enough of me to make me part of a special-
ops unit and then a city manager in Japan after the war.
At Macy's, I oversaw one design project after another, and
everyone seemed happy with the results, both customers and
bosses. The other employees and I made a good team. I was

able to be creative and use my imagination. Celebrities like
singer Linda Ronstadt and San Francisco TV host and newspaper columnist Pat Montandon sought out our department
for assistance in designing their homes.

There were a lot of wonderful and strange people working
at Macy's. No one else came close to a woman named Betty,
a saleslady in the furniture department. She used to visit my
office all the time. Betty and another employee, Libby, helped
out when I needed letters typed and errands run. A short,
round woman, Betty resembled comedian Totie Fields, and
somewhere in her past I believe she'd been a stand-up comic.
I was told that she was gay and had a live-in girlfriend. Betty
could tell jokes by the hour, one after the other. She loved to
create a scene, so to speak. She'd say to me, "Let's go to lunch."
On our way past the jewelry counter, she'd ask loud enough so
that everyone nearby could hear, "Honey, when are you going
to buy that ring you promised me?" Or she'd say the awfulest
things, like "*Well*, that's the last time I'm going to bed with
you if you don't buy that ring you promised!"

There was also a nice guy named Roman who worked
in Macy's furniture department, and I came to know him in
a secondhand way. The cost of parking was so high around
Macy's that I used to park in the Tenderloin, a mostly seedy
district nearby. After a while, walking from the Tenderloin
to Union Square each morning, I noticed another Macy's
employee walking the same way. Roberta was her name, and
she was a pretty young woman in her twenties. We began
to walk together. She'd always say, "Have you seen Roman?
What's Roman doing?" I only vaguely knew who he was, and
I wondered what on earth she wanted with a man as old as
I was. Next thing I knew she married Roman. Lucretia and
I invited the couple to dinner at our home, and they both
turned out to be good people. Roman had grown up poor
in Switzerland and had childhood stories to tell kind of like

mine. He'd been married before and had four kids. He told us about the time he and his family were driving through Texas and were pulled over for a traffic violation. He was hauled before a judge who fined him more money than he had. Roman told the judge, "I can't pay the fine, so I guess you'll have to put me in jail." The judge sentenced him to ten days. "Okay, your honor," said Roman. "Out there are my wife and four kids. You can take care of them while I'm in jail." They let him go.

A while after I landed the job at Macy's, Lucretia was hired on at Hardisty's Homewares, a big housewares store on Fifth Street in downtown Santa Rosa. She loved working there and soon became manager. Actor Raymond Burr, star of the television show *Perry Mason*, was a frequent customer. He gave Lucretia the phone number at his home up the road in Healdsburg so that if something he wanted came in, she could let him know. They became friendly, and he even invited us to Thanksgiving dinner at his home, although we didn't go. We didn't think we'd fit in. Actor Harry Morgan, known for *M*A*S*H* and *Dragnet*, also had a home in Sonoma County, and Lucretia got to know him as well.

A new development at Macy's in the mid-1970s made me love my job even more. Department heads at our store were asked to join forces to generate publicity ideas. Someone came up with idea of creating a show that would run several weeks and draw large crowds. We would make the seventh floor into an African rainforest, specifically the Ivory Coast, Upper Volta, and Cameroon. We'd run the show for several weeks, charge a fifteen-dollar entrance fee, donate the proceeds to charity, and generate great publicity for Macy's.

The west Macy's building was a block square, so the
seventh floor was a very large space in which to work. Three
of us from the design studio were assigned to fly to Africa to
gather artifacts. I was really excited about making this trip.
We would travel into the bush by Jeep to find people who
made masks and pottery and totems representing family, clan,
and first ancestors.

Sure enough, the trip to Africa was exhilarating. My
youth on the road had given me a lifelong love of travel, no
matter if it was rugged. An interpreter drove with us on dirt
roads to remote inland villages where we slept in grass huts
or longhouses. Mostly we located masks—the beautifully
made ones, not junk from middlemen—and bought carloads
to ship back to San Francisco. Leaving Upper Volta, our little
plane almost didn't make it off the ground, overloaded as it
was with all we'd bought. The pilot lifted off the pounded-dirt
airstrip, but the plane struggled to stay in the air and climb at
the end of the runway. We breathed again when he took us up
and out over the bush at the last moment.

Back in San Francisco we removed everything from the
seventh floor, including partitions and office enclosures, and
brought in shrubs and trees. The design studio arranged the
African artifacts among the greenery. You wouldn't believe
how authentic it looked. We even had a river run through
the space—and live animals, including lions and monkeys.
The animals were caged, but you couldn't see the cages. They
lived on the seventh floor a few weeks and then went back to
whatever zoo they'd come from.

The event was such a success that we held shows like this
with various themes for several years to come. In advance of
each show's opening, we called in curators from the de Young
Museum so they could select artifacts for their galleries. By
inviting curators to choose items for free, we were able to
write off the cost of the entire project. Before each event we

threw a nighttime grand opening party to which we invited every big wheel in San Francisco and the rest of the Bay Area. Artifacts not already selected for the de Young were offered for sale beginning that night. We drew large crowds, both for the champagne opening and during regular store hours for the duration of each show.

For the second show, I went with a few other employees to search for artifacts in the highlands of Papua New Guinea, and the following year we traveled along the upper reaches of the Amazon.

In New Guinea we looked for headhunter masks, totems, and spears. The trip lasted only a few days. I wasn't afraid for my life, although in certain places there was still head-hunting. We did our best to stay away from locales where head-hunters were known to be active. To this day, in New Guinea, there are probably places that haven't been touched by outsiders because the jungle is so dense and the highlands steeply mountainous. It was memorable, exotic territory. We glimpsed birds of paradise that did fantastic dances and bow-erbirds that built extraordinary, elaborate nests.

Lucretia was able to accompany me on the trip to the upper Amazon. That was the beginning of us traveling overseas every year on vacation. For the Amazon trip, we journeyed by boat with two other store employees. Our craft was a wooden vessel with an outboard motor; it resembled a native craft but was big enough to carry a lot of cargo. We looked mostly for pottery as well as some masks and spears. The pottery ranged in size from tiny to enormous.

It tickled me that, on the night of our grand opening party, a woman bought one of those pots for $1500. It wasn't one of the huge ones, but it wasn't tiny either, maybe ten inches in diameter and sixteen inches tall.

She said, "I could have bought this for fifteen cents when I was there recently."

I asked why she hadn't.

"Shipping is so tricky and costly that it's worth the $1500 to me now."

I saw her point. We'd carried our purchases out of the Amazon by boat, employed local people to carefully package the pottery so that it wouldn't be damaged, and then sent the goods back to San Francisco by air.

Local excitement eventually wore off, and show attendance slowed, so we held a culminating event: We built a replica of the Oval Office on the seventh floor. I didn't participate in creating that show because it wasn't really the kind of thing I did. The event was more cut-and-dried and handled by someone who knew the right channels for approaching the government to gain detailed information on the president's office. However, the expertise of the craftsmen who created the displays fascinated me, and I liked to observe them as they constructed a dead ringer for the Oval Office, including huge, hand-carved, ceiling cornices. In addition, the furnishings were actually some of those used in the White House. In the process of organizing this show, Macy's discovered that We the People of the United States did not own the furniture in the White House. It was all on loan from various museums and individuals. Macy's determined who the owners were and talked them into selling much of the furniture and art to our store, even, I think, a picture of George Washington by Gilbert Stuart. Afterward Macy's donated the furniture and art back to the White House so that U.S. citizens would own it.

We held one more, smaller show on the seventh floor. It didn't require taking apart the floor and redoing it in the way we'd done previously. At the time there was a design trend toward rustic pine furniture. A Macy's employee went to Scotland and bought up tons of rustic pine furniture and shipped it back. We set it up making use of the floor's preexisting center aisle to install a lawn with English-style bowling.

The following year, one of my decorators came up with the idea of a major annual fashion show on the seventh floor. That's when I learned models don't wear underwear in order to avoid having panty lines show beneath their clothing. The young women changed right near my office, which became a very popular observation point for my male colleagues.

It was 1989 or 1990, during the end of my employment at Macy's, when our son Willie stopped talking to us. His letter came as a terrible shock. He didn't believe that we loved him. This was inconceivable to me. And then Jerry stopped communicating, and that was also horrible.

It's clear that my years with the Walters molded my behavior toward my children. I'm not a huggy-kissy kind of person, and I know that I didn't say "I love you" enough. I'm sure I said it once or twice to each of my kids, but they needed to hear it more. Also, I've been told I'm puritanical in certain ways—for instance, when it comes to praise. I tended not to praise my kids for their achievements or good qualities, and when they talked about themselves with pride, I discouraged this as bragging. I still see it that way. Let other people say you're great, not you. If you want to say that my attitude comes from living with two adults who never had a kind word, not even for each other, I won't argue with that.

I wish my kids could have understood me better. I doubt they ever registered how low I was made to feel by the Walters, what living with those people did to me. I tried to tell my children stories about my early days but soon learned not to. I'd start in, and they'd interrupt with, "Yeah, yeah, we know, you told us, you suffered." I wanted them to know about the experiences that shaped me. Not the absolute worst of it; I didn't want to speak about that to anyone. My kids' lack of interest was deflating and depressing. I don't think I pulled that old "You think you have it rough, this is nothing compared to what happened to me" sort of thing. At least I don't think I did. To my children I guess it was all past history, and they weren't living that kind of life and couldn't relate. Or maybe they didn't want to hear painful details.

Events in my childhood gave me an anger that simmered inside. It's still there, but it shows itself verbally, never physically, thanks to Lucretia and what she demanded of me. If things don't go my way, I find it hard to accept. Sometimes I got riled at our kids when they were young and said harsh things, and afterward I'd hear my wife tell them, "You know your dad loves you. He didn't mean what he just said."

I don't recall ever hitting my kids. Dorothea tells me that occasionally there were spankings, but she also points out that when she and her brothers were growing up in the 1950s, it was acceptable for parents to spank their kids. Dorothea doesn't think that anything untoward happened in our home. Certainly there was nothing like what the Walters did to me with a horsewhip and other forms of punishment. I was determined not to let my kids experience brutality.

I thought I'd shown my children that I loved them in my own way, and I knew that Lucretia had openly expressed her love, so I didn't understand how we could lose our sons entirely. That hurt, and it made me angry. I was shocked they weren't at Lucretia's side when she was dying.

It wasn't long after we received Willie's letter that I quit Macy's. It was 1990, and I was sixty-five. It had been a good run: twenty-one years in a job that I hadn't even considered myself prepared for. A lot of exciting adventures had come my way thanks to Macy's, as well as a number of people I really liked. The work itself was satisfying, and those were good times, in spite of the way they ended.

Yes, I was mad at my co-worker, and I used that as a reason to quit, but also the management of Macy's had changed, and I'd been fed up with the way things were being run there for a while. When I was hired, Macy's ran efficiently under Edward Finkelstein, who first was president of Macy's California, then became president of Macy's New York, and eventually was chairman of the nationwide R. H. Macy & Company. But by the late 1980s it looked like Macy's was in financial trouble, and there were too many hands in the pot, too many people giving orders. I had a reasonable pension, retirement was no problem, and I was done with the place. I quit and gave no notice. Macy's management could care less. I think I was highly regarded by those who knew me, but other than that, it didn't make any difference to the company.

After I left Macy's, Lucretia and I took many wonderful trips together. Before she became too ill to travel, we saw about thirty-five countries on six continents and various islands. We'd saved our money over the course of our working life, making it possible to do a lot of travel. Usually we chose to go in September because temperatures in many parts of the world were milder at that time of year. Lucretia was good at organizing our trips, but maybe half the time we took tours, depending on the place and the conditions there. For example, tours in Russia and China were mandatory when we visited.

We tried not to be tourists in the usual sense and instead looked for adventure without planning each and every step. Beforehand we read up on regional history and points of interest but after that tried to be relatively spontaneous. For Europe we usually purchased Eurail passes and went from town to town, found a hotel, looked around to see what we could see, and moved on if none of the sights captured our imagination. Lucretia was good about rolling with the

punches. She was the perfect companion and never gave me
a bad time about anything. She was a little shy with strangers but had a winning way and became bosom buddies with
everyone.

It was during this time that I got back in touch with Art
Reidhead. Dorothea was working for a California winery, and
one day while she was using Dunn & Bradstreet to research
customer leads, she ran across a listing for Art Reidhead in
Snowflake, Arizona. He owned a sand and gravel business.
She'd heard me talk often about the Reidhead-Harrises and
knew I'd loved my days with them, so she wrote to the man.
He wasn't the Art Reidhead I'd known six decades before,
but he belonged to a distant branch of the same family. He
passed along Dorothea's letter to another family member,
who said, "Yeah, that's my grandfather. He's up in Utah." That
second person took Dorothea's letter to Art in Utah, and
he contacted me. This was when I was surprised to learn
that Art had dedicated his life to religion and had become
a Mormon bishop. No matter, it didn't get in the way of our
friendship. Art and his wife and Lucretia and I visited with
one another several times over the next years, and Art and I
continued to correspond. The last I knew, he had seventy-one
grandchildren.

When Lucretia and I weren't traveling, I often spent
my time working on our house in Santa Rosa. I did a lot of
construction, including a new bay window to create a dining
room off the kitchen and a new sunporch out back. I continued to do a bit of upholstery for our friends. Neighbors
found out and word got around, which brought more furniture refinishing and antique restoration jobs my way. Later I
enjoyed building model ships. Once or twice a week I'd play
golf with three other guys.

Retirement was good for Lucretia and me. It was never a
problem being home with each other all day. We never got on

each other's nerves. After Lucretia became seriously ill, she said, "When I get out of the hospital, you and I are going to live a quiet, peaceful life together. We'll just enjoy each other." Not that we didn't before that, but maybe she was thinking of all the travel we'd done and realized we'd no longer be able to. Once she was ill, she often sat beside me while I made replica boats or carried out other projects. Or she watched English television programs. She especially liked Jane Austen adaptations and *Masterpiece Theatre.*

Lucretia had a stroke in 2000, but at first it didn't seem life-threatening. Dorothea was home for a visit, and one morning the three of us got up to have breakfast. Lucretia said she didn't feel so good and lay down on the couch. I sat with her and realized as we talked that this wasn't my normal Lucretia. Her answers were vague or didn't make sense. Dorothea and I decided to take her to the hospital. Lucretia argued that she didn't want to go, but we called an ambulance. The paramedics took a look at her and chose the hospital with a trauma center.

The physician on duty—a Dr. Janian, a wonderful doctor—told us that he didn't know what type of stroke Lucretia had experienced, so we had a choice. He could give her one of two injections: If he guessed wrong about the kind of stroke, the injection would kill her, but if he was correct, the injection would prevent paralysis. Dr. Janian said Lucretia had to decide whether she wanted to take the risk. Lucretia said she did, and knowing My Mama, I agreed we should risk it because she wouldn't want to be paralyzed. He gave her the correct injection. She wasn't paralyzed, but that was the beginning of the end. Over the next eleven years she faced a series of awful health crises.

I blame myself for what happened to Lucretia toward the very end. We were at home together, and I was taking a nap in a recliner chair. Lucretia decided to do the same on a nearby couch. At that point she was able to move about with a walker. Lucretia lay down, then said she'd meant to turn out the light. I said I'd get it, but she rose up first. The curtains were drawn; the room was dark. On the way back to the couch Lucretia tripped over a coffee table, fell, and fractured her spine. That was it. She was in such pain. An ambulance took her to the hospital. Our family doctor, Marty Rubinger, who always took great care of Lucretia, called in a spine specialist. His colleague said he could cement the spine together to relieve the pain, but afterward Lucretia wouldn't be able to move around. That's what they decided to do. Cement was injected into her spine, and Lucretia went into a coma from the anesthetic. She was out for several days. They put her in the ICU, and I begged her day after day to wake up. Our doctors even called the University of California, San Francisco, Medical Center to find out what might be done for her.

Finally Lucretia woke from the coma. She was in a lot of pain. Marty transferred her to a convalescent hospital where they required her to do therapy. Dorothea has gone through agonies over this because she forced her mother to get up and do therapy so she'd be able to come home. I did the same thing. The exercises caused even more terrible pain. It was an awful hard time for Lucretia.

Lucretia was at the facility for maybe a month when I noticed a lump on her shoulder. A doctor visiting the premises looked at her shoulder and used a needle to draw pus out of the lump. He transferred her back to the hospital and scheduled surgery the next day to remove the fluid that had accumulated in her shoulder. She was also given massive doses of antibiotics to fight the infection. Dorothea and I cautioned the doctor about Lucretia's reaction to anesthesia, and they were very careful not to give her too much.

At this point, whenever Dorothea and I were in the room with Lucretia, we had to stay completely enclosed in special sanitary clothing and masks, to keep other sources of infection away from her. No one else was allowed in her room except for medical workers dressed the same way. Following this surgery Lucretia was fairly lucid. She was transferred back to the convalescent hospital, and a few days later I spotted another lump. She was diagnosed with sepsis, the infection having traveled in her bloodstream. The doctor informed us that the antibiotics weren't working for her and that there was no point trying to remove more fluid with another surgery.

Then Lucretia became incoherent off and on. She wouldn't let anyone feed her except for me. I was by her side almost around the clock. Dorothea relieved me, and I relieved her.

Sitting beside Lucretia, I thought about all the hard times she experienced after marrying me. She never complained about any of it, but I felt bad thinking back over it, how difficult her life had been because she chose to be with me. And it was terrible to see the way she was suffering now.

Lucretia was my best friend. There was a feeling of oneness between us. Marty, our doctor, told the nurses in the hospital, "Treat these two people as one person. They are like one person. Whatever she wants, she's going to get, as far as he's concerned, and they make their decisions together."

Passion burns out with the passage of years, and you become two old people, but our relationship was closer than ever—the affection we had for each other, the thoughtfulness. I loved to share things with her. We knew what the other was thinking half the time. There was a comfortable feeling of this special person being there alongside me, having faith in her and she in me. Over all the years, we never worried that the other would stray, even when outsiders tried to pose temptations, which happened from time to time and made us laugh.

As I sat beside Lucretia, my failure to say "I love you" haunted me. I'd told her these past few years, when I saw I might lose her, but all along I should have said it. I should have told Lucretia how lucky I felt about being able to marry her. How deep my feelings were. She made me a better person. She completed me. She eased my way in the world. I had failed over and over to say the three words she would have liked to hear and that were true. Now when she was awake, I said them, but it seemed like too little.

During moments when she was lucid, Lucretia told me she loved me. "I couldn't have made it through this without you," she said. I had taken care of all her needs when she was still at home and helped in the hospital any way I could, but that wasn't difficult because of the love I felt. None of it felt like enough.

A couple of days passed after the doctor ruled out surgery and antibiotics. I went to feed Lucretia, but she didn't respond. She didn't react to anything I did or said. It dawned on me that she was dying. I called hospice, and they came to the convalescent hospital. I hoped against hope Lucretia would survive. A bed was set up for me alongside Lucretia, and I stayed with her for four days, and then she died.

It was January 4, 2012. We had been together for more than sixty-five years. After she was gone, I didn't know how I would go on without her.

Epilogue

During the first two years that William told me his story, he often appeared morose over his loss of Lucretia, and well into the second year his depression deepened. All of his life, he said, he'd had faith in the future, but not now. The present and the future were empty voids. He hinted at thoughts of suicide.

William relied heavily on his daughter, Dorothea, for companionship, but she was employed full time and couldn't provide the level of constancy he required. Or improve his mood during the hours she did spend with him. Day and night Dorothea was on call for her father for any kind of reason, medical or otherwise, and they had frequent dinners and lunches together, but he wanted and needed more. She invited him to move in with her. He refused.

Dorothea and I urged visits to a therapist. William briefly gave one and then another a try. He didn't like either and let the matter drop.

Yet he managed to draw upon the inner strength that had carried him far. He decided to seek distraction. Diagnoses of kidney cancer, COPD, and heart failure were not allowed to be obstacles. (A doctor at San Francisco's veterans hospital identified his renal cell carcinoma as the type seen in people exposed to radiation at Nagasaki and Hiroshima.) William still drove his own truck and, in spite of his advanced age, continued to be an able motorist. He looked for opportunities to do volunteer work. Nothing turned up, although it didn't help that, when asked by a hospital volunteer coordinator whether he had a criminal record, he smiled and said he'd been in jail a number of times. When he turned his attention to travel, his doctors didn't object, although they did nix a trip with a tour group to Machu Picchu because of the strain high altitude would place on his heart. That verdict took William by surprise. Next he looked into flying lessons and was annoyed when that was ruled out as well for age and health reasons. As far as he was concerned, he was fit.

In search of a traveling companion, William posted his profile on Match.com, making it clear that he didn't want romance, only friendly company. A woman thirty years his junior came forward, happy to visit New Orleans and then Italy with him. At this woman's urging, and to his surprise, they became lovers, and he credited her with making him feel comfortable for the first time about confiding what had happened with Eleanor Walters. She even initiated contact with his son Gerald, helping to dispel the misunderstandings that had kept father and son apart for many years, which eventually also led to a reunion with son Will and his family. Amid a number of warning signs, though, William asked this woman to move in with him. The relationship became rocky and turned out to be a terrible mistake, with the result that William had to obtain legal help to evict her. The gnawing loneliness that had taken hold of him in childhood and that was eased for more than six decades by Lucretia, returned full force.

William didn't give up. Within the year he met another woman, but once again the relationship led to more unhappiness than solace. It wasn't long before a diagnosis of terminal cancer brought William even lower.

During his final year, weakened and mostly confined to his home, William was thrilled when his family dropped by for visits. Dorothea, as always, was in frequent contact, showing up to help her father in any way she could. She, Will, Susan, and their daughter, Heather, who was now a young woman, avoided talking with him about the problems of the past, all of them having agreed that there was no point in rehashing old business. (Heather's brother, Brandon, lived with his wife and young daughter several hours away in northern California.) If Dorothea and Will reminisced with their dad, reported Dorothea, it was to wonder how she and her brothers didn't get killed as children recklessly riding their go-carts or jumping off the roof. "We always did stupid things," she said, more with fondness than anything else. Over the years, William had amassed a large coin collection, and while visiting, he and his granddaughter sat together putting coins in rolls, an activity that helped break the ice for conversation with shy Heather. Although son Gerald made plans to fly to California for a visit, a sudden need for surgery caused Gerald to postpone, and Gerald's continuing health problems blocked trips afterward, although he kept in touch with William and the others by phone.

Privately, Dorothea and her brother Will discussed family events of the past couple of decades. When Lucretia had her stroke, Dorothea had called her brother Gerald to let him know about their mother's health crisis, and he had passed along word to Will. At that point Will and William "had not spoken in a very long time," said Dorothea. Will now explained to Dorothea that he had called his father, who angrily told him that he didn't want him or Susan coming to the hospital to see Lucretia. Years later, when Lucretia died, William announced to Dorothea that he absolutely did not want Will or Gerald to come to Lucretia's funeral, and that if they did, they would be asked to leave. As a result, Dorothea did not call her brothers with the news. Will and Susan learned about Lucretia's death from other people, and Gerald didn't learn about it until William sought reconciliation with him.

After her father died, Dorothea explained, "In the five years after Mom passed, Dad told people, 'Can you believe my sons didn't show up at their own mother's funeral?' I never corrected him when he told people that because he would have eaten me alive." Dorothea had reason to think he'd throw the full force of his fury at her, because he often yelled at her when unhappy, whether she had anything to do with his displeasure or not. He allowed the old, boiling anger to find regular release like steam from a hydrothermal vent.

However, as cancer took its toll, awareness of the limited time left to him appeared to transform William's relationship with his daughter. He became more expressive, and Dorothea felt closer to her dad than ever before. William told her, "I just can't believe what I put you through," acknowledging the many times in the recent past when she'd tried to help and he'd shouted at her. "I could not deserve a better daughter," he said. Often unable to stand easily, he grabbed her hands to cup them in his own and kissed them. Or, if he managed to stand, he might hug her. In spite of how William once described himself, he had become a huggy-kissy person.

If William's long life illustrates anything at all, it gives evidence for theories that the first four or five years of human life are crucial in the formation of a healthy, intact adult. In his first home, William knew loving-kindness and experienced the pleasures of backyard play and relative freedom, and those experiences seemed to have given him enough confidence and fortitude to persevere through abuse and other serious challenges that followed. Eventually William was able to love in his flawed way and to be loved by members of the family he helped create. For sixty-five years he felt the devotion of a remarkable wife. He was able to serve his country with pride during dangerous times, to land and hold an administrative job for twenty-one years, to express artistic creativity, and to satisfy a love of travel and adventure. The terrors and deprivations that began with William's journey on an Orphan Train may have scarred his psyche in certain ways, but in his life, it can be said that William was the victor.

Orphan Trains in America

Beginning in 1854, Orphan Trains in the United States relocated hundreds of thousands of children from eastern cities to new homes in the Midwest, West, and South. Today, the National Orphan Train Complex in Concordia, Kansas, estimates that 200,000 to 250,000 youngsters were put on those trains during an approximately seventy-five-year period. By the time the last Orphan Train left its eastern station in the early 1930s, controversy surrounding the trains made the phenomenon one that Americans preferred to forget.

Recordkeeping concerning the identities and numbers of children carried by Orphan Trains was sketchy, as were accounts of what happened to youngsters once they left the trains. This chapter in our history remained largely obscured until late in the twentieth century, when films, books, and scholarly works began to bring the orphan transports to light, sometimes treating the subject with nostalgia and other times offering a more complete, disturbing story.

Methodist minister Charles Loring Brace first conceived the idea of orphan trains in the mid-1800s. His idea to send children away from urban street life and institutionalization was noble in purpose and fit nicely with the presence of new train routes extending westward across the continent. Lori Halfhide, head researcher at the National Orphan Train Complex, told me in a February 21, 2017, phone call that eventually thirty charitable organizations in the East followed Brace's model and sent orphaned and abandoned children as well as destitute immigrant youngsters to rural families living along rail lines. While these agencies' intentions were honorable, and some children did find loving homes, the consequences of relocation were often disastrous for the youngsters involved, exposing them to virtual slavery, sexual and other physical abuse, and new abandonment in rural America. Furthermore, many of the children were removed from poverty-stricken parents who thought their children would be gone only temporarily and then discovered the removal to be permanent.

Why the perceived need for Orphan Trains and "placing out" children to homes primarily in the West? Around 1830, European immigration to the U.S. exploded and so did the number of homeless children in large eastern cities serving as ports of entry for the foreign arrivals. The wave of foreign immigrants found themselves competing with thousands of other newcomers for jobs in urban factories. This was because people living in rural America were relocating in significant numbers to big cities, drawn by the prospect of factory, trade, and shop work. If urban newcomers were fortunate enough to obtain jobs, the pay was meager, factory work dangerous, and the threat of starvation a constant. Families often found themselves crowded into a room or two in cold-water tenements. To make matters worse, in those earlier times, when a husband was badly injured or died, his widow had few options for making a living, and her children might be forced to work or beg. Also, given the lack of effective birth control, two healthy but impoverished parents sometimes thrust children age six or seven out of their home and onto the streets to fend for themselves when new brothers and sisters were born. By 1850 in New York, according to Andrea Warren's 1998 article "The Orphan Train" in the *Washington Post*, when that city's population was approximately half a million, it is believed that 10,000 to 30,000 children lived on the streets or in more than two dozen orphanages.

Brace first responded to the crisis by founding the Children's Aid Society (CAS) in New York in 1853. The son of a prominent Connecticut family, he had traveled to Europe after graduating from Yale and, while abroad, probably became familiar with the English and German practice of placing out orphaned children to new homes. Later, while he attended Union Theological Seminary in New York City, Brace was horrified at the plight of thousands of homeless children—from toddlers to teens—roaming that city's streets. Called "street Arabs" by many, they begged, sold matches and rags and newspapers, and became prostitutes in order to survive. In that time and place, the law treated a child of seven or older as an adult. Police arrested many of these youngsters as vagrants and threw them into jail cells with adults. If convicted of theft, a child twelve or older could face hanging.

Within its first two years, Brace's Children's Aid Society in New York City initiated what would become the Orphan Train movement and also created an industrial school for poor children, the first free school-lunch program in the United States, and a lodging house for homeless boys, including boys who barely got by hawking newspapers on the streets. The CAS relied upon charitable donations to finance its activities. Through his writings and speeches, Brace raised money from churches and charitable groups and occasionally was able to inspire wealthy donors to underwrite entire trainloads of children being relocated to the West.

In the 1850s, "the West" was what we think of today as the Midwest, but with the passage of time, the increasing reach of train lines, and participation by additional charitable agencies, Orphan Trains dispatched youngsters across the continent to the South, Southwest, and far West. In the earliest days of the Orphan Trains, the new transcontinental railroads agreed to discount fares for the children and the agents who accompanied them, in the hope that the youngsters' relocation to rural areas would further encourage development of population centers along railroad routes.

In the mid-1800s, rural America was thought to nurture wholesome values. At the same time as rural areas were losing population to urban America, the U.S. was expanding westward and needed people to work its farms and businesses. In the West, Brace believed, solid, God-fearing homes would be found for the children. Living on farms, breathing clean country air, the youngsters would have enough food to eat and the opportunity to develop a good work ethic. As explained on the National Orphan Train Complex website, the thinking was that, as they augmented the rural workforce, the children could grow into mature, responsible adults able to care for themselves. Families who selected children off the trains were expected to treat the newcomers as they would their own children; the CAS demanded that they provide schooling and teach the children the work of their family farms or businesses.

CAS agents scrubbed the youngsters, dressed them in new clothing, and put them on trains with a Bible in hand. Accounts vary regarding the number of children sent on each Orphan Train accompanied by at least one adult agent. The National Orphan Train Complex reported that 10 to 40 kids were transported by the CAS at one time, although other sources cited as many as 150 children on a train. In most cases, the children were allowed to leave the train only for the viewings by strangers who might take them home. The display of children at designated stops often took on the feeling of spectacle and even an auctionlike atmosphere. Competition could be stiff, with the greatest demand for babies, who might be as young as one month old. Farmers sought out children who would make good field hands, but it was not unusual for a couple who had suffered the death of a child to seek a baby or toddler on an Orphan Train. Theoretically, teens could quickly become productive farm hands, but older youngsters were usually harder to place because it was feared they had bad habits that were firmly established.

In advance of sending a carload of children through designated towns, the CAS communicated by mail with those locales to establish screening committees so that a panel of upstanding citizens could identify decent local people to foster the children. These citizen screening committees proved to be inadequate at best, given the reluctance of a town's residents to disapprove openly of their neighbors. A CAS agent was supposed to check on each placement yearly, but there were only a small number of agents and thousands of kids. Adequate follow-up became impossible. According to Marilyn Irvin Holt in *The Orphan Trains: Placing Out in America,* "Additionally, follow-up visitations were casual, if they occurred at all. During its early years, the Aid Society relied almost exclusively on correspondence, not visitations, to keep track of the placed out and to learn of their new home conditions. This proved unreliable and the society lost contact with many children or failed to transfer those in unsatisfactory homes" (p. 53).

Children taken off Orphan Trains were often passed from home to home by host families when they were found unacceptable for one reason or another. Brace had envisioned the transported children doing farm work in their new, healthier lives and did not expect them to become indentured servants. Many did. Rather than being incorporated within their host families and provided the schooling required by the CAS as if they were sons or daughters, many were put to work for long hours and given only minimal room and board. Following the Civil War, unknown numbers of older youngsters were used as replacements for newly outlawed slave labor. The extent of abuse to all of the relocated children is unknown. Many ran away and were reported drifting from place to place. They joined gangs, ended up in reform school, or managed to return to the urban centers from which they had come.

Even when transported youths did find loving homes, they were often thought of as outcasts by the larger community, most painfully by other kids at school. Unused to anything but city life, the newcomers stood out because of their accents and their lack of knowledge about rural culture and work. Frequently the newcomers were accused of having "bad blood" because it was assumed they were the children of unmarried mothers, prostitutes, and criminals or simply because they had been born to foreigners.

Eventually the CAS developed a working relationship with numerous charitable agencies that took in children, including a host of orphanages that supplied riders for CAS-sponsored trains. Other charitable organizations sponsored their own train cars as well, including the Sisters of Charity of St. Vincent de Paul and their New York Foundling Hospital, which concentrated on placing Catholic children in Catholic homes. The Sisters of Charity became second to the CAS in the number of children sent on trains. After they established their Foundling Hospital in 1869, the Sisters are believed to have relocated at least 40,000 babies and toddlers to Catholic communities in the West, according to Edward Gray in "The Orphan Trains," a 1995 documentary for the PBS series *American Experience*. Boston's Baldwin Place Home for Little Wanderers sent many orphans westward, as did Philadelphia and Chicago organizations that transported thousands more.

A significant number of children who traveled on Orphan Trains were not actually orphans, according to Rebecca S. Trammell in her article, "Orphan Train Myths and Legal Reality" in the fall 2009 issue of *Modern American*. Citing a Children's Aid Society 1864 annual report, Trammell says that the CAS described seeking children for the trains who were abandoned or homeless or "in such a state of poverty as to be improved by being taken to good homes in the country." According to Trammell, CAS volunteers or paid employees "roamed the streets of New York and other large eastern cities looking for neglected, vagrant, and destitute children. Inducements were not to be used to obtain the parents' agreement to a Western placement. Instead visitors were to explain to the children and their parents the advantages of going West, and obtain a written or witnessed verbal agreement to such placement from the child's parent or parents, or from a truly orphaned child" (endnote 49).

Historians who have studied the records of the Children's Aid Society have concluded that the largest number of Orphan Train children were sent by impoverished parents with the intent of temporarily transferring or sharing them but not giving them up. It appears that those parents had no intention of losing track of their children or placing them permanently for adoption, although this is, in fact, what often happened. According to the Adoption History Project website at the University of Oregon, recipient families were in many cases reluctant to pass along mail to children from their parents back East, and of course, for the many so-called orphans who ran away from their placements, maintaining contact with their birth families became even more difficult once they hit the road.

In *The Orphan Trains*, Holt explains that in the latter years of Orphan Trains, the CAS actually cautioned children against contacting their relatives back home, but there were many instances of sons and daughters corresponding with or even visiting their parents after being placed out. Others who were placed out were visited by parents who showed up to reclaim them (p. 130).

When the Orphan Train movement began, its aim was not to encourage adoption but to fulfill a dual purpose: obtain foster care and add to the rural workforce. By 1900, however, attitudes toward child labor had changed, and the sponsoring agencies stated a single goal of finding children "good homes." In reality, though, says Holt in *The Orphan Trains*, the children were still commonly used for farm labor (pp. 138–39). Adoption wasn't a widespread practice in the U.S. until after 1900, when various child protection laws were passed and adoption procedures clarified.

By the time the last Orphan Trains carried children away from eastern cities, the American public had come to favor public assistance for immigrants and other Americans living in poverty, and this, added to the growing sentiment against child labor, is cited for the decline of Orphan Trains. Also, the need for farm labor in the Midwest had declined. In the twentieth century, the emphasis on what childhood should look like shifted from the benefit of work to the benefit of play, from children's economic value to their families to their emotional needs in growing to be successful adults.

The Children's Aid Society sent its first Orphan Train to Dowagiac, Michigan, in 1854 and its last to Sulphur Springs, Texas, on May 31, 1929, according to the National Orphan Train Complex website. Other agencies continued to relocate children this way into the early 1930s, but it is not easy to determine which agencies continued the practice after 1929.

At his death in 1890, Charles Loring Brace was lauded as the most significant child-saver of the nineteenth century. Many have credited him as the father of modern adoption practices and America's foster care system. However, by 1930 there was a growing outcry over the Orphan Train movement and the ills to which it led. "The orphan train movement and orphan train placements were not the driving force for modern adoption laws, foster care practices, and child welfare laws," writes Trammell in "Orphan Train Myths and Legal Reality." "Instead, many of these reforms came about specifically to oppose orphan train practices."

The irony is that crediting Brace with fatherhood of modern foster care in America does not necessarily bestow an honor on him. Sadly, our nationwide foster care system today is fraught with almost as many serious problems as the earlier Orphan Trains. Journalist Cris Beam writes in *To the End of June: The Intimate Life of American Foster Care*:

> *I didn't know how we could be spending billions on foster children in the United States and yet see half of them with chronic medical conditions, eighty percent with serious emotional problems, and then abandon nearly a quarter of them to homelessness by their twenty-first birthdays. I didn't know how we could be failing them so spectacularly.*
>
> *Federal investigators recently spent three years looking into seven fundamental criteria for successful foster care in all fifty states. They examined the basics: things like kids being protected from abuse and neglect, being safely maintained at home whenever possible, and receiving adequate services for educational and physical health needs. No state met more than two of the seven criteria. (xvi)*

In an April 2010 article in *Family Court Review*, "Disrupting the Pathway from Foster Care to the Justice System—a Former Prosecutor's Perspectives on Reform," Miriam Aroni Krinsky stated that 25 percent of former foster youth end up incarcerated in the U.S. within a few years of leaving the foster care system.

And so the problem of children suffering from poverty, neglect, and abuse in the United States continues in a large way to this day. As a volunteer at a group home for foster kids in Santa Rosa, California, I had a chance to understand the situation more clearly. For several years I participated at an enlightened variant of the foster care system: The Children's Village, which housed twenty to twenty-four boys and girls. At the time, the Village was one of the more exemplary homes for foster children in California; it has since closed as a result of a new California law directing children away from group homes and toward placement with foster families. Many of the kids who arrived at the Village had sustained awful psychological damage at the hands of their biological parents, adoptive parents, and foster parents, and it was the children's great good fortune that the Village was able to provide multiple resources to help them, including social workers, therapists, tutors, activities director, surrogate grandparents, and house parents, as well as volunteers who offered everything from storybook time to cooking lessons to bicycle journeys. Nevertheless, Village staff and volunteers faced extreme challenges when the most severely injured children acted out or engaged in self-destructive behavior.

As I glimpsed both the highs and lows of Village life, I came to understand more clearly why the typical foster family with good intentions but without those multiple resources often faces overwhelming difficulties when it welcomes a foster child. Sadly, it is all too common for foster children to bounce from placement to placement because exasperated or defeated foster parents find they cannot cope. To make matters worse, foster youth in our country who reach the age of eighteen are very often set adrift by the system with little or no assistance in making the transition to self-sufficient adulthood. We may have moved beyond the primitive efforts of the Orphan Trains, but we have much farther to go.

Which Orphan Train carried William and his brother westward? The Sisters of Charity's New York Foundling Hospital used Orphan Trains to place orphaned Catholic children with Catholic families. In *The Orphan Trains*, Holt reports that in 1904 they expanded their train coverage to the Arizona Territory, which meant that their trains passed through New Mexico and that the Sisters of Charity did engage in southern and southwestern placements (pp. 136 and 158). However, Holt reports that the Sisters of Charity are said to have abandoned their placing-out program in 1927 (p. 162).

Lori Halfhide at the National Orphan Train Complex explained to me in our February 2017 phone call that the Sisters of Charity tried to avoid at all costs placing Catholic children with families who were not Catholic. As a result, it is not likely that William and Jared were sent from the East Coast on a train sponsored by the Sisters of Charity, because the Walters were not Catholic (even though they later had William baptized in a Catholic church). Jared was raised by nuns after his abandonment by the couple who took him off the Orphan Train, but nothing is known about the religion of the couple with whom he was first placed.

Amanda Wahlmeier, curator at the National Orphan Train Complex, confirmed to me in a June 26, 2013, email that the last Orphan Train is generally regarded as the one to Sulphur Springs, Texas, in 1929. "However," she noted, "orphans were still sent out on trains (usually in prearranged circumstances) into the 1930s." As of this writing, the sponsoring agency for William and Jared's (Gerald's) train remains a mystery.

William's Parents

During the last years of Lucretia's life, when she was weakened by illness, William concentrated on projects that could be accomplished at home and allow him to stay by her side. In the year 2000, he wrote to Susquehanna County's Historical Records/Archives department to see if he could learn anything more about his original family.

A historian in Susquehanna sent a small amount of information but referred him to the Susquehanna County Historical Society and Free Library Association, which provided more detail based on a search of U.S. census data and local tax records. I supplemented that information in 2013 with my own online search of census records and newspaper accounts. The following information suffers from multiple variations in name spellings, which are given here according to the way they were recorded in the original documents.

WILLIAM'S MOTHER

The historical record provides minimal information on William's mother, Dorothea Quick, and almost none after she met his father. There is enough evidence, however, to make me think that Dorothea Quick was a pretty, charming woman whose attractiveness endured into middle age. Photos of William as a boy and young man reveal a strikingly good-looking male with blond hair and slim build. The fact that Dorothea was able to marry, have three sons and a daughter, divorce an abusive husband after nine years, and remarry a man six years her junior when she was in her mid- to late thirties is one indicator of her appeal, plus the fact that her second husband appears to have become a father to the children from her first marriage. When that second husband exited her life, Dorothea lived with a third man, who may or may not have become her husband and with whom she had two more sons.

Dorothea Quick was born to Mr. and Mrs. Frank Quick in New York City in 1883 and next shows up in 1899 living with her parents in Oakland Township, Pennsylvania, across the Susquehanna River from the Pennsylvania railroad town of Susquehanna Depot. As a fourteen- or fifteen-year-old Dorothea was employed as a domestic by a Mrs. Maggie Parliman across the river. A newspaper article on May 19, 1899, in the *Independent Republican* reported a "Dastardly Outrage" involving "A Young Lady Assaulted by an Inhuman Brute." (There is a discrepancy between the birth year supplied by the Susquehanna County Historical Society and the age supplied by the newspaper in the article below; probably the newspaper is incorrect because the birth year agrees with Dorothea's age as reported in the 1920 Census.)

> *On Sunday night, between 9:30 and 12 o'clock, Susquehanna was the scene of a dastardly outrage against law and decency, the details of which are revolting, says the* Transcript.
>
> *Shortly after nine o'clock Miss Dorothea Quick, aged 14 years, daughter of Mr. and Mrs. Frank Quick, left Mrs. Maggie Parliman's on Jackson street, where she is employed as a domestic, and started for the home of her parents in Oakland.*
>
> *While passing under the Exchange street culvert of the Erie railroad, Miss Quick was met by a devil in human form named John Buckley, who grabbed her and told her at the point of a revolver that if she made an outcry he would kill her.*
>
> *From the culvert the innocent and unwilling victim was forced to accompany her abductor westward along*

the railroad track and subsequently to his board-
ing place, where, while he was endeavoring to gain
entrance, she managed to escape.

Buckley is a man about thirty years of age. He
arrived in Susquehanna the last of March, and had
since been emploped [sic] by Geo. Albee as a painter
and paper-hanger.

Soon after Miss Quick made her escape the assault
became known, and officers searched the railroad yard
for Buckley, to prevent, if possible, his departure on
outgoing trains.

It was learned, however, that he boarded a west-
bound freight train between twelve and one o'clock.

Telegrams were sent to neighboring points and Chief
McMahon soon got trace of the fugitive, finally captur-
ing him at Owego on Tuesday morning. Buckley was
arrested as a fugitive from justice and committed to the
Owego jail, from whence, as soon as requisition papers
are secured, he will be brought to the Montrose jail.

Dorothea Quick was twenty-five when she married James
A. Cokely in Auburn Township, Susquehanna County. They
had four children: sons Harris, Francis, and Duane, and
daughter Marian. The family held together seven years, until
1915, when James left his wife and children. Using the services of attorney John Ferguson, Dorothea filed for divorce in
1917 citing physical abuse by her spouse. At the time of the
divorce, Dorothea lived in Oakland Township and James lived
in Hallstead. The divorce was granted that same year and
required some bravery on Dorothea's part, because divorce
was considered a major scandal in the early 1900s and was far
less common than it is today. James died a pauper while living
with his brother six years after his divorce.

Three years after the divorce, Dorothea still resided in Oakland Township with her four children and was recorded in the 1920 Census remarried to a man named John Ross. At the time, she was thirty-seven and he was thirty-one. The 1920 Census indicates that Ross was able to read and write but that Dorothea was not. He worked as a laborer, and his three oldest stepchildren attended school.

Four years later, Dorothea appeared in the tax records of Susquehanna Depot as Dorothea VanSteinburg, listed beneath the name of Almon VanSteinburg. She was assessed an occupation tax of fifty dollars in 1924 for her work as a housekeeper. The same record indicates that Almon was a carpenter.

Next, Dorothea can be found in the April 1930 Census as Dorothea Van Steinburg, head of a family living at 323 East Main Street, Susquehanna, a domicile she rented for twenty-five dollars a month. At age forty-six she reported that she was married and working as a baker in a bakery, although the Census states that she was employed "on her own account" and not for wages, which may mean that she owned the bakery. Children living with her were listed as Harris Cokely, age twenty, employed as a house painter; Verna M. (Marian?) Cokely, age eighteen, student; Francis Cokely, age sixteen, student; Jared E. Van Steinburg, age seven, student; and William D. Van Steinburg, age four. A boarder named Fred Edwards lived with them; he was a widower, age fifty-six, employed as a stonecutter at a quarry.

The 1930 Census data states that William was living at home with his mother and siblings in the spring of that year. Dorothea must have become too ill to work after April 1930 and died within the next few months. (No death certificate for her has been found.) Orphan Train runs terminated in the early 1930s, and William believes that he came to live with the Walters shortly before or after turning five in September 1930.

As of April 1930, Dorothea's husband (or ex-husband), John Ross, is shown in the Census to be living at the National Soldiers Home in Elizabeth County, Virginia. At age forty-one, he listed himself as married and a veteran of the World War.

Did Dorothea divorce John Ross and marry Almon VanSteenburgh? No records of a divorce or remarriage were found, but the county courthouse in Montrose, Pennsylvania, which may have held these records, was partially consumed by a 1922 fire during which documents were destroyed. Also, no birth certificates survive for either Jared or William.

WILLIAM'S FATHER

William's father was married twice before Dorothea came to live in his home. It is not clear whether Almon's first two marriages ended in the death of a spouse, annulment, divorce, or separation. Only a few years before Dorothea and Almon resided together and Jared and William were born, Almon had been a married man living with his wife and five young children.

Almon VanSteenburgh was born in March 1870 in New York State. It appears that his parents were George and Mary VanSteenburgh, although the Susquehanna historical researcher who corresponded with William said that the record was not entirely clear on that fact. By 1900, Almon was a thirty-year-old living in Middletown, Delaware County, New York, with his wife, Rilla. They had been married ten years and had no children.

Almon next appears in the tax records of 1919 as a resident of Susquehanna Depot, where he had a home in the

Third Ward. The 1920 Census showed that he was forty-nine, worked as a house carpenter, had moved to the Second Ward, was married to a wife, Agnes, and that they had five sons (ages five months, two years, four years, six years, and seven years). His residence continued to be the Second Ward through 1922.

Almon next appears in the tax records as living in Susquehanna's First Ward in 1924. Directly below his name is Dorothea VanSteinburg's, as mentioned above, with the indication that she had been taxed for her work as a housekeeper. It was unusual for women to be listed in the tax records at that time, and the probable reason, according to a researcher for the Susquehanna County Historical Society, was that she was Almon's wife and was working outside the household. Or, it is possible that she was not married to him and was employed by him, and yet took his name because by that time she had given birth to a son by him.

What became of Almon's children with his second wife, Agnes? Only four years had elapsed between the 1920 Census, when he was shown living with his wife and young children, and the 1924 tax record, in which only Dorothea was mentioned. At that point, Jared (AKA Gerald) had been born to Dorothea and Almon.

My speculation is that Dorothea was not married to Almon, since her maiden name and not VanSteenburgh or any variation of that last name was listed on a baptismal certificate William obtained from a church in Gallup while searching in that city for more information on his origins. On the baptismal certificate dated May 8, 1953, attesting to William's baptism on July 16, 1933, William Delos Walters is listed as the child of "Almon Norval Van Steenburg" and "Dorothy Quick." Both parents' names may have been supplied to the Walters in a birth certificate or other information given to the couple when they took him off the Orphan Train.

Consider, too, that Dorothea's most recent husband, John Ross, resided far away in a veterans hospital in 1930 but was listed as married. Also, it can be asked why William was not baptized shortly after his birth; if he was born out of wedlock, a Catholic priest who was acquainted with his mother's situation would not have agreed to do so.

It is possible that Almon predeceased Dorothea, because William had no memory of his father. As is the case with William's mother, no death certificate for his father has been found. If my speculation is correct about Dorothea living with Almon out of wedlock, it could explain why Dorothea's two youngest children were put on an Orphan Train after her death. William and Gerald's half-sister, Marian, who cared for them as well as their mother in Dorothea's final days, may have been a single young woman with little means to support herself and two little half-brothers. Given the stigma attached to Dorothea's divorce (or divorces) and the possibility that she may not have been married to Almon, she may have alienated her three older sons by James Cokely to the point that they refused to take in her youngest sons.

I imagine Dorothea Quick/Cokely/Ross/VanSteenburgh's good looks in addition to her multiple marriages made her seem threatening to other women in a small town of that day and age. Thus the old woman's words to William years later upon his return to Susquehanna that his mother had been a "lady of ill repute." Furthermore, if Dorothea was, in fact, not married to Almon, and if his wife, Agnes, had left him in a huff, taking their five young children with her, tongues may have wagged in their small town about the home-wrecking beauty who became pregnant out of wedlock.

THE WALTERS

In a search of Archives.com, I discovered more about the couple who adopted William. I could not find 1920 or 1930 census information about them, but they do appear in the April 1940 Census for Winslow, Arizona, as well as in newspaper articles published in the *Gallup Independent, Albuquerque Journal, Las Vegas Daily Optic,* and *Santa Fe New Mexican.*

In 1940 the Walters owned their home in Winslow and reported that they had lived there in 1935 as well. Henry was fifty and Eleanor was sixty in 1940, so the couple was forty and fifty, respectively, when William first came to live with them. William often said that in his mind's eye the Walters reminded him of the couple in the Grant Wood painting *American Gothic,* and it is easy to see why the two appeared old to him as well as austere, especially since, unlike the woman in the painting, Eleanor had grey hair.

Besides the gap in the Walters' ages, there was a marked difference in their education levels. The Census shows that Henry Walters had an eighth-grade education whereas Eleanor completed four years of college. He was born in Kansas City and she in Pennsylvania. Henry Walters gave his occupation as conductor for a steam railroad, and Eleanor Walters described herself as engaged in home housework, although William heard that Eleanor had once been a schoolteacher. Henry worked fifty weeks in 1939, earning $2400. The couple reported that they had no income from sources other than Henry's job.

Upon learning from me that Henry had been a train conductor, William said this explained the man's repeated absences from home, often over periods of several days or more. The differences in the couple's ages and education levels also struck a chord with William, for it seemed to him that Eleanor took a leadership role in their household. With her frequent reports of misbehavior, she was the one who brought down most of the beatings on William, and years later, when William contacted the Walters before going off to war, Eleanor was the one to write a letter rejecting contact.

Eleanor's repeated references to William's "Uncle Clifford" and the couple's insistence that he call them "Aunt" and "Uncle" led William to wonder if he was related to Eleanor Walters. The fact that Eleanor was born in Pennsylvania might reinforce the idea of a family connection between William and Eleanor, but the Susquehanna County Historical Society researcher found no link between Dorothea Quick and anyone named Eleanor or Clifford Quick. I was not able to find information on an Eleanor VanSteenburgh or any variation of that name for the appropriate time period. It is possible that the couple wanted William as a replacement for a son who had died. As noted by Holt in *The Orphan Trains*, "Childless couples or those who had lost a child through death wished to take into their homes younger children. This quest for a child to replace one lost was not unusual" (p. 141).

Newspaper articles of the 1920s and 1930s reported on Henry's progression in local Republican politics. Beginning in 1928 he was nominated and then appointed a trustee on the Gallup town board. In 1929 he became chairman of that board and by the end of the year was mayor of Gallup. In 1931 it was reported that he gave up his position on the town board because of private business; family friend George Miksch was named as his replacement. In 1930 Eleanor ran for superintendent of schools, but the text is obscured in a way that makes it hard to know the outcome.

The *Gallup Independent* reported in December 1934 that Henry Albert Walters was declared bankrupt in U.S. District Court. William reported having been somewhat aware of the Walters' declining financial situation, and it may have been the bankruptcy that precipitated the Walters' move to

Winslow. William returned from Boys Town to live with the Walters in 1936 or 1937. The promised trip to Honolulu for the three of them around that time may have been the couple's pipe dream; when the trip was abruptly canceled, the Walters may have found it convenient to blame cancelation on William rather than their own difficult finances.

Henry shows up once more as a participant in the region's political life in the 1950s. A March 23, 1952, article in the *Santa Fe New Mexican* mentions him in passing as "former county manager."

No information on the deaths of Henry and Eleanor Walters was found.

Isidor Goldberg

For a sunny period just following World War II, Isidor Goldberg was William's employer at Meadowbrook Farm. The two were unaware of the fact that they both had lost their mothers when only four and then been removed from the first homes they had known. Isidor was born in Manhattan, New York, in 1893. The death of Isidor's mother in 1897 left his father unable to care for Isidor and his two infant sisters, and Isidor was taken in and raised at the Hebrew Sheltering Guardian Orphan Asylum in New York City. According to the "Guide to the Records of the Hebrew Sheltering Guardian Society of New York," at the Center for Jewish History website, by 1912 that institution "was able to relocate 500 children from orphanages in New York City to a new country setting in Pleasantville, New York, where both cottage residences and a school were created for them." This appears to be the nearby orphanage that regularly brought children to the Goldberg estate for parties during the late 1940s, when William worked for Goldberg. Through much of his adult life, Goldberg maintained ties with the orphanage in which he was raised, including serving on its board of trustees.

Goldberg had an impressive career as an inventor and was important in creating radio communications equipment for the United States and its allies during World War II. In 1945 the U.S. military recognized his company, Pilot Radio Corporation, with its prestigious Army-Navy "E" Award for excellence in production of war equipment. In addition, Goldberg was a leader in developing and introducing an array of peacetime communications and entertainment products, including TV and radio.

As a teen in New York, Goldberg graduated from the Hebrew Technical Institute in mechanical arts. He was only seventeen when he became a test pilot for Curtiss Aeroplane and Motor Corporation. At age twenty-two he received a U.S. patent for his first known invention, an emergency lamp. Just a few years later he founded Pilot Electric Manufacturing Company in Brooklyn, New York, to manufacture parts and kits for home radios. The name of the company was later changed to Pilot Radio and Tube Corporation and then to Pilot Radio Corporation. His company was the first to introduce a civilian shortwave radio and a portable, battery-powered radio. In 1929 Pilot sponsored the first scheduled TV broadcasting and offered TV receiver kits for sale. By 1937 the company produced ready-made televisions and ten years later marketed the first portable TV receiver. By the late 1930s, Pilot products were being sold in more than ninety countries, and eventually the company would become known in particular for the reliability and affordability of its high-fidelity (hi-fi) products. Pilot worked closely with RCA and enjoyed huge success until losing out to lower-priced Japanese manufacturers in the 1970s. Goldberg was president of Pilot from its inception until his death in 1961 at age sixty-eight.

An ardent Zionist and philanthropist, Goldberg was co-founder of the United Jewish Appeal in the United States and a member of the Zionist Organization of America. After establishing a subsidiary of his company in Tel Aviv in the late 1940s, he supplied communications equipment to the new Israeli army. Prior to the founding of a Jewish state, Goldberg helped Technion — Israel Institute of Technology to acquire land in Haifa. He also supported Technion with funds for research scholarships.

Isidor Goldberg had three children with his first wife, Rose Goldberg Lenitz. In 1936, Goldberg married his second wife, Joan.

BIBLIOGRAPHY

Beam, Cris. *To the End of June: The Intimate Life of American Foster Care*. Boston: Houghton Mifflin Harcourt, 2013.

"The Children's Aid Society" and "FAQs." National Orphan Train Complex. Accessed June 26, 2013. http://orphantrain depot.org/history/the-childrens-aid-society/ and http://orphantraindepot.org/history/faqs/.

"Dastardly Outrage: A Young Lady Assaulted by an Inhuman Brute." *Montrose (PA) Independent Republican*, May 19, 1899.

"A Finding Aid to the Isidor Goldberg Papers, Manuscript Collection No. 599, 1908–1992." Jacob Rader Marcus Center of the American Jewish Archives. http://collections .americanjewisharchives.org/ms/ms0599/ms0599.html.

Gray, Edward. "The Orphan Trains." *American Experience*, season 8, episode 4, directed by Janet Graham and Edward Gray. Aired November 1995. PBS Home Video, 2006. DVD, 60 min. This episode was part of a PBS history series and is available from Netflix.

"Guide to the Records of the Hebrew Sheltering Guardian Society of New York, undated, 1879–1972, 1995." I-43. Reprocessed by Dan Ma and Marvin Rusinek, April 2008. American Jewish Historical Society, Center for Jewish History. http://findingaids.cjh.org/?pID=251734.

"History of Firsts." Children's Aid Society. Accessed October 9, 2013. www.childrensaidsociety.org/about/history/history-firsts.

Holt, Marilyn Irvin. *The Orphan Trains: Placing Out in America.* Lincoln: University of Nebraska Press, 1992.

Krinsky, Miriam Aroni. "Disrupting the Pathway from Foster Care to the Justice System—a Former Prosecutor's Perspectives on Reform." *Family Court Review* 48, no. 2 (April 2010): 322–337. Available at Constitutionproject.org.

Martin, Douglas. "Consuelo Crespi, Aristocrat of Fashion, Dies at 82." *New York Times,* October 23, 2010.

————. "Edward Finkelstein, 89, Dies; Took Macy's to Its Highs and Lows." *New York Times,* June 3, 2014.

"Orphan Trains." Adoption History Project, Department of History, University of Oregon, Eugene. Last updated February 24, 2012. http://pages.uoregon.edu/adoption/topics/orphan.html.

Pendleton, Nat. "Pilot Radio Corp. History." Early Television Foundation and Museum. Accessed January 18, 2013. www.earlytelevision.org/pilot_history.html.

Riley, James Whitcomb. "The Preacher's Boy." In *The Works of James Whitcomb Riley.* Vol. 5: *Rhymes of Childhood.* New York: Charles Scribner's Sons, 1899.

Sousa, Joe. "Pilot: TV37; Electrical Repair and Operational Details." Radiomuseum. February 14, 2015. www.radiomuseum.org.

Trammell, Rebecca S. "Orphan Train Myths and Legal Reality."
Modern American 5, no. 2 (Fall 2009): 3–13. Available at
http://digitalcommons.wcl.american.edu/tma.

Warren, Andrea. "The Orphan Train." Special to the
Washington Post, 1998.

ACKNOWLEDGEMENTS

Thanks above all to William Walters, who was willing to tell me both the stories he enjoyed telling as well as the ones that were painful to speak aloud. Listening to William and finding ways to ask the right questions became a writing exercise unlike any other I've known, because what he had to say ranged from fascinating to horrific and because he found it hard to describe his emotions. William certainly taught me more about World War II than I thought I'd ever want to know, and he made it interesting. (All of the information he supplied is not contained in this book for reasons of length.) In the writing of William's book, I immersed myself hour after hour in another person's life to an extent I will probably never experience again.

My thanks go to William's daughter, Dorothea Shipp, who agreed to be interviewed, was always available for questions, and served as liaison with her brothers.

Editor and friend Linda Gunnarson served above and beyond the call of duty in reading this book six times, acting as developmental editor, line editor, and copyeditor. A consummate professional, she also bent with good grace to my stylistic oddities. Linda, you are a marvel. Your questions and corrections were essential to my goal of doing justice to William's story.

My husband, Alfred White, served as my first reader each time I produced a new draft of the book, catching mistakes and offering important feedback. He, too, read the book six times! How lucky I am, dear Alfred, to have you as my partner and my love.

This book achieved its present form with crucial help from numerous people willing to critique the manuscript as it evolved. I offer my thanks to Travis Berg, David Calloway, Dee Cope, Carol Katzoff, John Meislahn, Susan Mitchell, Anthony Mohr, Bob Pettit, M.D., Dorothea Shipp, and Cate White. Input from literary agents Michael Congdon at Don Congdon Associates, Annie Hwang at Folio Literary Management, and Clare Mao at Lippincott Massie McQuilkin was invaluable. When it came time to query agents, Joan Giannecchini was helpful in crafting a query letter and perking up what was, at the time, the book's subtitle.

Various individuals contributed by phone and email or in person to my research: Lori Halfhide, head researcher, and Amanda Wahlmeier, curator, at the National Orphan Train Complex in Concordia, Kansas; Melissa Eleftherion Carr and Jannah Minnix, librarians at the Ukiah, California, public library; Christy Bradshaw, education coordinator at the American Hereford Association in Kansas City, Missouri; Nathan Huegen, assistant director of education at The National World War II Museum in New Orleans; and Tom Lynch, historian at Boys Town.

William's story might never have been recorded if it were not for my friend Carol Katzoff. Shortly after she lost her husband and our dear friend Richard, Carol attended a hospice grief group where she met William Walters and was deeply impressed by the story he told while introducing himself to the group. It was Carol who insisted that I meet William and who arranged a meeting with him and Dorothea. I will be forever grateful.

ABOUT THE AUTHOR

Victoria Golden earned a degree in sociology from the University of California, Los Angeles. A former public relations writer, editor, and book reviewer, she is the author of *Independent Photography* with photographer Robert Foothorap and *The Readers' Choice: 200 Book Club Favorites.* For several years she was a volunteer at a group home for foster children in Santa Rosa, California. She lives with her husband in the northern California wine country, where she is currently writing fiction.

Dear Booklover,

Thanks for reading my book. I hope you enjoy it.

If you'd like to offer feedback or ask questions about the writing of *A Last Survivor of the Orphan Trains*, it would be fun to meet with your book club via Zoom. You can arrange this through my website: victoriagoldenauthor.com.

Best,

Victoria Holden

Made in the USA
Middletown, DE
24 August 2020